D1135454

Once Again to Zelda

Once Again to Zelda

Fifty Great Dedications and Their Stories

MARLENE WAGMAN-GELLER

PICADOR

First published 2008 as a Perigee book by Penguin Group (USA) Inc., New York

This revised edition first published in Great Britain 2009 by Picador
an imprint of Pan Macmillan Ltd
Pan Macmillan, 20 New Wharf Road, London N1 9RR
Basingstoke and Oxford
Associated companies throughout the world
www.panmacmillan.com

ISBN 978-0330-51135-3

1 3 5 7 9 8 6 4 2

A CIP catalogue record for this book is available
from the British Library.

Printed and bound in the UK by
CPI Mackays, Chatham ME5 8TD

Visit www.picador.com to read more about all our books
and to buy them. You will also find features, author interviews and
news of any author events, and you can sign up for e-newsletters
so that you're always first to hear about our new releases.

To my Js—
And to the writers whose fictionalized worlds
have forever enriched our own.

Contents

Introduction

My first gift and my last, to you
I dedicate this fascicle of songs—
The only wealth I have:
Just as they are, to you.

—ROBERT LOUIS STEVENSON

When people discover that you have written a book, one of the first questions you're inevitably asked is, "How did you come up with the idea?" I well remember the conception of *Once Again to Zelda*.

I had just finished reading Grace Metalious's *Peyton Place* and was fascinated by her depiction of a small New England town of the 1950s. On the surface it appeared very Christian and very conservative. (This was in keeping with the era, when TV sitcom couples were always shown in twin beds.) However, once you scratched the surface, you found alcoholism, abortion, rape, incest, adultery, and illegitimacy. Flipping through its pages upon its completion, I happened to glance, once more, at its dedication: "To George—for all the reasons he knows so well." I was immediately intrigued. Who was George? And what were the reasons he knew so well? I started to research the answer, and the story rivaled that of the novel.

Enthralled at the story behind the story, I soon found myself in the role of Dedication Detective. I started looking at other book dedications and researched the interplay between authors and recipients of the writers' tributes. This was an intriguing pursuit, as it proved an encapsulated biography of the author at the time when he or she penned their books. Moreover, it also shed insight into the lives of the people whom the author cared the most about.

In some instances, the research cast me in the role of Sherlock Holmes. This was the case with a book where I was perplexed, as the dedication surprisingly wasn't even written by the author. The story that unfolded was equal parts mesmerizing and heart-rending. As it turned out, the writer had been murdered and her manuscript had lain hidden in a locked suitcase for sixty years. When it was finally published, the dedication was written by the deceased's daughter, in tribute to her lost mother.

In the case of *Schindler's List*, I knew Schindler's story because of Steven Spielberg's classic film; however, when I looked at the dedication in Thomas Keneally's book, it was not only "to the memory of Oskar Schindler" but to Leopold Pfefferberg as well. It was fascinating to learn how the Los Angeles store owner was the driving force who prevented his savior's name from being relegated to the dustbin of history.

The 1960s film *The Graduate* made Mrs. Robinson a part of American pop culture. However, when I researched the Eve of Charles Webb's tribute, his ex-wife and present live-in lover definitely qualifies as the most unforgettable character.

Under the Tuscan Sun, the memoir about Frances Mayes's years in Italy, was also popularized because of the movie version. However, the work was dedicated to Ann Cornelisen, someone who was not mentioned in either the film or the book. It was interesting to learn about the Vassar-educated girl who left the States for the remote areas of post–World War II Italy and forever changed the lives of the villagers, as well as her own.

One author, who dedicated his novel to his wife, met her when she was wearing a wolf's mask. She brought him solace when his father was killed by Bolshevik assassins and his brother was murdered in a Nazi concentration camp, where he had been imprisoned for homosexuality.

Another novel dedicated to a wife revealed that the spouse was one whose own life rivaled even that of a fictional one. Before her marriage to her current husband, her former one had been assassinated by members of an Apartheid-centered regime; this horror took place in front of her two young daughters.

My research also gave me new insight into history, a discipline I have always found an engaging pursuit. One book was dedicated to four sisters, with whose names I had not been familiar. However, I was to discover that they are revered martyrs in their native Dominican Republic, which has several shrines to the women, who sacrificed their lives to save their country from the tyranny of its dictator.

The dedications spanned the spectrum: to family members, lovers, friends, romantic interests, and heroes. In two works, they were to beloved dogs. In another, the dedication proved ironic. This was the case when one woman had the *chutzpah* to dedicate her magnum opus to both her husband and her lover. When the latter dumped her in favor of a younger, more beautiful woman, "the woman scorned" had his name expunged from all subsequent editions.

The common denominator was that in each dedication, the

authors led the reader into the antechambers of their personal lives. This was especially gratifying in the case of reclusive writers such as Harper Lee: in her dedication she lifted the curtain of her reclusive life, wherein she revealed the two people she had revered the most. The same sentiment holds true for the extremely private Dan Brown in his dedication to *The Da Vinci Code*: "For Blythe . . . again, more than ever."

I discovered that what precedes the opening line of a novel can serve as a crystal ball as to what is to follow the turning of the pages. When F. Scott Fitzgerald wrote "Once Again to Zelda," he was referring to the love, and the bane, of his life. The nuances of this dedication are echoed in *The Great Gatsby* when one uncovers the similarities between the fictional relationship between Gatsby and Daisy and their nonfictional counterparts.

Exploring each dedication was akin to prying open a clam; it unearthed a pearl of fascinating tales. Moreover, each also revealed troves of literary trivia. I learned about a Nobel Prize–winning dramatist whose daughter married a 2008 Academy Award recipient; two classic American authors who shared more than just a love of literature; why a book had to be written from the confines of a bed; the Ayatollah's forgotten victim; the eighteen-year-old who dedicated her classic tale of horror to her father rather than her poet husband; which V always dedicated his books to another V; why a Californian author, while living in Switzerland, had a knife held to her throat for twenty minutes by an enraged mother who threatened to murder her. At one point it occurred to me that fellow bibliophiles might share an interest in these stories, and *Once Again to Zelda* was born.

The entries are arranged in chronological order, based on the dates of first publication. The authors' names are given as they appeared on their respective books, followed, within parentheses, by their birth names. The dedications were replicated so that they are in the same format and the same style as on the original editions.

Literary dedications had their origin in the eighteenth century; at the time, they were mainly obsequious, courting the favor of wealthy patrons. However, in the past one hundred years they have become more autobiographical; in them writers truly enter the confessional, giving us unique insight into the authors whose words we cherish and the people whom they loved. I hope readers will enjoy the stories behind the dedications as much as I did unearthing them.

Marlene Wagman-Geller
San Diego, California
2008

Post Script: As I'm still enjoying my work as a Dedication Detective, feel free to visit my website at www.onceagaintozelda.net or email me at onceagaintozelda@hotmail.com to let me know of any of your favorite literary dedications.

1

Emma

Jane Austen
1815

TO

HIS ROYAL HIGHNESS
THE PRINCE REGENT,

THIS WORK IS,

By His Royal Highness's Permission,

Most Respectfully Dedicated,

BY HIS ROYAL HIGHNESS'S

DUTIFUL

AND OBEDIENT

HUMBLE SERVANT,

THE AUTHOR

Writing a book is akin to giving birth: one can never predict the path the progeny will tread. This was the case with Jane Austen in her novel *Emma* and the story of its ironic dedication.

More often than not, authors use their own traumas and dramas as material for their plots. However, Austen did not follow this pattern. As her nephew James Edward Austen-Leigh wrote

of his aunt, "of events her life was singularly barren: few changes
and no great crisis ever broke the smooth current of its course."
Jane was born in a rectory in Steventon in Hampshire; she had an
adored, elder sister, Cassandra, and six brothers; her favorite was
Henry.

The first pivotal event in her life occurred when she was twenty-
one and fell prey to what would be one of the most prevalent
subjects of her books: romance. The man who won her heart was
Tom Lefroy, a nephew of one of her neighbors. From her letters to
her closest confidante, Cassandra, it is apparent the two of them
spent a great deal of time together. They had shared interests such
as mutual admiration of Henry Fielding's *Tom Jones*; another
commonality was their sense of ironic humor. While her family
was thrilled she had found love, his did not share the sentiment.
Lefroy's family was not pleased he was courting a girl without a
dowry or other financial prospects, and as he was dependent on
them for money in order to finish his education and help estab-
lish his future legal career, he departed for London, leaving his
romantic interest behind. Jane never saw him again. Perhaps
one of the reasons she, unlike her fictional heroines, never heard
the wedding bells peal for her was because the torch she carried
for Tom was never extinguished. On the other hand, Tom, who
became the chief justice of Ireland, later admitted to his nephew
that when he was young, he had been in love with Jane Austen
but that "it was boyish love."

Six years later, Jane was to receive her only marriage proposal.
Harris Bigg-Wither asked for her hand, and she accepted. She had
known him for many years and being his wife would save her
both from being an old maid and from her precarious financial
situation. However, the next morning, deciding she was not for

sale to a man she was not in love with and who was not her intellectual match, Jane withdrew her acceptance. She realized there was too great a price to pay for a union not based on a meeting of minds. As she later wrote to her niece, "Anything is to be preferred or endured rather than marrying without Affection."

Without having any income or any other prospects at marriage, Austen tried her luck at publishing her novels and was both surprised and thrilled when *Sense and Sensibility* was well received. This book, like all her subsequent ones, declined to name her as author and instead was simply attributed "By a Lady."

George Augustus Frederick was the uncle of Queen Victoria and the eldest of George III's fifteen children. His father, rather than viewing his son as his successor, regarded him as his usurper, and their relationship was always contentious. By the age of eighteen, barred from any active role, the prince's main preoccupations in life were self-indulgence: food, gambling, wine, women, and luxury. His weight burgeoned, as did his debts, and he was nicknamed the Prince of "Whales," the Playboy Prince, and the Prince of Pleasure.

Parliament agreed to bail George out if he agreed to marry his cousin, the Protestant Princess Caroline of Brunswick. Although he was at that time wed to Maria Fitzherbert, the king had refused to acknowledge their union as legal because it was undertaken without his permission, and because she was a Catholic, it was declared not legal. Predictably, the union between George and Caroline proved a recipe for a royal disaster. Soon George became a serial adulterer and had several illegitimate children. One of his mistresses, the actress Mary Robinson, had to be paid off with a handsome sum when she threatened to sell his letters to the newspapers.

When his father went insane in 1811, George was appointed the Prince Regent, a role he held until his father's demise in 1820, when he assumed the throne as George IV. At that time so great was his antipathy toward his wife that he banned her from attending his coronation. His act of stopping Caroline from entering the doors of Westminster Abbey turned the people against him from the onset of his reign.

Jane Austen felt nothing but disgust for George; she loathed his excesses, adultery, and mistreatment of his wife. Her antipathy showed in one of her letters: "Poor woman [Caroline], I shall support her as long as I can, because she *is* a Woman, & because I hate her Husband . . . a Man whom she must detest." Little did Austen dream that the man who she despised would soon cross her path.

In 1815, Jane traveled to London to care for her ill brother Henry at his home, Hans Place. His physician was Dr. Baillie, who coincidentally also happened to be the Prince Regent's doctor. On one of his visits, Baillie informed Jane that the prince was a great admirer of her novels and had a set of them in each of his homes. Although Jane had published them anonymously, word had recently leaked she was indeed the author. Before he took his leave, Baillie informed Jane that she should expect a visit from the prince's personal librarian, James Stanier Clarke. Instead, Clarke invited Jane to the prince's opulent Carlton House, where he informed her she was at liberty to dedicate her forthcoming novel, *Emma*, to the Prince Regent. Austen was aghast at having to dedicate her book to a man whom she felt possessed very little sense or sensibility. Her initial thought was to ignore the invitation; however, she feared that doing so might have dire consequences for herself and her siblings. This worry was based on the fact that Leigh and John Hunt, editors of the *Examiner*, had been fined £500 and jailed for two years on a charge of libel when they described the royal heir as "a libertine head over heels in debt and disgrace, a despiser of domestic ties, the companion of gamblers and demi-reps [women of doubtful reputation]."

After much consideration, Jane decided she had no choice but to comply. However, she would do so in her own ironic fashion. With pen in hand and tongue in cheek, Jane set out to have the last laugh.

Princess Caroline, in a scathing letter to her husband that she later made public, had repeatedly addressed him as "His Royal Highness." Austen used the same title, three times, well aware that exaggeration is a satirist's best friend. By merely signing herself as "author," she emphasized her own modesty by contrast. The novel itself served as a veiled barb, as the prince had proclaimed himself "The First Gentleman of Europe," and *Emma* explored the concept of what constitutes a true gentleman—none of which traits remotely resembled the future king.

The royal's debauched lifestyle had contributed to a multitude of health problems such as gout, cataracts, and arteriosclerosis, as well as alcohol and laudanum addictions. He began to descend into insanity, as his father had before him. He told people he had been a soldier and had fought in the Battle of Waterloo. He became more and more of a recluse in Windsor Castle, where he died in 1830.

George Augustus Frederick lent his name to the Regency era, which produced a distinctive style in fashion, architecture, and literature. There were many monuments erected during his life to commemorate his reign, including a bronze statue of him astride his horse in Trafalgar Square, but the more surprising remembrance can be found upon reading the words of a retiring minister's daughter, in her thrice repeated "tribute" to "the first gentleman of Europe:" His Royal Highness.

2

Frankenstein or
The Modern Prometheus

MARY SHELLEY
(MARY WOLLSTONECRAFT GODWIN SHELLEY)
1818

TO

WILLIAM GODWIN

Author of Political Justice, Caleb Williams, &c.

THESE VOLUMES

Are respectfully inscribed

BY

THE AUTHOR

THREE men would forever impact author Mary Shelley's life, as well as the history of Gothic literature: her father, William Godwin, the radical anarchist atheist philosopher; her husband, Percy Bysse Shelley, the doomed Romantic poet; and her creation, Victor Frankenstein, the tortured modern Prometheus.

William Godwin met his future wife, Mary Wollstonecraft, at a dinner party in London. He found himself extremely irritated by the woman who kept interrupting one of the guests, Thomas

Paine, in order to disagree with the eminent writer on nearly every subject.

William and Mary were not to see each other for many years; however, when they met again at the home of Mary Hays, William's initial irritation was replaced with passion. Although they both were, in theory, against the "slavery of marriage," when Mary discovered she was pregnant, William asked her to marry him because he wanted his baby to be legitimate. Although Godwin was an atheist, they were married in St. Pancras Church.

Their union, however, did not mean conventionality; they moved into two adjoining households, which they called the Polygon, so that they could retain their individual autonomy. The Godwin–Wollstonecraft relationship was an extremely close one; unfortunately, it was only of six months' duration. Ten days after the birth of Mary Wollstonecraft Godwin, her mother died from complications stemming from the delivery. Godwin was devastated and wrote to his friend Thomas Holcroft of his grief, "I firmly believe there does not exist her equal in the world. I know from experience we were formed to make each other happy. I have not the least expectation that I can now ever know happiness again."

As a catharsis to his grief, he wrote *Memoirs of the Author of A Vindication of the Rights of Woman*. Godwin meant it as a tribute to his lost love; however, the public's reaction was to brand Mary as licentious. Victorian society was not prepared to accept her, to put it mildly, unconventional lifestyle. Some of the tell-all tidbits Godwin included were her relationship with Henry Fuseli, who ultimately rejected Mary in favor of his wife, as well as her affair with an American, Gilbert Imlay, with whom she became pregnant (she had a daughter named Fanny), and several suicide attempts. The inadvertent effect of William Godwin's book was to undermine for the next century the intellectual feminism his beloved wife had championed. Moreover, it tarnished his reputation as well. Robert Southey accused him of "the want of all feeling in stripping his dead wife naked."

William was now the sole guardian of Fanny and Mary, the latter of whom he adored. He called her his "pretty little Mary" and was also extremely proud of her exceptional intelligence, which he took care to foster. When Mary was a child, her father took the girl to her mother's grave in St. Pancras Churchyard. There he taught his daughter to read and spell her name by tracing the inscription on the headstone. He continued to educate Mary from home, and made sure her education was far superior to what the average eighteenth-century girl received. Not only did she have one of the foremost writers and philosophers of the time as her tutor, she was also present when the leading intellectuals of the era came to visit her illustrious father. She was introduced to the works of Coleridge, Wordsworth, and Blake—by the authors themselves.

When Mary was nine, she was enthralled when Samuel Taylor Coleridge came to visit and read his *The Rime of the Ancient Mariner* to Godwin. In *Frankenstein*, when the creature goes into the cabin in the woods, he finds the Coleridge poem in one of the books there. Similarly, Victor Frankenstein quotes from the poem when he recites, "Like one, that on a lonesome road/Doth walk in fear and dread/And, having once turned round, walks on/And turns no more his head/Because he knows a frightful fiend/Doth close behind him tread."

Godwin also fostered his daughter's early interest in writing, and when she was eleven, she wrote a story called "Mounseer

Nongtongpaw," which her proud father published. Its main character used the catchphrase "I don't understand you."

Life for the Godwins continued until the advent, four years later, of "the evil stepmother." A neighbor, who had not yet made the walk up the aisle although she had two children, set her sights on William. He agreed to wed Mary Jane Clairmont so his daughters would have a mother figure; however, his good intentions signaled the beginning of problems for Mary. The new wife was extremely jealous of the close bond between William and Mary, one which she tried, though did not succeed, in breaking. Their household included Fanny and Mary, Mary Jane's son, Charles Clairmont, and daughter, Claire Clairmont, as well as the child they had together, William Godwin Jr.—five children from five different pairs of parents. Yet even the birth of another biological child did nothing to diminish the strong father–daughter ties.

When Mary was sixteen, she found someone other than her father to love. In 1812, the Romantic poet Percy Bysshe Shelley, then nineteen, discovered that Godwin, the author of *Political Justice*, was living in London, and, in awe of the older man's political philosophy, visited the Godwin bookstore. There he became even more awed with the author's daughter, Mary Godwin. She, in turn, was infatuated with Percy, who reminded her so much of the father whom she idolized. Percy soon began joining her outside of the bookstore, away from prying parental eyes. The poet also accompanied Mary on her frequent excursions to her mother's grave, where she would sit and read her mother's works, most notably *A Vindication of the Rights of Woman*. It was there that the two first declared their love.

Upon discovering their relationship, Godwin forbade his

sixteen-year-old daughter to see Percy again. Not only was Percy married, his wife, Harriet, was pregnant. However, when the poet threatened to commit suicide if Mary abandoned him, she agreed to continue their affair. As a result, one early morning in 1814, Mary and Percy Shelley ran away to France. Although Shelley, by living with the woman he loved, was complying with the principle of free love as outlined in *Political Justice*, Godwin was livid. Upon their return several weeks later, Godwin refused to speak to either one, a silence that would extend for two years.

When the couple returned to England, Percy told his wife that he wanted to continue his love relationship with Mary, but that Harriet and the baby could live with them as well. Harriet declined. Instead, she chose the alternative path of drowning herself (several months pregnant) in the Serpentine in Hyde Park. London society was scandalized, and the ostracized couple fled to Switzerland. They were joined by Mary's stepsister, Claire Clairmont.

In Switzerland, the three became guests of Lord Byron, who had rented a castle overlooking Lake Geneva. One evening during their stay, there was a thunderstorm. The guests devised a contest to see who could come up with the best horror story. Mary retired to her room, and had a waking nightmare. In it she saw "the pale student of unhallowed arts kneeling beside the thing he had put together." It was the start of her masterpiece, *Frankenstein*. The creature's demands for his maker to create a mate to help ease his loneliness may have been an echo of Mary's own father's loneliness at losing the love of his life, Mary Wollstonecraft.

After a few weeks at Byron's castle, Mary, Percy, and Claire (who was now pregnant with Byron's baby) returned to England. With Harriet's death, Percy was free to wed Mary. William

Godwin attended his daughter's wedding, satisfied that it was now going to be church-sanctioned. Perhaps the fact that Percy had become William's chief financial backer also secured the reconciliation.

The rest of society was not as forgiving, and the newly married couple, plagued by scandal, fled to Italy. Tragically, sorrow was a shadow, and heartache continued to pursue Mary. Mary's first child, a daughter, died shortly after birth. Her second child, her son William (named in honor of Mary's father), died when he was three. This was followed by the death of Percy Bysshe Shelley, who drowned in a storm at sea. During this time, Mary must often have implored God with the recurring phrase from her juvenile story, "I don't understand you."

In dire financial straits, and unable to earn money in Italy, Mary and her only surviving child, son Percy Florence Shelley, eventually returned to England and her father. There she worked as a professional writer, and used her money to support not only her son, but also William, who was now dependent on her income. Godwin, who had always acted as his daughter's literary agent, was most likely the one who convinced Mary to change her original draft of *Frankenstein*. In it, Victor and Elizabeth were brother and sister who became lovers; in the published edition, Elizabeth was adopted. The topic of incest appeared again in Mary's novella *Mathilda*, which this time involved father–daughter sexual relations. William vetoed the publication of *Mathilda*, which contained obvious autobiographical undertones. It was only released posthumously, in the 1950s.

Because Mary Jane Clairmont had sent Mary to Scotland for a time to get her away from William, and because of the recurring theme of incest in her two books as well as their lifelong extremely close relationship, there is conjecture as to whether or not Mary shared more than just her name with her mother. Was she, like Hamlet, "too much i' the sun?" William might have figured that the Godwin Wollstonecraft Shelley family had already displayed enough of their skeletons, what with adultery, illegitimacy, and suicides, to add incest to the mix. However, what is known is that when it came to dedicating her masterpiece, it was not to her lover but to her father that she bestowed that honor.

Mary died in 1851 and was buried in St. Peter's Churchyard in Dorset. Her son arranged for the remains of Mary's mother and father to be transferred from the Old St. Pancras Churchyard in London to their daughter's final resting place so she could be interred between the mother she never knew, Mary Wollstonecraft, and the father whom she adored, William Godwin.

3

Jane Eyre: An Autobiography

Charlotte Brontë
1848

To

W. M. THACKERAY, Esq.

THIS WORK

IS RESPECTFULLY INSCRIBED,

BY

THE AUTHOR*

CHARLOTTE Brontë, writing under the pseudonym Currer Bell, dedicated *Jane Eyre* to another eminent Victorian author, William Makepeace Thackeray, because of his enthusiastic review of the first edition of her novel, and because she was a great admirer of his writing. Thackeray denounced social and religious hypocrisy in his novels, as she did in her own. However, as Charlotte was later to discover to her great surprise and mortification, her dedication was to prove an ironic postscript to *Jane Eyre*.

When *Jane Eyre* first came out, Thackeray's literary views carried great weight because of his standing as an eminent author

---

* Found in the second edition of *Jane Eyre*.

in his own right. On October 23, 1847, he wrote to Mr. W. S. Williams, "I wish you had not sent me Jane Eyre. It interested me so much that I have lost (or won if you like) a whole day in reading it...I thought the man & woman capital." In fact, he had ignored his own publishing deadline, unable to tear himself away from Brontë's novel. Thackeray ended his letter by relating the following anecdote. He explained that when his butler had brought in coals, the man was shocked to see his employer crying while reading the novel. He said the love passages were so moving they had reduced him to tears. Mr. Williams, knowing that Brontë would be thrilled, forwarded excerpts from the letter to her. She was so gratified by the praise she decided to dedicate the second edition of *Jane Eyre* to Thackeray, never dreaming that her tribute would prove to be one that would launch a sea of gossip in London society. She wrote in her preface that he was a "Titan of the mind" and an "intellectual boa-constrictor." Other laudatory praises were "Why have I alluded to this man? I have alluded to him, Reader, because I think I see in him an intellect profounder and more unique than his contemporaries have yet recognized.... Finally, I have alluded to Mr. Thackeray, because to him—if he will accept the tribute of a total stranger—I have dedicated this second edition of JANE EYRE." Thackeray said of the dedication that it was "the greatest compliment I have ever received in my life." The lavish praise was not only salve for his ego. In addition, it also increased interest in the work he was publishing in serial format, *Vanity Fair*, which was in the twelfth of its nineteen monthly installments.

As fate would have it, however, the mutual admiration between the two novelists carried unpleasant aspects in its wake. Charlotte Brontë had written *Jane Eyre* while she lived in

Haworth Parsonage, which was an isolated locale on the moors of Yorkshire. The family had moved there when their father, Patrick Brontë, an Irish Anglican clergyman, had been appointed as church curator. The plot and characters of her novel were purely fiction. Indeed, the three Brontë sisters, Charlotte, Anne, and Emily, growing up without friends, had always relied heavily on imagination to make up for the lack of excitement in their everyday lives.

Ironically, the events and characters in *Jane Eyre* mirrored the actual lives of both Brontë and Thackeray. Charlotte, like Jane, had been sent to a boarding school that was physically and mentally abusive. After leaving the nightmare that was school, both women went to work as governesses.

Thackeray's wife, Isabella, had gone into a deep depression after the birth of her third child, one from which she never recovered. Indeed, her mental condition deteriorated to such an extent that she attempted to drown her three-year-old daughter, Annie; however, possessing a remnant of sanity, she ended up saving her. Disgusted at the conditions in state-run asylums, Thackeray confined Isabella to their London home, under the care of two women attendants. In *Jane Eyre*, Mr. Rochester has his mad first wife, Bertha, locked in an attic.

Another eerie similarity is that Mrs. Thackeray, while on a trip to Ireland, had tried to commit suicide by jumping into the ocean. Mrs. Rochester, after setting fire to Thornfield, plunges from the burning roof to her death.

Just as Rochester hires Jane Eyre, Thackeray, after locking up his wife, employed a governess to care for his children. Both Mrs. Rochester and Mrs. Thackeray had become mad after four years of marriage, "both were given to manic bursts of laughter," and "both were at times violent and even homicidal."

These coincidences led to public speculation that the novel was based on Thackeray's domestic situation and Brontë's own life. Victorian London was abuzz with unfounded rumors that Brontë had worked as a governess for Thackeray's children when his wife went mad, and that the two of them had an illicit affair, conducted under the very roof where his wife lived. They surmised that because Charlotte was still in love with William, she dedicated her novel to him. Further fueling the fires of innuendo was the original title of Brontë's novel: *Jane Eyre: An Autobiography*. Charlotte, aghast at the inadvertent mimicking of fiction and fact, "was torn between amazement and mortification," apologized profusely to Thackeray, and wrote in a letter to Mr. Williams, "Well may it be said that Fact is often stranger than Fiction! The coincidence struck me as equally unfortunate and extraordinary."

Unfortunately, the lives of the two authors did not fare as well romantically as did that of the orphaned governess, Jane. Thackeray's wife languished in institutions for thirty years, outliving her husband, never able to shake off her mental illness. The last line of *Vanity Fair* says, "Come, children, let us shut up the box and the puppets, for our play is played out." Charlotte's play ended at age thirty, in the first year of marriage, while she was pregnant. However, to the devout Christian, death held the promise of reunion with her beloved sisters Anne and Emily, and a release from a world whose rumors and cruelties had truly proved itself a Vanity Fair.

4

Moby Dick*

HERMAN MELVILLE

1851

IN TOKEN

OF MY ADMIRATION FOR HIS GENIUS

THIS BOOK IS INSCRIBED

TO

NATHANIEL HAWTHORNE

MELVILLE did not merely dedicate *Moby Dick* to Hawthorne because of his admiration for his genius. He also did so because it was through Hawthorne's mentorship and guidance that his novel changed from a lighthearted yarn about a whaling ship to one of the classics of world literature. In addition, his praise was in gratitude because, for at least a brief moment in time, their friendship prevented Herman from being Ishmael.

The meeting of the twain occurred in August 1850, in Massachusetts, on the occasion of a picnic organized by David Dudley Field. That year, Melville had purchased an eighteenth-century farmhouse, Arrowhead, in Pittsfield; Hawthorne had a home six

---

*Originally published as *The Whale*.

miles away in Lenox. Although the two men had not met, they had favorably reviewed one another's work with mutual admiration. The forty-six-year-old Hawthorne had praised Melville's *Typee* in *The Salem Advertiser* in 1846, and the thirty-one-year-old Melville had just completed a warm review of Hawthorne's *Mosses from an Old Manse*, a copy of which his aunt had given him a few weeks before. During the picnic, a thunderstorm forced the excursion indoors, whereupon the two men became acquainted. The strangers quickly became friends. Two days later Hawthorne wrote to a friend, "I liked Melville so much that I have asked him to spend a few days with me." Melville, in awe of his literary neighbor, was only too happy to oblige. The visit would be the first of numerous ones, and when the two men were apart, they corresponded through mail. Melville's letters survive; however, Hawthorne's to Melville have either been lost or destroyed.

The two men reveled in each other's company, both feeling that they had found their soul mates, as well as their intellectual equals. Sophia Hawthorne was pleased her husband had someone with whom to communicate. She said, "Mr. Melville, generally silent and uncommunicative, pours out the rich floods of his mind and experience to Nathaniel, so sure of apprehension, so sure of a large and generous interpretation, and of the most delicate and fine judgment." This friendship helped ease Melville's lifelong feeling of alienation, one he shared with his character Ishmael, who also took to the sea to escape the confines of a society from which he felt adrift.

On one meeting, Melville showed Hawthorne a draft of *Moby Dick*. Hawthorne, himself currently completing *The Scarlet Letter*, persuaded his friend to rework it from a tale of the high seas to an epic allegory that told not only a tale, but probed the defeats and triumphs of the human spirit. Melville delayed his submission to his publishers until it could meet Hawthorne's exacting standards. When it did, Hawthorne at last pronounced that the tragic tale was "cooked in hellfire." It was the praise Melville had sought. However, later documents have left many scholars wondering if their relationship involved only a meeting of minds.

In the summer of 1851 Mrs. Hawthorne took a three-week trip to Boston to visit her relatives. She left behind her husband and their five-year-old son Julian. In his memoir, *Twenty Days with Julian and Little Bunny by Papa*, published in 2007, Hawthorne writes about his summer idyll with his son. He paints a picture of childhood innocence: picking currants and looking after a pet rabbit called Bunny. However, and this was not mentioned in the memoir, which was essentially written for Mrs. Hawthorne, Melville became a frequent guest during this time. Indeed, he even chose to spend his birthday with his friend rather than his own family. Hawthorne wrote of one of these evenings, "Melville and I had a talk about time and eternity, things of this world and next, and books, and publishers, and all possible and impossible matters, that lasted pretty deep into the night." This might be construed as nineteenth-century guy talk, but on examining some of Melville's letters to Hawthorne, one can find a decidedly romantic tone. Melville wrote, "I felt pantheistic then—your heart beat in my ribs and mine in yours, and both in God's. Whence come you, Hawthorne? By what right do you drink from my flagon of life? And when I put it to my lips—lo, they are yours and not mine." The conversations and the letters are fraught with romantic and sexual overtones between the two men, suggesting that *The Scarlet Letter*'s Dimmesdale was not the only one to harbor a secret.

Two years after the first encounter between Herman Melville and Nathaniel Hawthorne, the latter abruptly severed the relationship. At the same time, Hawthorne sold his farm and moved away. The reason for the termination is a matter of conjecture. One theory is that the puritanical Hawthorne was no longer comfortable with the nature of the younger man's feelings toward him. This may have been because he was heterosexual and therefore spurned his advances, or, being a product of the century in which homosexuality was cryptically referred to as "the love that dare not speak its name," would not reciprocate. Hawthorne, a respected literary figure and a family man, whose ancestor had been a judge in the Salem witch trials, had no desire to himself wear the scarlet letter *H*. Whatever the nature of their physical relationship, it is clear that Melville was distraught at its end. In *Moby Dick*, when Captain Ahab drops his pipe into the ocean, it symbolizes the loss of future pleasure. The same held true when Hawthorne abandoned Melville, making him a solitary Ishmael once more.

Tragically, after Melville lost Hawthorne's friendship, he lost much more as well. His oldest son, Malcolm, committed suicide after an argument with his father. His second and only other son, Stanwix, died after a long and agonizing illness. One of his daughters, who suffered from a mental disorder, passed away at a young age. Beset by personal loss and financial hardships, his marriage, never strong, reached a breaking point. However, with the persistence of Captain Ahab, Melville took a job as a New York City customs inspector, which he held for nineteen years. For someone who had sailed the seas and then devoted himself to writing, his job as a bureaucrat must have been purgatory, but that was a place with which Melville was well acquainted.

In 1856 the two men met once more. Hawthorne had moved to England, where he had accepted a post as a U.S. consul. Melville dropped in to see him, en route to a trip to the Holy Land. Of their time together, Hawthorne wrote in his journal, "We soon found ourselves on pretty much our former terms of sociability and confidence." He also mentioned that Herman had not been well lately, and that he looked, "a little paler, and perhaps a little sadder." He recounted their activities, which mainly consisted of sitting on the sand hills, staring at the sea that both of them loved so well. While they did so, they smoked cigars and talked endlessly into the night.

Although it was their last meeting and they never again corresponded, Melville never forgot Hawthorne. He continued to annotate Hawthorne's work after his lost friend died in 1864. With his passing, the country mourned the death of its literary lion. On the contrary, when Melville died, he received only one line in the *New York Times*. Moreover, his name was misspelled as "Henry" Melville.

Although Melville ended his days in obscurity, his work largely forgotten, posterity has proved a far kinder audience. *Moby Dick* is now considered one of the masterpieces of world literature. And, because it was his friend who had convinced him to turn his whaling adventure into an allegory that plumbed the depth of the human heart, readers, too, must share in Melville's admiration for the genius of Nathaniel Hawthorne.

5

Adam Bede

GEORGE ELIOT

(MARY ANNE EVANS/MRS. HENRY LEWES/MARY ANNE CROSS)

1859

Marian Lewes
March 23, 1859
To my dear husband, George Henry Lewes,
I give this M.S. of a work which would
never have been written but for the happiness
which his love has conferred on my life.*

IF one were to free-associate with the term *Victorian England*, the first thing that might come to mind is sexual repression. This, of course, emanated from the queen herself, who had all the piano legs in her palace covered with cloth because they were too suggestive of female anatomy. In addition, there is her memorable advice to her daughters on the eve of their weddings: "Lie back and think of England." However, the story behind Eliot's

---

*This dedication is in the original manuscript in the British Museum. Because her marriage was not church-sanctioned, her publisher would not print this dedication.

dedication suggests that Victoria's world was not as proper as her palace's pianos.

On an intellectual plane, nature had sown its gifts on Mary Anne Evans. She was able to easily grasp philosophy, politics, the classics, religion, and languages. (She was fluent in French and German.) However, what she possessed in intelligence she lacked in looks. Henry James, in a letter to his brother, used the adjective *equine* to describe her appearance. Upon the death of her father, her inheritance was so slight that, unlike her married pretty sisters, she had to seek, as the expression goes, gainful employment. Scorning the options open to a woman of her class (work as a governess or as a companion to an elderly woman), Mary Anne took the unconventional road of moving to London, where she obtained work as a journalist for the *Westminster Review*, a newspaper owned by the radical publisher John Chapman. Mary Anne was not only employed by Chapman; she also began to live in his house. John began to visit her in her room, where she would play the piano for him and teach him German. The lessons soon turned from the vertical plane to a horizontal one. When his wife and mistress (who also lived in the same home) learned of this, they demanded her immediate expulsion. John agreed to let her go with the words that though he admired her mental beauty, he found her lacking in physical charm. On the rebound, she soon became smitten with the single Herbert Spencer; however, he would not marry her because he was a confirmed bachelor.

Alone in London, at the age of thirty-two, her two romances failing to lead to a lasting relationship, Mary Anne became extremely depressed. She confided to her friend Charles Bray how terrified she was at the "horrific disgrace of spinster-hood." She wrote at this time, "My only ardent desire is to find some possibility of devoting myself to some one and making that one purely and calmly happy." The gods must have heard her prayer, for later in the year, John Chapman (with whom she had remained friends) took her to William Jeff's bookstore, where he introduced her to the man to whom she would dedicate *Adam Bede*, as well as her life: George Henry Lewes. Ironically, she at first was not attracted to him because of his looks. She described him as "a sort of miniature Mirabeau in appearance," in reference to his short stature and homely face. Lewes's friend Charles Dickens had once quipped that it was his appearance that had caused his wife to desert him and then finally drove her into insanity. However, Lewes and Mary Anne soon fell in love. They both shared the commonalities of plainness of features and brilliance of mind. Moreover, they both were unconventional. William Makepeace Thackeray once remarked that if he were "to see Lewes perched on a white elephant in Picadilly he should not be in the least surprised." His friends knew something was up when he trimmed his whiskers, started combing his hair, and bought new clothes. Her friends knew something was up when she told them from henceforth she wanted to be referred to as Mrs. George Lewes.

Unfortunately, the couple could not legally wed, as the mad, estranged first wife was still alive. When they took the defiant step of going against the church by living together as man and wife, there were immediate repercussions. Her brother and two sisters said that she was never to contact them, and Mary Anne was shunned by polite society. She was portrayed as a husband stealer, and his legal wife, Agnes, as the victim. This was unfair because Agnes had become pregnant, four times, with George's friend Thornton Hunt. However, Mary Anne was willing to risk everyone for her special someone. She wrote to John Chapman of her decision: "I do not wish to take the ground of ignoring what is unconventional in my position. I have counted the cost of the step I have taken and am prepared to bear, without irritation or bitterness, renunciation of all my friends. I am not mistaken in the person to whom I have attached myself." To escape the scandal, the Lewes fled to Germany, where George could work on his biography of Goethe. Mary Anne considered the trip her honeymoon. While there, they met the composer Franz Liszt, who was living with a married woman without raising eyebrows.

When they returned to England, to distract her from society's disapprobation, George encouraged her to write. With his belief in her ability, and with his editing skills, she wrote her first novel, *Adam Bede*. She published it under the nom de plume George Eliot because they felt that the novel would not sell if there was a social embargo against its author. She explained to her friend John Cross that she chose the pen name because "George was Mr. Lewes's Christian name, and Eliot was a good mouth-filling, easily pronounced word." The novel proved so popular that literary London became enthralled with the mystery writer. Charles Dickens immediately guessed that it had been penned by a woman, and Elizabeth Gaskell was flattered when she was asked if she was its author. Queen Victoria, who had been introduced to the book by her daughter Princess Louise, was also a fan. Indeed, the queen admired the novel to such an extent that she commissioned two paintings based on two of its scenes. Finally, Evans admitted authorship, and over the next few years, with the popularity of her book, society slowly began to welcome her into its circle once more.

After the publication of *Middlemarch*, which deals with the theme of common-law marriage, the Lewes purchased a magnificent home from her royalties, The Priory, near Regent's Park. They hired Owen Jones (the chief designer of the Crystal Palace) to decorate their sumptuous living room, where they entertained the most celebrated people of the day, such as Ralph Waldo Emerson, Ivan Turgenev, Richard Wagner, Charles Darwin, Aldous Huxley, and Henry James. However, her siblings, still disapproving of her church-unsanctioned relationship, continued their estrangement. It was because of disapprobation such as this that Mary Anne, although now financially and romantically secure, held steadfast in her determination not to have a child. Having been a victim of scandal, she was unwilling to bring an illegitimate baby into judgmental Victorian England.

After a time, the Lewes began to tire of their constant stream of visitors and hired John Cross to find them a country home. There they discovered that they preferred to be just with one another, and their only regular visitors were George's son Charles and their business agent, Cross, whom they took to referring to as "their dear nephew." As they took long walks together, they often repeated the phrase, "So much better than Society!"

However, their country idyll came to a tragic end in 1878, when George began to suffer from horrific nightly pains. He tried to conceal his illness from Mary Anne, but she was able to discern the truth. One month after the onset of his symptoms, Mary Anne's spiritual spouse passed away. She was so distraught that she was not able to attend his funeral and did not leave her home for a week; furthermore, she would not allow anyone to visit. She wrote, "Each day seems a new beginning—a new acquaintance with grief." For comfort she filled her diary with quotations from Tennyson's poem *In Memoriam*, which is what Queen Victoria did after the death of her beloved Prince Albert.

Mary Anne spent the next two years in mourning, devoting herself to editing George's works and establishing a student trust in his memory. As fate would have it, a few days after George's death, the Lewes's business agent, John Cross, a forty-year-old bachelor who had always lived at home, was confronted with his mother's death. In mutual grief, he and Mary Anne found themselves reading Dante together, which segued into a proposal of marriage. Desperate not to spend her remaining years alone, she accepted. Society was shocked at the age discrepancy, as she was sixty-one and he was forty, but Mary Anne was far too inured to scandal to care.

Now that Mary Anne was married, her brother, Isaac, finally came around and sent a letter of congratulation. Charles Lewes gave his father's lover away at St. George's in Hanover Square. The newlyweds honeymooned in Italy, where, sadly, John either accidentally or in an attempted suicide plunged from his hotel balcony into the Grand Canal in Venice. He survived, however, and the couple returned to London. Shortly after their arrival, Mary Anne became ill and died as a result of a kidney infection. John attempted to bury his wife in Westminster Abbey so that she could spend eternity in the proximity of other literary luminaries such as Charles Dickens, but the church refused because she had lived with George Lewes in sin.

Cross eventually buried his wife in Highgate Cemetery, in the section reserved for religious dissenters. He had her tombstone inscribed: "Here rests the body of 'George Eliot' (Mary Anne Cross)." Ironically, her epitaph does not mention the name that she always believed to be her true one: Mrs. George Henry Lewes. However, the plot next to her is that of another dissenter: George Lewes. It was fitting that the author would spend eternity with the one who had always seen her inner beauty and whose love had "conferred happiness upon her life."

6

Alice's Adventures in Wonderland

LEWIS CARROLL

(CHARLES LUTWIDGE DODGSON)

1865

Alice! A childish story take,
And, with a gentle hand,
Lay it where Childhood's dreams are twined
In Memory's mystic band,
Like pilgrim's wither'd wreath of flowers
Pluck'd in a far-off land.

ONE of the most cryptic dedications in literature is the poem Lewis Carroll wrote in *Alice's Adventures in Wonderland*. When the fictional Alice fell through the rabbit hole into an alternate reality, she said, "Curiouser and curiouser." It is a phrase that readily comes to mind when examining the relationship between the middle-aged college professor and the eleven-year-old Alice Liddell.

Their paths first crossed when Charles Dodgson became dean of Christ Church, Oxford, where Alice's father, Henry Liddell, was a mathematics professor. Liddell invited the thirty-year-old bachelor, who lived alone, to his home, whereupon Dodgson became very friendly with his children, especially his daughter Alice. From that day onward, the lives of the middle-aged teacher and the young girl would be forever intertwined.

On July 4, 1862, Dodgson, along with the Reverend Robinson Duckworth, took the three Liddell children, Lorina, Alice, and Edith, for a rowboat ride on the Thames River on their way to a picnic. To keep the youngsters entertained, he told them the adventures and misadventures of a fictional character he christened Alice, after the middle sister. The children were delighted with the stories, especially the ones that involved them. Alice was so enthralled with the tale that she begged Charles to write it down for her. That year, for Christmas, he gave her the handwritten manuscript, called *Alice's Adventures Under Ground*; alongside the script were Dodgson's illustrations. (All the members of the boating party make an appearance in chapter 3 of the book: Alice is the protagonist, Dodgson the dodo, the Reverend Duckworth is the duck, the lory is Lorina Liddell, and the eaglet is Edith Liddell.)

Encouraged by the reaction of the Liddell girls, Dodgson elaborated on the story and sent his manuscript to publishers under the pen name of Lewis Carroll. He did not want to use his own name as he felt that it would not be seemly for an Oxford professor to write a children's fantasy. The book was indeed published and became so popular that Queen Victoria contacted Dodgson and asked him to dedicate his next book to her. Hence children's literature became populated with some of its most unforgettable characters: the Mad Hatter, the White Rabbit, the Cheshire Cat, and the Queen of Hearts, to name but a few.

Around this time Dodgson took up photography, and one of his favorite subjects was Alice Liddell. One of the most well-known pictures he took shows her scantily clad; it was named "Beggar Maid."

The relationship between Dodgson and Alice came to an abrupt and caustic end when Mrs. Liddell told him he was to have no further contact with either her or her children. The news was devastating enough to make even the Cheshire Cat lose its grin.

Because Mrs. Liddell never publicly spoke about her reasons, they are open to conjecture. Similarly, Dodgson's diary, which could have shed insight into the termination, had the pages of this period ripped out by his heirs after his death. Some theories are Mrs. Liddell was upset with the pornographic nature of his photographs of her young daughter and that Dodgson was spending an unseemly amount of time with Alice. Another theory is that her breaking point came when Dodgson said he wanted to marry Alice some day. Not only did she forbid further contact, she also burned all letters that he had written to her daughter. It is safe to assume that the Queen of Hearts was not the only one to proclaim, "Off with 'his' head!"

Lewis Carroll's next publication was *Through the Looking-Glass and What Alice Found There*. This book's lengthy dedication is also to Alice, and is much more autobiographical than the first. It is also more poignant, as the two were no longer in contact. He alludes to this fact when he writes, *"No thought of me shall find a place / In thy young life's hereafter."* Here he also blames their separation on their age difference, *"and I and thou / Are half a life asunder."* The most intimate of all the verses in the dedication is the last stanza where he writes,

And, though the shadow of a sigh
May tremble through the story,

For "Happy summer days" gone by,
And vanish'd summer glory-
It shall not touch, with breath of bale,
The pleasance of our fairy-tale.

We can merely surmise what Charles Dodgson saw when he peered at himself through his own looking glass. However, what we do know for certain is that Alice Liddell was Charles Dodgson's inspiration and muse and, to whatever degree the Fates permitted, his life's Queen of Hearts.

7

The Brothers Karamazov

FYODOR DOSTOEVSKY
(FYODOR MIKHAILOVICH DOSTOEVSKY)
1880

Dedicated to
Anna Grigorevna Dostoevsky

D OSTOEVSKY once wrote, "To love someone means to see him as God intended him." This quotation helps one understand how the beautiful young Anna could have fallen in love with Fyodor, who was a sickly, destitute, epileptic gambler. And when chance brought them together, even great misfortune was not enough to drive them apart.

If one were to describe the forty-four-year-old Fyodor Dostoevsky, the adjective *fortunate* would not have been the most apt word. Tragedy surrounded the author from a young age. When he was a child, his drunken father so enraged his serfs that they murdered him by forcing copious amounts of vodka down his throat. Although the young Dostoevsky had always had an acrimonious relationship with his father, he felt guilty about his murder, perhaps because on a subconscious level he had desired for it.

Dostoevsky's first wife succumbed to tuberculosis, which was followed two months later by the death of his beloved brother from liver disease. His own health had always been precarious, stemming from the epilepsy that had first manifested itself when the author was nine years old. His fortunes were in shambles; he was always in debt, which mainly stemmed from his uncontrollable gambling problem.

In addition, when he was in his twenties, he had been arrested on orders of Czar Nicholas I for plotting against him and was sent to Siberia for execution. In his hands was placed a bible, *The Gospels*, so that he could attain peace with his Maker. When he was in front of the firing squad, he was saved by a last-minute royal reprieve. The shock of his imminent execution was to haunt him for the remainder of his life. His death penalty was commuted to four years of hard labor in Omska Gulag, Siberia. He was brought there in ten-pound ankle chains, via a sled ride that lasted for two weeks in minus-forty-degree-centigrade temperatures. This horror was followed by another five years of compulsory military service. Into this man's despair-filled life, however, was soon to come a desperately needed ray of light: Anna Grigorevna Snitkina.

In October 1866, Dostoevsky's life was at critical mass, as he was tens of thousands of rubles in debt. Ever the gambler, he had made a bet with his publisher that he would submit his next novel within the next eighteen months. The consequence for his failure to meet the November 1 deadline was he would lose his publishing rights for all his works, including all past, present, and future novels. One month was left and the author, plagued by depression, epilepsy, and obsessive gambling, had not managed to put down a single word on paper. A friend suggested he hire a stenographer to help with his problem. Dostoevsky contacted a business college in St. Petersburg, and they sent over a twenty-year-old stenographer,

Anna Grigorevna Snitkina. When she knocked at his apartment door on Malaya Meshanskaya Street, little did she dream that her fate lay over the threshold—and what a fate it would be.

During the next four weeks, the two of them worked at a feverish pace to finish the novel in time. While Dostoevsky poured out a torrent of words from his ever-tortured soul, Anna, in her unique style of shorthand, committed his ravings to paper. During this time, working every day and long into the evening, the author found his emotions toward his young employee evolving from business to friendship to romance.

Together they completed *The Gambler* before the deadline. The writer was anxious that their relationship continue; however, feeling that the pretty young girl would have nothing to do with an older, sick, and depressive man, he was afraid to reveal his affection. He decided instead to couch his romantic interest in the guise of a projected idea for a new novel. He asked Anna if she thought that a plot involving the romance between a tormented, ill, older man and a beautiful, uncomplicated girl was psychologically probable. When she replied that she thought it possible, he revealed that the two of them were who he really had in mind. She answered that she knew.

Dostoevsky and Anna were married in February at the Trinity Zmailorsky Cathedral. However, the bride did not have the wedding most girls envision. Dostoevsky consumed such a vast quantity of champagne during the festivities that it led to an extremely violent epileptic attack. As their horrified guests looked on, the author writhed on the floor in agony, frothing at the mouth. Anna, in her wedding dress, sat on the floor and placed his head in her lap for several hours, until his convulsions subsided. This was the first time that she had witnessed his condition. When it was over, he was utterly incoherent and carried on like a madman. Later he confided to her that he believed that he was going to die during one of these seizures, and, for the rest of his life, when he had one, Anna would not leave his side.

Although the new couple was madly in love, their marriage was dampened by financial difficulties. Creditors constantly knocked at their door, demanding that Dostoevsky make good on his promissory notes. Once again, Anna saved Fyodor. She pawned everything they owned and arranged for herself and her husband to flee Russia, thereby escaping their disastrous financial situation. She hoped that in a new place, Fyodor would have the peace of mind to write and recoup their finances. They planned on being away for four months but ended up staying away for four years. Unfortunately, if there was one thing that they did not attain in their time in Europe, it was peace.

Initially their sojourn abroad started out in a promising fashion. Secure and happy in his marriage, Doestoevsky was able to write *The Idiot*. However, the lure of the roulette table was too strong an attraction, and he often strayed from his home to the gaming tables. His ardor did not match his success, and he lost such large sums that he had to pawn Anna's jewelry. Once he even had to trade her wedding ring, but he was able to win it back at a later date. He returned it with champagne, flowers, and remorse. His usual pattern after losing at gambling was to throw himself at his wife's feet and beg forgiveness. It was always forthcoming.

In 1867, the Dostoevskys were overjoyed when Anna gave birth to their daughter Sonya. Because fatherhood had come late in life, and he had suffered so many losses, the new father doted on his child's every move. They were devastated when, at three months old, Sonya developed a cold that led to her death. Heartsick, Fyodor longed for the familiarity of his homeland, but they were unable to afford the passage back to Russia. Then, in Germany, Anna gave birth to another daughter, Lyubov, and two sons, Fyodor and Alexi. Tragically, Alexi died at age three, after an epileptic seizure. Finally, borrowing money from friends and relatives, the Dostoevsky family returned home.

Once back in St. Petersburg, after publishing *Crime and Punishment* and *The Brothers Karamazov*, Fyodor was finally the famous writer he had always dreamed of becoming. In a strange twist of fate, the czar now hired the man whom he had once condemned to death as a tutor for his royal nephews and welcomed him in the Winter Palace. To complement his professional life, Fyodor was content in a home filled with the love of Anna and their children.

However, his long-awaited serenity was to have a short lease. In 1881, after an acrimonious conversation with his sister regarding a family inheritance, Fyodor began to hemorrhage from this throat. Two days later, Anna awoke late at night to find him wide awake. He informed her that the next day would be his last. She tried to reason with him, but to no avail. Ever the writer, he was determined to script his own demise. He told her to get *The Gospels*, the same one he had received on the eve of his Siberian execution. She read him the parable of the Prodigal Son. This time he was unable to avoid his appointment with death.

At Dostoevsky's funeral, forty thousand people came to pay their respects to St. Petersburg's own prodigal son. On his tomb Anna had inscribed the biblical words from the frontispiece to *The Brothers Karamazov*: "Verily, verily, I say unto you. Except a corn of wheat fall into the ground and die, it abideth alone: but if it die, it bringeth forth much fruit" (John 12:24).

Anna never ceased mourning the loss of her husband, and devoted herself to recording the shorthand notes she had faithfully kept during her marriage, in order to pen her memoirs. Of her fourteen-year marriage, despite often dwelling in an abyss of despair, she stated that they were the happiest years of her life.

8

The Adventures of Tom Sawyer

MARK TWAIN

(SAMUEL LANGHORNE CLEMENS)

1884

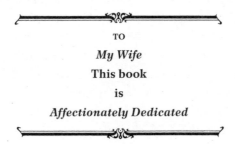

TO

My Wife

This book

is

Affectionately Dedicated

THE genesis of the dedication to *The Adventures of Tom Sawyer* was not, as one would assume, born against the backdrop of the Mississippi River, but rather in the mid–Atlantic Ocean. It began with an object that fit into the author's hand.

Samuel Langhorne Clemens was, to use the adjective commonly associated with an unmarried man, a *confirmed bachelor*. As he wrote to his old Hannibal friend William Bowen, "Marry be d _ _ _ _d. I am too old to marry. I am nearly 31. I have got gray hairs in my head. Women appear to like me, but d _ _ _ _ d, they don't love me." Another reason why he did not want to embark on the road to holy matrimony was he felt that he was not rich enough to wed. His philosophy was a wife was supposed to be a companion, and that was to be her only job. He stated, "I don't want to sleep with a three-fold Being who is cook, chambermaid and washer-woman all in one." Clemens, however, should have paid attention to the Bernard Shaw adage "We men chase women—until they catch us."

Clemens's desire to remain a bachelor changed in 1869, when, in his role as a reporter, he was aboard the ocean liner *Quaker City*, on his way to tour Europe and the Holy Land. One evening, he went to the luxurious suite of Charles Langdon, a man he had met during the voyage. While there, Charles showed him a miniature ivory portrait of his sister Olivia. King Pygmalion fell in love with a statue; Samuel did the same with a portrait.

It was understandable, then, when he accepted Charles's invitation to have dinner with his family at the old St. Nicholas Hotel once they returned to New York City, where the Langdons were vacationing. Shortly afterward, Clemens took Olivia, whom he called Livy, to Steinway Hall, where Charles Dickens was giving a reading. Years later Clemens was able to recall most details from that memorable night. The famed British author was dressed in a black velvet coat, which contrasted with the red flower in his buttonhole. The text he read from was *David Copperfield*; the scene featured the storm in which the character James Steerforth dies. However, Clemens remembers he was far more impressed with his date than with Dickens. He was thrilled that Olivia's personality matched the perfection promised in her portrait. Long afterward he remarked of that evening, "It was forty years ago. From that day to this she has never been out of my mind." Throughout their marriage he often remarked how Olivia was indistinguishable from the angels.

The New York City rendezvous was followed by a visit to

the nearby town of Elmira, where, within two weeks, Samuel declared his love. However, her response was that he was going to have to reform his ways before she would have him. Specifically, she wanted him to stop smoking, swearing, and drinking, and to start attending church. The last lines of *The Adventures of Huckleberry Finn* show Huck's reluctance at getting tamed: "But I reckon I got to light out for the Territory ahead of the rest because Aunt Sally she's going to adopt me and sivilize me and I can't stand it. I been there before." However, for Olivia, Samuel was willing to embark upon the road of reformation.

After a period of two years, in which they exchanged hundreds of letters, Clemens was ecstatic when Olivia agreed to become Mrs. Samuel Clemens. They were married in her family's lavish parlor, and then moved to Buffalo into a house that was a present from his wealthy father-in-law. The year following their marriage was a happy one. The new couple enjoyed setting up house, and Samuel worked as a journalist for the *Buffalo Express,* a newspaper of which he was a partial owner. During this period, Clemens began to receive proofs from *The Innocents Abroad* (which was a memoir of his trip on the *Quaker*). He gave these drafts to his wife, who diligently edited every word, a labor of love that she would continue to do until the months before her death. Samuel wrote, "Mrs. Clemens has kept a lot of things from getting into print that might have given me a reputation I wouldn't care to have, and that I wouldn't have known any better than to have published."

What added to their happiness during this time was the birth of their son Langdon and their daughter Olivia Susan. However, when their daughter was a newborn, a series of three tragedies occurred. First, Livy's father died, which was followed by the death of her close friend who was staying at their home.

Then, Langdon, who had been a frail, premature baby, passed away at two years old from diphtheria. Their love for one another and their daughter helped them get through this heartrending period.

Fortunately, good times soon appeared on the horizon. Having made a substantial amount of money, Clemens was finally able to purchase a home that was the equivalent of the one his Livy had grown up in. His mansion in Hartford, Connecticut, was the biggest and most elaborate in the city. It boasted five bathrooms and nineteen bedrooms (where he could indulge in his constant cigar smoking without irritating his wife). He smoked as many as forty cigars a day, but, as he told Livy, he "never smoked more than one at a time." The marital bed was black and decorated with engravings of the angels, of whom he joked his Livy was one. The bedrooms were soon occupied by their three daughters: Olivia Susan (Susy), Clara Langdon, and Jane Lamton (Jean), as well as the Clemens's many cats, some of which the author often carried on his shoulders. Their names were Lazy, Pestilence, Famine, Satan, and Sin. On the occasions when he felt sad, he played hymns on the piano. Their neighbor, who lived in a modest cottage, was the person whom President Lincoln had referred to as "the little woman who had started that big war," the author of *Uncle Tom's Cabin*, Harriet Beecher Stowe.

Content with his children, wife, and luxurious lifestyle, which was far removed from his childhood home in Hannibal, Clemens, writing under the pseudonym of Mark Twain, enjoyed his greatest literary output: *The Adventures of Tom Sawyer*, *The Adventures of Huckleberry Finn*, *A Connecticut Yankee in King Arthur's Court*, and *The Prince and the Pauper*. The latter novel's dedication is "To

Those Good-Mannered and Agreeable Children Susie and Clara Clemens This Book Is Affectionately Inscribed By Their Father." One of his later and lesser-known works, *Personal Recollections of Joan of Arc*, was dedicated to Olivia: "To My Wife Olivia Langton Clemens This Book is tendered on our wedding anniversary in grateful recognition of her twenty-five years of valued service as my literary adviser and editor 1870–1895 The Author."

However, the cloud that hung over the mansion was a financial one. Although Clemens was making money from the sales of his books, his elaborate lifestyle, especially his home, was causing a financial strain. Another problem was Clemens was a far better writer than he was an investor. In one misbegotten venture, he invested $200,000, losing the entire amount. Ironically, when he had the opportunity to invest in Alexander Graham Bell's new invention, the telephone, he declined.

Whenever Clemens was in a financial straitjacket, however, he was able to go on a world lecture tour, and thereby pad his bank account. In 1891, Clemens shut down his expensive Hartford home and took his wife and three daughters to Europe, where they lived for a decade in various countries such as France, Germany, Switzerland, and Italy. While there they met some of the greatest luminaries of the era: Kaiser Wilhelm II, Prince Edward (the Prince of Wales), Mahatma Gandhi, Sigmund Freud, Emperor Franz Josef I, and Winston Churchill, to name but a few.

Samuel Clemens had derived his pen name "Mark Twain" from a nautical term used by ferrymen on the Mississippi River. Marking the twain meant that the water was at least two fathoms deep, thereby safe for a journey by water. Tragically, in the 1890s, the waters of Clemens's life had reached a dangerously low level. In 1896, while on another European tour, the Clemenses were notified that their eldest daughter, Susie, who had remained in the States, had died from meningitis. In his autobiography he wrote of his daughter's demise, "It is one of the mysteries of our nature that a man, all unprepared, can receive a thunder-stroke like that and live."

Still reeling from this devastating blow, Livy became extremely ill. On her doctor's recommendation, she moved to Florence, Italy, in the hope that the mild climate would restore her health. It did not, and in 1904 it was her time to truly join the angels.

Two years later Clemens published *Eve's Diary*. At Eve's passing, Adam said, "Wheresoever she was, there was Eden." After Olivia's demise, life was the equivalent of a lost Eden to her bereft husband.

The third loss was the death of his youngest daughter, Jean, in 1909. These threefold tragedies bring to mind the Shakespearean quotation, "When sorrows come, they come not in single spies, but in battalions."

Deeply depressed, Clemens stopped writing. Instead he would spend hours at the piano, playing a dirge for his lost loved ones. In this state of mind, his health began to rapidly deteriorate. When Samuel Clemens was born, Halley's Comet had streaked across the sky. It did not reappear until the night of his death, seventy-four years later. Clemens was buried in the family plot in Elmira, where he lies beside the woman with whom he had fallen in love, before he had even met her. On the tail of Halley's Comet, he was able to return to his Eden, and to his Eve.

9

The Wonderful Wizard of Oz

L. Frank Baum

(Lyman Frank Baum)

1900

This book is dedicated to my
Good friend & comrade.
My Wife.
L.F.B.

In *The Wonderful Wizard of Oz*, Dorothy tells the Scarecrow, "There is no place like home." What made home so wonderful for author L. Frank Baum was the presence of his wife, Maud Gage Baum.

Maud met Frank when she was a student at Cornell University, where she shared a room with Josie Baum. In true matchmaker fashion, Josie had insisted that her friend meet her cousin Frank Baum. At a Christmas party in 1881, Josie's mother, Josephine, was the one to actually introduce them. She did this by taking Maud by the arm over to where Frank was standing and saying, "This is my nephew, Frank. Frank, I want you to know Maud Gage. I'm sure you will love her." His response was, "Consider yourself loved, Miss Gage." Her rejoinder was, "Thank you, Mr. Baum.

That's a promise. Please see that you live up to it." Frank spent his life dedicated to that promise.

When Frank proposed to Maud, her mother, Matilda Joslyn Gage, opposed the marriage. She told her daughter that Frank was an impractical dreamer who would never make a living. However, when she realized that her daughter was going to get married with or without her blessing, she relented, and the reception was held in the parlor of Matilda's home.

At the beginning of their marriage, Frank worked in the world that he loved best, in theater in New York. However, when Maud became pregnant, he decided that he had to make a steady living for his wife and child, and moved to South Dakota, where they opened a dry goods store. Because he extended too much credit to his poor customers, the store went bankrupt. (Drought-ridden South Dakota was later to become the prototype for gray Kansas in *The Wizard of Oz*.) The Baums moved once again, this time to Chicago, where Frank worked as a newspaper reporter. The family now consisted of four sons, and Maud's mother, Matilda, often stayed with them.

One evening, while the family was gathered around the fire-place in their den, Frank began telling the story of a young boy who was carried away by a cyclone to a magical land. When one of his sons asked the name of the magical land, Frank, glancing at the filing cabinet labeled O–Z, replied, "Oz." With his wife's encouragement, he started to write down his stories, with an eye to publication. Maud was, in this manner, the mother of Oz.

During this time Maud went to visit her sister Helen, whose daughter Dorothy Louise Gage was seriously ill. After the baby's death, Maud was inconsolable. She had loved the baby as the daughter she never had. Frank, to comfort his wife, changed the gender of his protagonist and named her after the little girl, just substituting her middle initial in her surname. Frank, in his fashion, had given Maud back her Dorothy. Aunt Em was named after his mother-in-law, who always signed her name *M* for Matilda, and Uncle Henry was named after his father-in-law. When *The Wonderful Wizard of Oz* was published in 1900, Frank was finally freed from the Atlas burden of financial fear.

Because of Frank's precarious health, the Baums moved from Chicago to California. At first they settled in Coronado, California, where they often dined at the historic Hotel del Coronado. Because of this, oftentimes at Christmas, the hotel places a giant tree in its lobby, covered with ornaments from the movie version of *The Wizard of Oz*.

The Baums' last move was to Hollywood, where they bought a house they christened Ozcot, and obtained a puppy, of course named Toto. Frank covered an entire wall of their home with his favorite pictures of his wife, taken from various times during their thirty-two-year marriage. He christened it his "Yard of Maud." On the back of one picture of himself, he wrote the inscription, "To my own Sweet Love. The image of your baby. December, 1899."

In *The Wonderful Wizard of Oz,* the most poignant line is spoken by the Wizard, after the Tin Man approaches him to request a heart. "I think you are wrong to want a heart. It makes most people unhappy. If you only knew it, you are in luck not to have a heart." The truth of his words was something Maud could understand all too well because her husband lay dying. With his passing, she would forever more be denied entry to the Emerald City. Frank's last words to her were, "Now we can cross the shifting sands." His solace, at the end, was that he was with his "good friend & comrade—his wife."

10

De Profundis

OSCAR WILDE
(OSCAR FINGAL O'FLAHERTIE WILLS WILDE)
1905

Dear Bosie,

DE Profundis is the longest and most heartfelt letter ever published. The entire text is dedicated to Lord Alfred Douglas, who lifted Oscar to the most dizzying heights of love, only to plunge him to the lowest rung of despair. It was for this reason its name was derived from the Latin translation of Psalm 130, "from the depths." Wilde's "The Ballad of Reading Gaol" states, "Yet each man kills the thing he loves," and that is what Bosie did to Oscar, with a Judas kiss.

Alfred was the third son of the ninth Marquis of Queensberry and his first wife. He was idolized and overindulged by his mother, of whom he was the favorite, and it was she who gave him the nickname of Bosie, which stuck for the rest of his life. As much as Alfred idolized his mother, he detested his father, who likewise felt extreme contempt for his effeminate son. The marquis, a man's man interested in boxing, race horses, and fox hunting, was repelled by his son who was interested in clothes, poetry, and other men.

The man who would forever alter Alfred's life—Oscar—was born in Ireland, the son of Sir William Wilde, a renowned ear and eye surgeon, and Jane Francesca Elgee, a successful writer. After graduating from Oxford University, Oscar returned to Dublin, where he met and became interested in Florence Balcombe. However, she bypassed his attention for another Irish writer, Bram Stoker. Oscar, his ego more bruised than his heart, left for London, where he met and married Constance Lloyd. Wilde probably was aware of his homosexual proclivities at the time of his wedding but hoped that marriage would "cure him." The couple had two sons, Cyril (who was killed in France in World War I) and Vyvyan (who would later write his memoirs of his infamous father).

Oscar Wilde met Lord Alfred Douglas when the two were introduced in Chelsea by the poet Lionel Johnson. Alfred was a twenty-two-year-old student, and Oscar was a thirty-seven-year-old man-about-town. Johnson brought along Alfred when he was invited to tea at Oscar's home. Wilde was a moth drawn to the flame of Alfred's blond hair and blue eyes, their mutual love of language, and Douglas's eminent family name. Oscar was later to write of him, "He is quite like a narcissus—so white and gold...he lies like a hyacinth on the sofa and I worship him."

Soon the two were a couple, being overtly affectionate while dining at London's finest restaurants and most luxurious hotels. They also took trips, vacationing in Paris and Algiers. In the summer they lived in an estate on the English coast. Of course, the flamboyant Irish playwright, dressed in outlandish clothes and accompanied by a member of the peerage, never went unnoticed. However, Wilde did not care. He wrote, "The only thing worse than being talked about is not being talked about." Apparently, "Wilde" was not merely a surname. Together they founded an informal gathering of "the Society for the Suppression of Virtue."

While the courtship of Oscar and Alfred continued for four years, the Marquis of Queensbury was infuriated his son was consorting with the most notorious homosexual of the era, whom he disparagingly referred to as "the high priest of decadence." He did everything in his power to break up their affair. One of his first moves was to show up at Wilde's house, accompanied by a champion boxer. They angrily shoved Oscar's servant aside and proceeded to the ground-floor study, shouting obscenities along the way. Wilde's reaction was to sarcastically inquire as to whether he owed the pleasure of the uninvited visit to the marquis's desire to apologize for the rude public remarks that he was making all over London about him. When the marquis finally left, he did so accompanied by Wilde's parting remark, made in reference to the boxing rules that the nobleman had recently endorsed: "I do not know what the Queensberry rules are, but the Wilde rules are to shoot on sight!" The marquis decided that the next round should be fought in the public arena.

On the opening night of *The Importance of Being Earnest*, the marquis bought a ticket, with the plan of making a scene whereby he would inform the audience about the moral bankruptcy of the playwright. However, as someone had tipped Wilde off, guards prevented the marquis from entering the theater. When that didn't pan out, armed with some rotten vegetables, he tried to get in through the stage door but was prevented by the police, who had also been alerted to his intentions. Ironically enough, the marquis was not the one who initiated the downfall of Oscar Wilde.

One night the marquis went to the Albemarle Club, which Oscar and Alfred frequented, and left a card with the porter. On it was written: "For Oscar Wilde, posing somdomite." (Apparently, spelling was not the lord's strong point.) When Alfred saw the note, he was incensed, and also saw it as an opportunity to destroy the father whom he abhorred. To this end, he cajoled his lover to charge his father with libel, citing the incendiary note. Wilde was reluctant to do so, and this feeling was shared by his fellow Irish friend Bernard Shaw. The playwright warned Wilde that it would be madness to take on someone with the power and prestige of the peerage. In addition, it was absurd for him to invoke the law when he knew, because of his sexual preferences, that he was living in defiance of it. However, unable to be rational when Bosie begged, he took the marquis to court.

Tragically, Oscar should have stuck with writing dramas rather than starring in his own. The calling-card libel suit became a cause célèbre as increasingly salacious details appeared in the press. The prosecution charged that the marquis's actions were justified, as Wilde was a homosexual corrupter of youth. He was also charged with the crime of sodomy, a shortened form of "the sins of Sodom," and, like the inhabitants of that biblical city, the Victorians felt he, too, deserved to be destroyed.

Oscar could have been saved if Alfred had testified on his lover's behalf, declaring the relationship was not coerced, but consensual. However, when the debris from the trial started to fly, Alfred fled England for Calais. Oscar dropped his charges, but he in turn was charged with acts of "gross indecency," which was the indictment of homosexuality—not only immoral, but illegal, in nineteenth-century England. Indeed, it was euphemistically referred to "as the love that dare not speak its name," which, incidentally, was a term coined by Alfred in one of his poems. Wilde was arrested and had to appear in court in chains. Moreover, when forced to repay Queensberry six hundred pounds for the latter's defense, Oscar went bankrupt and was forced to part with his editions of his first books as well as artwork by his friends Whistler and Bearsdley.

Wilde was found guilty and sentenced to two years of hard labor in Reading Gaol, where he was known as prisoner C.3.3. (he was incarcerated in block C, floor three, cell three). The erstwhile man-about-town had lost his liberty, his wealth, and his beloved Bosie. And more grief was to follow. Constance (now going by the surname Holland to distance herself from the scandal) came to deliver the heartrending news that his mother had passed away. Also, in the same tragic vein, the courts terminated his parental rights, and he lost custody of his two sons.

During his imprisonment, Oscar wrote *De Profundis*, taking advantage of prison stipulations that letters were the only form of writing that was permitted. However, when the fifty-thousand-word letter was completed, prison officials did not allow him to send it to Alfred Douglas. Instead, upon his release, Wilde gave it to his close friend and onetime lover Robert Ross to deliver to Bosie. Ross (the man to whom Wilde had dedicated *The Importance of Being Earnest*) ended up only giving a copy to Douglas, which the latter never acknowledged and probably destroyed.

De Profundis is one of the most unique letters in literature. On one level, it is a traditional love letter, which simultaneously pours out the author's equal amounts of affection and fury at Lord Alfred Douglas, interlaced with an impassioned plea for reconciliation upon his release. It also serves as an elegy for Oscar Wilde's own lost greatness. In a larger sense, Wilde made it not only an individual proclamation of love but also a universal meditation on human suffering.

When Wilde entrusted the letter to Ross, who was the truest love of Oscar's life, the author stipulated that it was not to be published until fifty years after his demise. However, Ross ended up publishing a greatly expurgated version (a third of it) in 1905, four years after Oscar's death. He shared more of the intimate contents of *De Profundis* when he issued *The Collected Works of Oscar Wilde* in 1908. After this, he donated the original letter to the British Museum, with the caveat that it not be made public, in its entirety, until 1960.

Bosie had effectively "killed the thing he loved." In Oscar's play *Salome*, after performing a provocative dance for her stepfather, Salome demanded in payment the head of John the Baptist. In this case, art imitated life; in reality it was the playwright's own head that had been severed, the unwitting architect, his lover, Lord Alfred Douglas.

Upon his release from prison, Oscar Wilde was a persona non grata in London. He was a convicted homosexual, his plays had been removed from all marquees, and he had become the person whom polite society shunned. In disgrace, he left for France, but, lonely and bored, he felt he had merely traded one prison for another. In exile, he went by the assumed name of Sebastian Melmoth, based on Saint Sebastian, who was martyred when his body was pierced by arrows. When he peered into the horizon of his future, he could not bear to see the emptiness that lay there.

It was into this bleak landscape that Bosie reappeared, and the two left to winter in Naples. However, the ghosts and sins of the past weighed too heavily between them, and they separated for the last time. Wilde finally was able to see the true face of Dorian Gray. Oscar returned alone to Paris, where he rented a cheap, dreary room in a Left Bank hotel. Bereft, he no longer had anything to live for. Reportedly, his last words, while looking at the ugly wallpaper of his rented room were "My wallpaper and I are fighting a duel to the death. One or the other of us has to go." It was there that he lost his last fight. On his deathbed, he was comforted by the ever-loyal Ross, who arranged for a Roman Catholic priest to administer the Last Rites. He hired a sculptor, Sir Jacob Epstein, to design Oscar's tomb in Pere Lachaise cemetery; in addition, he made arrangements for a small compartment where his own ashes could later be interred, which they were, in 1950. One of the tragedies of Wilde's life was, for all his great wit, he did not possess the wisdom to realize who his true love really was. It was the fatal flaw of not being able to distinguish the shadow from the substance that sealed his doom.

Hopefully, as the great dramatist lay dying, he was able to blot out not only the ugliness of the wallpaper, but the ugliness of his life: his trial, his imprisonment, the loss of his two sons, his career, and his lover. However, maybe death gave Oscar the mercy he had been denied in life and drew a curtain over the pain, so that when he departed this world for the next, he only remembered the time when he had been the toast of London, and basking in the limelight and his love was his "Dear Bosie."

11

The Murder on the Links

Agatha Christie

(Agatha Mary Clarissa Miller Christie Mallowan)

1923

**TO MY HUSBAND. A fellow enthusiast for
detective stories and to whom I am indebted
for much helpful advice and criticism.**

ONE of Agatha Christie's greatest mysteries emanated not
from her pen, but from the pages of her own life. In her later
years, she went missing—her disappearance instigating a national
search. Her literary sleuth, Hercule Poirot, once remarked, "It is
the brain, the little gray cells on which one must rely. One must
seek the truth within—not without." And while the exact details
of her disappearance are still unclear, it does not take a copious
number of gray cells to grasp that, on some level, the mystery of
Agatha's vanishing was connected to the one to whom *The Murder on the Links* is dedicated.

Agatha Mary Clarissa Miller was born in Torquay, a place
where she would—when not on her extensive travels—spend
most of her life. In her early years, she was home-schooled, which
suited her shy personality. Her extreme reticence stayed with her

throughout her life; she rarely spoke to strangers first. At age five, she taught herself to read, and later became an avid fan of Sir Arthur Conan Doyle. She also began writing stories, with the help of her nanny, dolls, and pets. Of this period Agatha recalled, "For some years I enjoyed myself very much writing stories of unrelieved gloom where most of the characters died." This childhood pursuit was to serve as the dress rehearsal for her life's calling.

Because of her propensity for music and dance, her doting mother, Clara, sent her to Paris when she was sixteen, with the hope that she might become an opera star or concert pianist. However, because of her intense stage fright, any type of public performance was out of the question. After her graduation, Agatha and Clara embarked on the exciting adventure of a three-month tour of Egypt, which was at that time a fashionable "wintering" spot for English society. When she returned, it was to another type of adventure—one of a romantic nature.

Agatha met Archibald Christie at a party for soldiers stationed in Exeter. He was a colonel in the Royal Field Artillery and had the allure of an intrepid aviator. They danced together for most of the evening. She described her partner as "a tall, fair young man, with crisp curly hair, a rather interesting nose, turned up not down, and a great deal of careless confidence about him." For the next few weeks, Archie made "frequent and unexpected appearances." On Christmas Eve 1914, after a whirlwind courtship, the two were married. A brief time later, her new husband was called to the Continent to fight in World War I. Upon his departure, the twenty-four-year-old Agatha began volunteering as a nurse at a Red Cross hospital in Torquay, where she took a post in the dispensary. There she gained an intimate knowledge of pharmaceutical drugs, material she would later employ in her books.

To help pass the solitary evenings, Agatha continued to indulge in her childhood pastime of reading mysteries. In 1916, she and her sister, Madge, were discussing Sherlock Holmes when Christie said she wanted to try her hand at penning her own. When Madge expressed skepticism, the dare proved the catalyst for Agatha. In order to obtain the right ambience, she checked into the Moorland Hotel in Dartmoor. In just three weeks she had completed her first novel, *The Mysterious Affair at Styles*; its dedication read, "To my Mother."

The book featured the debut of her famous Belgian detective Hercule Poirot, the quirky yet logical sleuth who became an icon of whodunit until his final appearance in *Curtain*. One of Poirot's quotations was, "Understand this, I mean to arrive at the truth. The truth, however ugly in itself, is always curious and beautiful to the seeker after it." In Christie's autobiography, she wrote that Poirot's nationality was arrived at due to the many Belgian refugees who were in Torquay during World War I.

When Archibald returned, their only child was born; she was christened Rosalind after the heroine in Shakespeare's *As You Like It*. To an outsider looking in, it appeared the Christies had an idyllic life. Agatha was an accomplished writer, the author of six well-received novels. She said she would plot them in a hot bath while eating apples. One of these was *Murder on the Links*, which she dedicated to her husband. The setting was inspired by their shared passion for golf and a course that was in close proximity to their magnificent home, Styles (so named after the success of Christie's debut novel). Her latest book, *The Murder of Roger Ackroyd*, had brought wealth as well as fame. Indeed, Agatha made more profit out of murder than any woman since Lucrezia Borgia.

In 1926, Christie became extremely depressed over the passing of her beloved mother after a brief illness, and went to France for a month to help distance herself from the pain. One morning over breakfast, she had an extremely acrimonious argument with Colonel Christie. The reason for the fight was his announcement that he was leaving for the weekend in order to spend it with his mistress, Nancy Neele, a younger woman with whom he had fallen in love. He then topped off that bombshell with another: he wanted a divorce. After the huge row, he left for his tryst. Agatha, always highly sensitive, and who had been of the persuasion her marital vows were truly "till death do us part" was shaken to her core. As one of her characters had stated, "But surely for everything you love you have to pay some price."

The evening of December 3 was the beginning of Agatha's own why-dunit, rather than a whodunit. At 9:45 p.m. she wrote two notes, a scathing one to her husband and the other to her secretary, telling the latter to cancel her reservations for lodgings in Yorkshire. She also sent a letter to the deputy chief constable in Surrey, stating that her life was in danger and she was in dire need of help. She went upstairs to kiss her sleeping seven-year-old daughter and then drove away in her black Morris Cowley sports car, carrying one small bag.

Her servants raised the alarm when she had not returned by the following morning. Later that day, her car was discovered in a small body of water, the Silent Pool, which had been part of the setting of one her novels. It was situated a few miles from Styles, near the hotel where her husband was with his lover. The vehicle was abandoned and covered in frost, with the lights left on. Inside was Agatha's expired driver's license, her fur coat, and her suitcase containing some clothing.

Because of Christie's fame, her disappearance made front-page news across the country and appeared on the cover of the *New York Times*. The frenzy to find the author was so intense that the home secretary, William Joynson-Hicks, put extra pressure on the police. The search marked the first time in British history that airplanes were used as part of a search party. Fifteen thousand volunteers combed the surrounding countryside, along with body-sniffing dogs. The celebrated crime writer Sir Arthur Conan Doyle was drawn into the investigation as well, in the hope that his literary sleuthing would find a counterpart in real life; he even took Christie's discarded glove to a medium in search of a clue.

When news of his wife's disappearance and his private indiscretion were made public, Archie found himself the object of intense suspicion, with his countrymen either conjecturing that he had murdered his wife or driven her to suicide. The phones at Styles were tapped and the police shadowed his every movement. His reaction was to play the part of the concerned husband, and he offered £500 for information. Rosalind was devastated by both her mother's vanishing and her father's suspected role in it.

Eleven days later, the Mistress of Mystery was found, but the discovery only intensified the enigma. She had checked in to the posh Harrogate Hydropathic Hotel (now the Old Swan Hotel). Bizarrely, she had registered as Mrs. Teresa Neele, taking the surname of Archibald's mistress, and informed fellow guests she was visiting from Cape Town. She took out an advertisement in the *Times* requesting, "Friends and relatives of Teresa Neele, late of South Africa, please communicate—Write Box R 702, EC4."

Guests later reported that "Mrs. Neele" did the Charleston to the strains of "Yes, we have no bananas," played bridge, did crosswords, and read the newspapers, where she was featured in the headlines. Several guests recognized her as the subject of the massive manhunt, but she denied she was the missing celebrity. However, as suspicion grew, one of the hotel's musicians contacted the authorities, and for his efforts received the hundred-pound police reward. Archie was notified and upon his arrival Agatha exclaimed, "Fancy, my brother has just arrived." On her return to Styles, she was photographed smiling.

Two main theories evolved after the eleven-day stunt. One was that the mystery writer had created a real-life plot, one where her philandering husband would be humiliated for his adultery and implicated for murder. Thereby the woman scorned would have exacted the perfect revenge. Another was that Agatha had suffered a form of amnesia, brought on by the twin traumas of her mother's sudden death and her husband's heartrending infidelity. Dame Christie (as she was called after the queen so honored her) never commented on the exception to her otherwise scandal-free years.

Agatha described her breakup with Archibald: "So, after illness, came sorrow, despair, and heartbreak. There is no need to dwell on it. I stood out for a year, hoping he would change. But he did not. So ended my first married life." Agatha had traveled far from the dedication page where she had paid tribute to her husband to whom she had been "indebted for much helpful advice and criticism."

12

The Great Gatsby

F. Scott Fitzgerald
(Francis Scott Key Fitzgerald)

1925

**ONCE AGAIN
TO
ZELDA**

The title of one of Fitzgerald's novels, *The Beautiful and the Damned*, could serve as an encapsulated biography of Scott and Zelda. Like the decade that Fitzgerald himself christened "The Jazz Age," their relationship started off in dizzying triumph and ended in stark tragedy.

The star-crossed lovers met during World War I, when Fitzgerald was stationed at Camp Sheridan in Alabama. In 1918, at a dance at the Montgomery Country Club, they first saw each other, and Scott was as enchanted as Romeo was when he first spied Juliet. However, whereas Romeo says of Juliet, "It seems she hangs upon the cheek of night / As a rich jewel in an Ethiop's ear," Fitzgerald referred to Zelda as the "top cat." He may have thus dubbed her because of her beauty, her wild personality, or her position in society: Her father was a judge on Alabama's Supreme

Court. Within a month, the smitten Scott was declaring his love. In the frontispiece to *The Great Gatsby*, Fitzgerald wrote a verse that echoes his passion for Zelda: "Then wear the gold hat, if that will move her; / If you can bounce high, bounce for her too, / Till she cry 'Lover, gold-hatted, high-bouncing lover, / I must have you.'" Zelda said she returned his love but would not consider him marriage material because of his bleak economic prospects. Before he left the training camp, his friends and Zelda presented him with the gift of a silver hip flask, with the engraving: "To 1st Lt. F. Scott Fitzgerald / 65th Infantry / Camp Sheridan / Forget-me-not / Zelda / 9-13-18."

Scott returned to his childhood home in St. Paul and began to work on *This Side of Paradise*. When it was accepted by Scribner's in 1919, Zelda agreed to become Mrs. Fitzgerald, and they were married in St. Patrick's Cathedral in New York City. With the popularity of Fitzgerald's novel, coupled with the fact that he was wed to the quintessential flapper, Scott, with his wife, became the toast of New York, and their every move—when they jumped into the Plaza Hotel fountain fully clothed, or when, for a party, they drained a swimming pool and filled it with bootleg liquor—was faithfully chronicled in the tabloids. In 1921, in St. Paul, Frances Scott Fitzgerald (Scottie) was born. However, the birth of their only child failed to bring emotional stability to their lives.

Throughout the 1920s, despite Fitzgerald's literary successes and the fact that Scott and Zelda were perceived as the golden couple, their lives were beset with problems. One of their demons was alcohol. Scott was so deeply dependent on the bottle that he had his own private bootlegger, and would typically binge-drink at a speakeasy until he would pass out and was sent home in a taxi. Another problem that added stress to their lives was of a financial nature. Although Fitzgerald was earning a great deal of money from the sale of his novels, the family was adept at spending more than was coming in. The Fitzgeralds typically went through $30,000 a year, which was an astounding amount at that time.

However, the greatest cloud that hung over their heads was Zelda's fight with the demons that threatened her ever-fragile mental stability. Partly to escape their troubles, they left the States for Europe, but sorrows, like Hemingway's Paris, proved "a moveable feast."

A further problem that plagued the author was his wife's obsessive jealousy. She was envious of her husband's writing ability, and revealed as much when she said in an interview, "It seems to me that on one page I recognized a portion of an old diary of mine which mysteriously disappeared shortly after my marriage and also scraps of letters which, though considerably edited, sound to me vaguely familiar. In fact, Mr. Fitzgerald—I believe that is how he spells his name—seems to believe that plagiarism begins at home." Even worse, Zelda's jealousy didn't end with her husband's writing.

In France the Fitzgeralds became part of a group of expatriate writers that congregated in the home of Gertrude Stein and her companion Alice B. Toklas. It was the former who coined the term "The Lost Generation," and no one fit the description as aptly as Scott and Zelda. While in Paris, Scott met Ernest Hemingway, and the two of them initially hit it off. However, Zelda despised Hemingway. She accused Hemingway of being a "fairy" and claimed he and Scott were having a homosexual affair. Perhaps in retaliation, Zelda began an affair with a young French aviator, Edouard Jozan, whom she met at the beach. When her husband found out, she broke it off, and, to prevent further dalliances, he locked her in their house. Later, Fitzgerald would write of this incident, "That September of 1924, I knew that something had happened that could never be repaired."

A year later, the Fitzgeralds had dinner with Sara and Gerald Murphy at a restaurant in Colombe d'Or, in Nice; the terrace on which they dined overlooked a valley. There they saw Isadora Duncan at another table, and Gerald took Scott over to introduce him to the famous dancer. As soon as he had done so, Scott fell to his knees at her feet. In response, Duncan ran her fingers through Scott's hair, simultaneously calling him "my centurion." Zelda's response to this scenario was to stand on her chair and leap across the table where she landed in the darkness. Sara Murphy rushed over. Gerald Murphy later reported of the dramatic dinner episode, "I was sure she was dead. We were all stunned and motionless. I've never been able to forget it." Scott, at the end, even though he wore "the gold hat," was not able to bounce high enough for Zelda. Perhaps no man could.

In 1930 Zelda suffered her first full-scale mental breakdown. Unable to care for her, Scott had to commit her to a mental institution and face the fact that she would never be mentally stable enough to live outside of one again. Her illness had been the drama/trauma that had dominated, and destroyed, their lives. In his notebook he wrote, "I left my capacity for hoping on the little roads that led to Zelda's sanitarium." His wife's madness would forever keep them physically estranged. However, Scott never stopped loving the memory of who Zelda had once been. And it was that fact that was to dominate the second act of Fitzgerald's life.

Zelda never forgot Scott; from the hospital she wrote him numerous love letters, in them recalling happier times. In her periods of lucidity, she also penned her only book, an autobiography, *Save Me the Waltz*. Refusing to put her in a public institution, Scott, desperate for money, moved to Hollywood, where he began working on scripts for Metro-Goldwyn-Mayer. It was there he began an affair with Sheilah Graham, a Hollywood columnist. At the age of forty-four, Fitzgerald collapsed while clutching the mantelpiece in Graham's apartment; his heart had given out. His funeral was attended by few people. One of the handfuls of mourners at his Hollywood funeral was Dorothy Parker, who, as she looked into his coffin, murmured the same words that Nick Calloway had spoken at Jay Gatsby's funeral, "Poor son of a bitch."

Seven years later, just after midnight, Zelda was locked in a room at the Highland Mental Hospital, where she was waiting for shock treatment that was to be administered the next day. A fire broke out, ending her life. In her room were the love letters that she had written to Scott. She had "saved him the waltz" as long as she had been able. One of Zelda's most poignant quotations was "Nobody has ever measured, not even poets, how much the heart can hold."

Their daughter, Scottie, had both her parents' bodies moved to a family plot in Saint Mary's Cemetery, in Maryland, where they share a single headstone. Their epitaph is a quotation from *The Great Gatsby*: "So we beat on, boats against the current, borne back ceaselessly into the past." Her restless parents were at last at rest. Scott and Zelda achieved in death what they could not in life, to be together, in peace.

13

Orlando: A Biography

VIRGINIA WOOLF
(ADELINE VIRGINIA STEPHEN)
1928

TO

V. SACKVILLE-WEST

T HE novel *Orlando: A Biography* was the product of the relationship between two famous, British, female, bisexual twentieth-century writers. What made their unorthodox relationship even more dramatic was the fact that Vita was a member of the British aristocracy (she could trace her lineage to William the Conquerer), and Virginia was an integral member of the infamous Bloomsbury Group. London never lacked for gossip with the two controversial literary ladies in its midst.

In 1922, the art critic (and Virginia's brother-in-law) Clive Bell introduced Virginia Woolf and Vita Sackville-West. They immediately forged a bond. Vita was dramatic and outspoken; Virginia was reticent and intellectual. Virginia was in awe of her new friend's aristocratic heritage. Virginia's background, though not possessing her lover's blueness of blood, was, however, rich in culture. Her father, Sir Leslie Stephen, was the widower of

William Makepeace Thackeray's eldest daughter and an eminent editor and critic. Her mother, Julia, a renowned beauty, was descended from an attendant of Marie Antoinette. Visitors to their home in Hyde Park were luminaries such as Henry James, George Eliot, and George Henry Lewes.

Despite the illustrious visitors, the family home held dark secrets. Virginia and her sister Vanessa were subjected to sexual abuse by their half brothers George and Gerald. Her mother suddenly died when Virginia was thirteen; the tragedy was followed by the death of her half sister Stella two years later. These events led to the first of her lifelong nervous breakdowns. One of the many symptoms that occurred in her throes of madness was hearing birds singing to her in Greek. During her marriage, after another bout, she remained in bed for two straight months. Her husband, Leonard, was later to recall of her mental breakdowns, "She talked almost without stopping for two to three days, paying no attention to anyone in the room or anything said to her... Then gradually it became completely incoherent, a mere jumble of dissociated words." Had it not been for his support, she probably would have been confined to an asylum for life.

Soon after Virginia and Vita met, they began an affair that was to last until the end of the 1920s, and a friendship that would endure for the rest of their lives. The fact that both women were married did not present a problem. Harold Nicolson, Vita's husband, also had many homosexual encounters, and they both respected each other's preferences. For his part, Leonard Woolf never interfered with his brilliant, tormented wife. It was enough for him that she could sometimes obtain fleeting happiness. The following year, Virginia and Vita took a holiday together, traveling to France and Italy. When they were unable to be together

(Vita had two young sons), they corresponded through letters and poured out the secrets of their souls to one another. In one letter, Vita writes, "I am reduced to a thing that wants Virginia. I composed a beautiful letter to you in the sleepless nightmare hours of the night, and it has all gone: I just miss you, in a quite simple desperate human way."

The novel *Orlando* was inspired by Vita; she even told Virginia that she fell in love with herself after reading it. The hero/heroine's life spans three centuries and shifts from male to female. In a letter dated October 1927, Virginia writes to Vita that she owed *Orlando* to her, "But listen; suppose Orlando turns out to be Vita; and it's all about you and the lusts of your flesh and the lure of your mind."

Nigel Nicolson, Vita's son, approved of both his mother's relationship with Virginia Woolf and the novel *Orlando*. He wrote that the book was "the longest and most charming love letter in literature." However, Vita's mother was not quite enamored of her daughter's skeletons leaving the closet. She wrote to the editor of *The Observer*, J. L. Garvin, begging him not to carry a review of the book. "Love is slipping off one's petticoats'...All that is so coarse and will be so shocking to the middle classes, mostly...I have spent years, *hiding*, what Harold and Vita really are. I am sorry to confess it. And it makes it twice as dreadful now and such food for indecent gossip." Mrs. Sackville-West was furious that the main character was based on her daughter. Moreover, the book was illustrated with photographs of Vita, all of them depicting her dressed as a man. The fact that the novel promoted lesbianism was not what Mrs. Sackville-West wanted associated with her ancient family peerage. Her fury was unleashed against Virginia Woolf, whom she thereafter referred to as "the Virgin Wolf."

However, Mrs. Sackville-West was hypocritical in her condem-
nation; she herself had innumerable times sidestepped her vows
of marital fidelity. The difference is she kept what happened in
the bedroom in the bedroom. The Vita–Virginia affair came to a
demise when Vita became infatuated with Mary Campbell, the
wife of the poet Roy Campbell. She was, in some aspects, her
mother's daughter, after all.

The semiautobiographical novel *Orlando* could reflect the type
of pain that Virginia felt when Vita preferred another lover over
her. When Orlando's heart is broken, his/her emotional distress is
echoed in the fury of nature: "Huge noises as of tearing and rend-
ing of oak trees could be heard. There were also wild cries and
terrible inhuman groanings." Virginia's mental stability, never
very intact, received a great blow at Vita's departure.

In 1941, her emotional fragility was exacerbated by the Luftwaffe bombing of London. During the Blitz, her own home had
been hit, forcing her to move to the south of England. There she
was isolated from her circle of friends, and Leonard, fighting his
own psychological demons, was not able to be there for her. Distraught over the madness of the Third Reich and her own personal depression, she felt herself slipping further into the arms of
the demons that were her ever-present shadows. Once again she
heard birds singing to her in Greek. She wrote Leonard a suicide
note stating, "I am certain that I am going mad again. It is just
as it was the first time." Not wanting to put her long-suffering
husband through more misery, she loaded her coat pockets with
stones and went on her last walk to the River Ouse, where she
committed suicide by drowning. Leonard Woolf buried her remains
under a tree in the garden of their home in Sussex. The birds,
singing in Greek, were at last silenced.

Tragically, there was no lighthouse to guide her through the darkness. Vita spoke of Virginia's death as "a loss that can never be diminished." However, perhaps Vita was later able to replace the image of her friend's last horrific hour with the memory of when they had first fallen in love, a love that had produced *Orlando*.

14

Lady Chatterley's Lover

D. H. LAWRENCE
(DAVID HERBERT RICHARDS LAWRENCE)
1928

For having published this book, Penguin Books were prosecuted under the Obscene Publications Act, 1959, at the Old Bailey in London from 20 October to 2 November, 1960. This edition is therefore dedicated to the twelve jurors, three women and nine men, who returned a verdict of "Not Guilty" and thus made D. H. Lawrence's last novel available for the first time to the public in the United Kingdom.*

SEVERAL world-famous trials were instigated when individuals challenged sacrosanct norms: in 1601, a court prosecuted Galileo Galilei for attacking the Church's precept that all heavenly bodies revolved around the Earth; in 1873, a court prosecuted Susan B. Antony for attacking the government's precept that women did not belong in a polling booth; in 1925, a court prosecuted John Scopes for attacking his school's ban on offering an alternative to the creation story. And in 1960, a publishing house

---

*The above dedication appears in the Penguin edition, 1961.

went on trial for overstepping the boundary of established mores of decency.

David Herbert Lawrence was one of five children of Arthur John Lawrence, a barely literate coal miner, and Lydia, a former schoolmistress. He later described his parents' marriage as "one carnal, bloody fight." His formative years were spent in Nottinghamshire, a locale that made such an impression on his life that he referred to it as "the country of my heart." Like Robin Hood, he was going to be one of Nottingham's most famous sons.

In 1912, Lawrence met the woman with whom he was to spend the rest of his life, a German aristocrat named Frieda von Richthofen, who stated that during their first meeting Lawrence talked about Oedipus and the effects of early childhood on one's subsequent years.

The relationship between Lawrence and Frieda was fraught with scandal. She was six years his senior, married to his former professor Ernest Weekley, and the mother of three. To avoid the tumultuous fallout of their liaison, they eloped to Frieda's parents' home in Germany, where Lawrence was arrested and charged with being a British spy. He was released at the intervention of his father-in-law.

Eventually they returned to England where they shared a house with writer Katherine Mansfield. In 1917, the couple fell under a cloud of suspicion, as Frieda was not only German but also the cousin of the German flying ace Manfred von Richthofen (aka the Red Baron). The couple was accused of signaling to German submarines off the coast of Cornwall, and the police routinely searched their home. The Defence of the Realm Act was used to officially expel them from Cornwall. In 1919, when they were finally able to obtain passports, they embarked on what Lawrence was to refer to as "his savage pilgrimage," his exile from "the country of his heart."

After a meandering odyssey through several countries, the couple made their home in a villa in Italy, where Aldous Huxley and Lawrence struck up a close friendship. He began to write full-time, and in Italy in 1928 he wrote his last major work, *Lady Chatterley's Lover*. Because of its highly controversial nature, it could only be printed in private editions in Florence and Paris. The established publishing houses did not pick it up because it broke too many taboos in its liberal use of profanity and depiction of graphic love scenes, which sent the post-Victorian world reaching collectively for its smelling salts. As if this were not enough, the main characters broke class barriers as well.

After launching his novel, Lawrence hoped the reactions would be positive. His optimism was conveyed in the book's opening line, "Ours is essentially a tragic age, so we refuse to take it tragically." The responses, however, were for the most part extremely hostile. One British headline read, "Famous Author's Shameful Book," and a reviewer wrote, "It is the most evil outpouring that has ever besmirched the literature of our country. The sewers of French pornography would be dragged in vain to find a parallel in beastliness." Another commentary stated, "The creations of muddy-minded perverts, peddled in back-street bookstalls in Paris, are prudish by comparison." One article called it "the fetid masterpiece of this sex-sodden genius."

Lawrence was heartbroken by the vitriolic attacks, and soon after developed a severe bout of tuberculosis and blamed the illness on the commentary. He passed away at the Villa Robermond in France. Despite the notoriety of his life, he was to gain even further infamy after his passing.

In 1960, to coincide with the thirtieth anniversary of the
author's demise, Allen Lane, head of Penguin Books, decided to
issue an unexpurgated edition of *Lady Chatterley's Lover*. His decision met unanimous opposition from his board of directors, who
feared Penguin would be charged with violating the Obscene Publications Act of 1959. The Act said that works of a pornographic
nature could be held legally liable; however, it added the caveat
that they could pass muster if the defense could prove the work
possessed literary merit. Lane explained his action to his brother
Dick, "I don't see myself in the role of a crusader, but I thought
that if ever a book had been designed to be a test book for the Act,
this was it."

After announcing his decision, the next step was for the pros-
ecuting counsel, Mervyn Griffith-Jones, to determine whether to
try the case. Asked by a colleague on what he was to base his
decision, Jones responded, "I put my feet up on the desk and
start reading. If I get an erection, we prosecute." The case became
Regina v. Penguin Books. The trial was going to prove one of the
most talked about affairs in publishing history, and its notoriety
made Lady Chatterley as infamous as Lady Godiva.

Jones's opening speech to the jury delineated the Obscene
Publications Act and then explained that if they found *Lady
Chatterley's Lover* not obscene and unlikely to "deprave and cor-
rupt," they must decide in its favor. He followed the opening
gambit with his personal bias, "Would you approve your young
sons, young daughters—because girls can read as well as boys—
reading this book? Is it a book you would have lying around in
your own house? Is it a book you would even wish your wife or
your servants to read?" He used the phrase "putting adultery on
a pedestal" thirty-two times. At the close of the proceedings, the

judge made obvious his disapproval of the book, and the jurors adjourned.

After five days of deliberation, the jury came back with a not guilty verdict. They had delivered a resounding blow to censorship.

The verdict made the novel a succès de scandale and garnered a fortune for Penguin Books when queues of the literate (and the nonliterate) lined up to purchase their copies, and three million were sold from bookstores.

The landmark trial also proved a literary turning point, and it paved the way for hitherto forbidden volumes such as the *Kama Sutra* to be removed from the list of banned books. Allen Lane was hailed as a trailblazing publisher, and D. H. Lawrence received posthumous vindication that *Lady Chatterley's Lover* was not just dirt for dirt's sake. However, amid the elation over this victory of literary expression, a number of the true heroes were overlooked. Allen Lane decided to right that wrong. When Penguin issued its second edition of *Lady's Chatterley's Lover*, it paid tribute to those who had made its birth possible: "This edition is therefore dedicated to the twelve jurors, three women and nine men, who returned a verdict of 'Not Guilty' and thus made D. H. Lawrence's last novel available for the first time in the United Kingdom."

15

Look Homeward Angel

THOMAS WOLFE
(THOMAS CLAYTON WOLFE)
1929

To A. B.

WHEN Thomas Wolfe dedicated his first novel, *Look Home-ward Angel,* he was compelled, because of circumstance, to merely refer to the woman he loved as A. B. Her initials proved symbolic, as they are the first two letters of the alphabet, and she was Wolfe's first, and only, love.

In August 1925, Wolfe, a university teacher, was returning home from his summer vacation in Europe aboard the ocean liner *Olympia.* On the last night of the voyage, a shipboard acquaintance invited him to join him at a final gala. Similarly, Aline Bernstein and her friend made their way to the same destination. Thomas's friend knew Aline's, and consequently the four shared a table.

The chemistry between Thomas and Aline was electric, and they soon abandoned the other two diners. They danced and drank, and then made their way to the ship's rail, where the stars and the lights of New York City served as a romantic backdrop to their passion. When Thomas suggested that they go back to his cabin where he had a bottle of brandy, she readily acquiesced. She was smitten by his good looks (he was six feet five inches tall), which, combined with his boyish face, proved irresistible. The next morning Aline left Thomas's third-class cabin for her first-class one. When they disembarked later that day, they both considered their shared evening a one-night stand, little imagining that it would be one that would leave its imprint on the rest of their lives.

After landing in New York City, Thomas went to his hometown of Asheville, North Carolina. He was shocked when thoughts of Aline kept drifting into his mind. His usual interaction with the opposite sex was to meet them at one of the innumerable Greenwich Village parties, disappear with them into a bedroom for an hour, and leave, their faces as memorable as a page number in a book. As one of these bedded and then discarded women said of the lone Wolfe, "He was intolerable and wonderful and talked like an angel and was a real son-of-a-bitch." When Thomas returned to New York City, like an infatuated schoolboy, he wrote Aline a letter, which he carried for several days in his pocket before he had the courage to mail it to his "one-night stand." She answered immediately and the next day they met on the steps of the New York City Public Library. From there they went out for lunch in order to celebrate Thomas's twenty-fifth birthday. The lunch was of a liquid nature for Tom, and Aline put her drunken date in a taxi, ignoring his pleas that she come home with him.

After another rendezvous and more magnetic sexual sessions, however, they decided to embark on a full-fledged affair, although their backgrounds made them very different. Thomas was Christian and Aline was Jewish; he was a struggling teacher and she was a wealthy woman; he hailed from a small Southern town while she was a native New Yorker; and she was twenty years his senior. However, an even greater impediment to their relationship was the fact that Aline was married and the mother of two teenaged children. Nevertheless, so great was their attraction that they were willing to open the Pandora's Box of a long-term adulterous affair.

A few months later the couple decided that they wanted to rent an apartment together. Aline told her wealthy stockbroker husband that she needed a studio where she could work (she was a theater set designer), and proceeded to lease a loft at 13 East Eighth Street in Greenwich Village. It was there that Thomas confided in Aline his dream of becoming a playwright. She astutely realized that her lover's talent was more suited to fiction, and she encouraged him to begin work on a novel. To this end, she purchased some red cloth notebooks, which he began filling with what was to become *Look Homeward Angel*. In addition, she began to support him financially, so that he could reduce his teaching schedule, thereby allowing him the time and energy to devote to his writing.

The following year was a busy one for Aline as she juggled her high-profile husband, two teenaged children, theatrical career, and demanding lover. In the summer of 1926, Thomas and Aline traveled to Europe. However, because of the demands of her other life, she had to return to New York while Thomas decided to stay. During the brutal months of separation, Aline wrote Thomas innumerable letters articulating her pain and loneliness. In one she wrote, "I am bleeding frightfully where I have torn myself from you." In another she stated that she wanted "to find some magician to make an elixir of Aline to send you in a flask." Equally histrionic, as he ate his solitary birthday dinner in London, Wolfe ordered an extra glass of sherry and placed it at the vacant seat at his table for Aline in absentia.

In 1929, when *Look Homeward Angel* was published, Wolfe dedicated it to A. B., the only woman he had ever loved. He gave Aline the first copy of his novel, with the following handwritten inscription:

> To Aline Bernstein: On my twenty-ninth birthday, I present her with this, the first copy of my first book. This book was written because of her, and is dedicated to her. At a time when my life seemed desolate, and when I had little faith in myself, I met her. She brought me friendship, material and spiritual relief, and love such as I had never had before. I hope therefore that readers of my book will find at least part of it worthy of such a woman. Thomas Wolfe, Oct. 3, 1929.

When Aline and Thomas had returned from their first European trip, it had signified the beginning of their affair. However, upon Thomas's return from his second trip abroad, it signified the beginning of its end. Emotionally, during their separation, Thomas had begun to withdraw; however, Aline was as committed to their relationship as ever. In an attempt to distance himself physically as well as emotionally from Aline, Wolfe rented his own apartment in Brooklyn, making sure that it was away from his old haunt, Greenwich Village.

The nature of his conflicted emotions toward Aline can be illustrated through two very different letters that he wrote to friends at this time. In the first he stated about his breakup, "Life is too short to be mixed up in nasty complications with other people."

And, to another friend he wrote, "Because I was penniless and took one ship instead of another, I met the great and beautiful friend who had stood by me through all the torture, struggle, and madness of my nature for over three years." These two sentiments were Thomas's attempt at eulogizing his life with Aline.

When his woman scorned read in the newspaper that Wolfe was back in New York, and had not contacted her, she was so distraught that she swallowed a number of sleeping pills. For three days she hovered on the brink of death and had to be hospitalized for several weeks. It is not documented how Mr. Bernstein felt about his wife's shared accommodation with her lover, their European trips, her financing of Thomas's writing, and her suicide attempt after his rejection of their continued relationship. Aline stayed married, though she had lost the passion in it. It is doubtful if even time itself was ever able to unbreak her heart.

After their breakup, Tom and Aline avoided running into one another, knowing that a meeting would be too painful. However, although New York City is a megalopolis, the artistic community is a small town, and they both knew that their paths would cross again. They never guessed that the next time they saw one another would be in the men's room of the Plaza Hotel at 3:00 a.m. Tom had become so intoxicated that he had passed out in the bathroom. The attendant who attempted to rouse him heard his plea that he would not leave until "Mrs. Bernstein came to take him home." He gave her number to the attendant, who called Aline. She met him in the bathroom, cradled him in her arms, and then put her giant, inebriated ex-lover into a taxi, ignoring his pleas to come home with him.

Although Thomas Wolfe had severed Aline Bernstein from his life, he was unable to do the same with his soul. In the mid-1930s, he and his friend and editor Maxwell Perkins, at the author's behest, made their way to the Greenwich Village apartment at 13 East Eighth Street, which Thomas pronounced his favorite place in the city. Through the fire escape, they entered the unoccupied apartment through a window, and wandered through the home where Aline and Thomas had lived and loved together in the first heady wave of their passion. Before they left, Thomas pulled a pencil stub from his pocket and wrote on the wall his sacred graffiti: "Thomas Wolfe lived here." Three years later, not yet forty, Thomas Wolfe lay dying from tuberculosis of the brain. Aline had wanted to join him at the end, but Perkins, knowing that Thomas's mother hated the woman whom she looked down upon as a Jewish, adulterous cradle robber, urged her to stay away, thereby avoiding a scene. A veteran of too many of them involving Thomas, she did as he requested.

Thomas Wolfe's final words, before sinking into a coma from which he never awoke, were, "Where's Aline?...I want Aline..."

16

The Thin Man

Dashiell Hammett
(Samuel Dashiell Hammett)
1934

**TO
LILLIAN**

Because Dashiell Hammett was a two-fisted drinker for most of his life, and because he and Hellman had a thirty-year relationship, it is easy to imagine the author, with raised glass, making his eternal toast, "To Lillian."

Hammett and Hellman met in 1931 in a restaurant in Hollywood, when she was twenty-four and he was thirty-six. The author was at the height of his success: he had written four novels and was the literary celebrity of both New York and Hollywood. Dorothy Parker's usually poisoned pen carried nothing but praise. She wrote of his *Maltese Falcon* in *The New Yorker*, "I went mooning about in a daze of love [for Spade] such as I had not known for any character in literature since I encountered Sir Launcelot."

Riding the book's success, Hammett went west to assist in the adaptation of its screenplay, which helped make him a very wealthy man. However, the money and the fame were only of minute, secondary importance to Dashiell, whose main guiding lights were principles and justice. It was partially for this reason that he scorned the bevies of Los Angeles beauties for the rather plain Lillian, in whom he found a kindred spirit.

At the time, Lillian was engaged in trying to organize her fellow screenwriters into a union. Later Hellman would write of the night when she met the man who would, more than anyone else, impact her life.

The five day drunk had left the wonderful face looking rumpled, and the very tall thin figure was tired and sagged. We talked of T. S. Eliot, although I no longer remember what we said, and then went and sat in his car and talked at each other and over each other until it was daylight. We were to meet again a few days later, and, after that, on and sometimes off again for the rest of his life and thirty years of mine.

The fact that both were married was not a factor in their relationship. Hammett was already separated from his wife, who was living with their two daughters, and Hellman divorced Arthur Kober a year later. Because of their often conflicting personalities and promiscuous natures, the two never married.

Lillian and Dashiell soon began living together in New York City, and these years were to become their golden ones. They were deeply in love, and both were achieving success with their writing. Under Dashiell's tutelage, Hellman started working on plays, and in 1934 *The Children's Hour* was produced. The fiercely private Dashiell joked with her about her newfound interest in writing that he was at least assured that she would never pen his biography, because, if she did, in her egocentricity the whole book would be about Lillian, with only "an occasional reference to a friend called Hammett."

That same year Dashiell published *The Thin Man.* (In the murder mystery, the "thin man" is the victim, a "thin man," euphemistically a skeleton.) Not only did he dedicate the novel to Lillian, he also based the main female character, Nora, on her, while the main character was patterned after himself. Lillian later wrote of her fictional counterpart, "It was nice to be Nora, married to Nick Charles, maybe one of the few marriages in modern literature where the man and woman like each other and have a fine time together." Dashiell, in the playful banter that they often used with another, told her not to be thrilled about his characterization of her, as he had also patterned the silly girl and the villainess after her as well. Ironically, just as Lillian came into her own as a playwright, Dashiell stopped writing.

In Hellman's introduction to an anthology of Hammett's five novels, she writes:

> I have been asked many times over the years why he did not write another novel after *The Thin Man.* I do not know. I think, but I only think, I know a few of the reasons: he wanted to do a new kind of work; he was sick for many of those years and getting sicker. But he kept his work, and his plans for work, in angry privacy and even I would not have been answered if I had ever asked, and maybe because I never asked is why I was with him until the last day of his life.

However, in retrospect, perhaps the reason why Dashiell stopped writing was because he had transferred his energies into the political arena.

In 1942, after Pearl Harbor, as a virulent antifascist, Hammett enlisted in World War II. Although he was forty-eight, and in ill health from his stints as both a Pinkerton agent and a World War I veteran, he insisted upon doing his part. When he was accepted for active service, he phoned Lillian to state it was the happiest day of his life. Sick with apprehension, she replied that it wasn't the happiest of hers.

When he returned from the war, he became, like many intellectuals of the time, involved in left-wing causes and joined the American Communist Party. In 1946, he became president of the Civil Rights Congress, and subsequently was subpoenaed and ordered to reveal the names of those who had contributed to its fund. Lillian, the night before his court appearance, frightened for his welfare, asked him why he wouldn't just say that he didn't know the names, which was, in actuality, the truth. He answered her with the words, "If it were more than jail, if it were my life, I would give it for what I think democracy is, and I don't let cops or judges tell me what I think democracy is." When questioned, Hammett repeatedly invoked his Fifth Amendment rights, with the result that he was cited for contempt of court and sentenced to six months in a federal penitentiary. Even in prison, his thoughts were more concern for Lillian than worry over his own plight. He sent the lawyer that Hellman had hired for him to her with an old envelope. On it he had written a note for the attorney to show her: "Tell Lilly to go away. Tell her I don't need proof she loves me and don't want it."

It was not long before it was Lillian's own turn to be persecuted; she received a subpoena to appear in front of the House Un-American Activities Committee. Her name had come up because

HUAC knew that she was the longtime lover of Hammett, and had been to the Soviet Union. When she was asked to name names of those whom she knew to have communist affiliations, Hellman delivered a prepared speech, one that was to prove a resounding slap to McCarthyism's face: "To hurt innocent people whom I knew many years ago in order to save myself is, to me, inhuman and indecent and dishonorable. I cannot and will not cut my conscience to fit this year's fashions." Although she was not sentenced to jail, she was blacklisted.

At the end of Dashiell's jail sentence, Lillian went to the airport to await his arrival. When she saw him walking down the ramp, even her worst fears were surpassed. He was emaciated, and so frail he had to lean heavily on the rail, periodically stopping to rest. It was then that Lillian realized that Dashiell himself was soon to be a "thin man." She was so overcome with emotion that she had to run back into the airport in order to compose herself, thus delaying the long-awaited reunion.

In 1972 Hellman was to write a memoir entitled *Pentimento*. She derived the unusual title from an Italian painting term. It refers to when an artist draws an image, and then, repenting, paints over it. Over time, the original image comes to the forefront, sometimes even obscuring the more recent image. As Lillian sat with Dashiell in his last days, as he fought for each labored breath, she may have, as her autobiography would later suggest, blocked out the horror of his deathbed with thoughts of the golden years, when they were first in love and the toast of Manhattan and Hollywood. Sitting there, she realized she would, as Dashiell had predicted, never agree to pen her reminiscences of her decades-long lover. As she was to write in *An Unfinished Woman*, "I will never write that biography because I cannot write about my clos-est, my most beloved friend." Nostalgically, she hearkened back to the days before the *Scoundrel Time* (her nonfiction account of the McCarthy era), before *C* had become America's Scarlet Letter, before the megalomaniac senator had turned American democ-racy into "the thin man."

17

Gone with the Wind

Margaret Mitchell
(Margaret Munnerlyn Mitchell)
1936

TO

J. R. M.

THE succinct dedication to *Gone with the Wind* is in sharp contrast to the 1,024-page American epic. And, after discovering Margaret Mitchell's story, one can understand Rhett Butler and his fiery, fictional counterpart, Scarlett.

Margaret, who often went by the nickname Peggy, was truly a daughter of the South. She grew up on the laps of Civil War veterans, who regaled her with tales of the conflict and its aftermath. Her knowledge of that time was encyclopedic, as relatives told her everything about the Confederacy's past, with the exception that it had lost the war. Indeed, she was ten years old before she learned about the omission of that truth.

The first influence for Rhett was Clifford Henry, a Yankee lieutenant she met at a party. When he received his order to be transferred overseas, the two became secretly engaged. Margaret was enrolled in Smith College when, on September 11, 1918, her roommate, Ginny, handed her a letter from Saint-Mihiel. It stated that while Clifford lay injured in a hospital bed he was awarded the Croix de Guerre. He died the same day. The next year her mother, Maybelle, died from the Spanish influenza, and, as her father was incoherent with grief, she returned home to nurse both her broken heart and her father.

Upon her return, Margaret was approved for membership in the elite Debutante Club because her grandmother, Annie Fitzgerald Stephens, was a pillar of Atlanta society. There she proved she was not Melanie, but Scarlett. During one of the debutante dances she came dressed as the antithesis of the proper Southern belle; she wore black stockings, a black satin slit-front skirt, and bright red lipstick. She danced in such a provocative manner that she scandalized the female members. Her grandmother's connections had got her into the club; her suggestive dancing got her out. In the same vein, when invited to a bridal shower, all the guests brought virginal white lingerie, with the exception of Margaret, whose present was a purple nightgown.

In 1922, Margaret met Berrien "Red" Upshaw, her second Rhett Butler. He had broad shoulders, was six foot two, with red hair, green eyes, and a cleft chin. An ex-football player and current bootlegger, his nickname for the diminutive Margaret was Short-Leg Pete. She appeared to be furious at this, but she could never disguise the fact that she was smitten. Her grandmother disapproved of the "bad boy," a sentiment Margaret did not share.

On one occasion Red introduced Margaret to his roommate, John Robert Marsh, a soft-spoken newspaper editor. He was a far cry from the handsome Red: he was stoop-shouldered, wore glasses, and had sandy-colored hair flecked with gray and a receding hairline. It soon became evident that both men were in love

with her. She chose Red, and John, heartbroken, still agreed to be
the best man at their wedding. On September 2, 1922, Margaret
Mitchell became Margaret Upshaw.

The marriage was a decision she would soon come to regret.
Red did not bring in a steady income and was physically abusive;
once he assaulted her in front of their guests. Margaret begged
John to return to Atlanta from Washington, where he was working, to talk to Red about his drinking, which was the cause of
most of their marital problems. John's sister later commented, "I
think he went back to Atlanta mostly because of his love for her.
It was a steady love as far as he was concerned. Maybe for her,
too. She realized that he would be what Red wasn't, you see. Red
was a wild creature." John talked to Red, but it did not have the
result that Margaret expected. The following morning Red told
Margaret that he was leaving for Asheville, North Carolina, and
she could go ahead and get a divorce because he was never coming back. Margaret turned to John for solace, and he was only too
happy to comply. He quit his job to remain in Atlanta. Margaret
filed for divorce and became Margaret Mitchell once more.

On July fourth she remarried, and this time John was the
groom instead of the best man. Their reception was held in their
new ground-floor apartment, a home Margaret would affectionately nickname "the Dump."

Margaret's occupation was as a reporter at the same newspaper where John was the editor. However, an ankle injury forced
her to be bedridden for several months. To keep his wife from
becoming bored during her convalescence, her husband brought
home historical books from the public library. One evening, after
finding she had gone through most of the library's historic works,
he jokingly said to her, "Peggy, if you want another book, why

don't you write your own?" The next day, instead of delivering his wife another book, he delivered a Remington typewriter, accompanied by the note: "Madam, I greet you on the beginning of a new career." When she asked him what she should write about, he answered with an editor's response: "Write what you know." Margaret, drawing on the stories of the Old South that she had grown up with and which had always fascinated her, decided to do that and began work on the manuscript that would become *Gone with the Wind.*

The only person Margaret allowed to look at the ever-increasing pages was John, who edited her work as he read. She came up with the title when her husband showed her the poem he had read over and over when Margaret had chosen Red over him. It was by Ernest Dowson, "Non Sum Qualis eram Bonae Sub Regno Cynarae." The third stanza was the one that resonated with her:

I have forgot much, Cynara! gone with the wind,
Flung roses, roses riotously with the throng,
Dancing, to put thy pale, lost lilies out of mind;
But I was desolate and sick of an old passion,
Yea, all the time, because the dance was long:
I have been faithful to thee, Cynara! in my fashion.

From its first line her novel's title was born. As she said, "It was the far away, faintly sad sound I wanted."

Interestingly enough, one of the greatest epics in Southern literature was only published by happenstance. After Margaret's ankle had healed, she put aside her voluminous manuscript and went back to what she felt was her real work, as a reporter. In

1935, Howard Latham, a publisher employed by Macmillan, came to Atlanta seeking to unearth new, Southern literary talent. He was introduced to Margaret by a mutual friend, and she agreed to show him around the city. He was enchanted by his escort, and he asked her if she had ever written a book. She answered in the negative. He then told her that if she ever did, she was to show it to him first. Learning of this conversation, an acquaintance of Margaret's said, "Imagine anyone as silly as Peggy writing a book!" Irritated at this comment, Margaret unearthed her work and took it to the Georgian Terrace Hotel, just as Latham was leaving for home. She thrust the manuscript, which seemed gigantic in the arms of the diminutive Margaret, at him and told him to take it before she changed her mind. The work was so thick that Latham had to purchase an additional suitcase to accommodate it. He read part of the manuscript on the train to New Orleans, and immediately forwarded it to New York. Once back home, the author had an attack of writer's remorse, and sent Latham a telegram directing him to send back her writing. Her pleas fell on deafened ears; Latham had read enough of the manuscript to know that he held a masterpiece. The novel and its blockbuster film were to make the diffident author the recipient of the Pulitzer Prize and to turn her into Atlanta's First Lady.

Margaret Mitchell did not revel in the role brought on by the phenomenal success of her novel and its spectacular movie version. She soon stopped granting interviews, claiming she was content to be Mrs. John Marsh. On an August night in 1949, tragedy befell the couple as they were walking to the local movie theater to watch a film version of *The Canterbury Tales*. When Margaret stepped off the sidewalk, she was struck by a drunk, off-duty taxi driver. She was taken to Grady Hospital, where she never regained consciousness. For the next five days, crowds waited outside the hospital for the legendary author's condition. President Harry S. Truman asked to be notified if there was any change. Margaret died in the arms of her husband.

J. H. M. was once more confronted with having to put "her pale, lost lilies out of mind." John had lost his wife and constant companion of twenty-four years. His happiness, like the world of the Old South, had become forever gone with the wind.

18

For Whom the Bell Tolls

ERNEST HEMINGWAY

1940

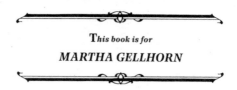

This book is for
MARTHA GELLHORN

IN light of the lives of Ernest Hemingway and Martha Gell-horn, the dedication in *For Whom the Bell Tolls* is extremely ironic. However, the title remains apropos because, after a few years, the bell inevitably tolled for them.

Martha and Ernest met in 1936, when Martha spent Christmas in Key West, Florida. They first saw one another in Sloppy Joe's bar, where Ernest was a regular. Over drinks they found they had a great deal in common: Both were writers and journalists. Moreover, they both felt passionately about the Spanish Civil War. Because Martha was blonde with amazing long legs, Ernest soon felt passionately about her as well. The fact that he was married already did little to dampen his ardor. For her part, most of Martha's boyfriends had been married. Another factor that must have endeared her to Hemingway was that she adored his work. She was especially fond of his novel *A Farewell to Arms*, where the hero tells a woman, "You're brave. Nothing ever happens to the brave."

After they met, they soon decided to travel together, in their official roles as journalists, to Spain to cover its war. Hemingway was working as a reporter for the *Toronto Star*, and Martha was working for the New York–based *Collier's*. They checked into the Hotel Florida, where they had two rooms on the quiet side, away from the constant shelling and bursts of cannon fire. They had their first fight the very next day when Hemingway proceeded to lock her in the room with the comment that he "didn't want her mistaken for a whore de combat." The feminist Gellhorn was livid. Later, she was to remark of the incident, "I should have known at that moment what doom was."

They spent that Christmas in Barcelona. In 1939, Martha moved in with Hemingway in his home in Cuba. When Hemingway's divorce became final, they married in 1940, in Cheyenne, Wyoming. Hemingway's friend Robert Capa photographed the ceremony for *Life* magazine. During that same year Hemingway published *For Whom the Bell Tolls*, and dedicated it to his new wife. He mentioned that to a certain extent the character of Maria was patterned after Gellhorn. When the book was made into a film, Martha was the one to suggest that Ingrid Bergman play the role of Maria.

The first years of their marriage were happy ones, and during them, when they were not busy writing, Hemingway taught Martha to do the things he loved, such as riding, shooting, and fishing. However, the marriage had weaknesses, one of which was sexual in nature. Gellhorn thought Hemingway was a "ghastly lover—wham bam thank you ma'am, or maybe just wham bam." However, she gave her own sexual prowess the same accolades when she remarked, "I daresay I was the worst bed partner in five continents."

Another major thorn in Martha's side was being viewed as "Mrs. Ernest Hemingway." She felt as a writer and a journalist she should receive her own recognition. When reporters wanted to interview her, she would agree to do so with the caveat that they ask no questions about her husband. She was adamant that she not be reduced to "a footnote in someone else's life." When people met Martha, and did not give her any recognition until after they discovered that she was married to Ernest Hemingway, she would wrap her hand into a fist, from which it would take a while to return to its natural state.

In 1941, when *Collier's* sent her to China to cover its war with Japan, she took her husband. Although preferring to remain in Cuba, he reluctantly agreed to go. His philosophy was, "What old Indian likes to lose his squaw with a hard winter coming on?" There they met General Chiang Kai-shek (of whom Martha remarked, "He has no teeth"). Gellhorn wrote a book based on their time there called *Travels with Myself and Another*. In the book she referred to her husband only as U. C., which stood for Unwilling Companion. While he mainly hung out at a hotel bar in Hong Kong, the more adventurous Martha explored the seamy side of the country: She visited opium dens, brothels, and sweatshops.

When they returned to Havana, Gellhorn rapidly became bored and was anxious for her next assignment. Hemingway soon became tired of having an absentee wife. In 1943, when she was off covering the Italian Front, he wrote her a letter asking, "Are you a war correspondent, or wife in my bed?" Gellhorn insisted on reporting on the war. As she said, "I followed the war wherever I could reach it."

Aggravated at his wife's "infidelity" to their marriage (preferring a career over him), Hemingway retaliated. His wife's magazine, *Collier's*, was allowed only one correspondent in Europe. He contacted its editor and offered to cover the war for them. They complied, as his famous name would prove a huge draw. Therefore, Hemingway was sent to cover the Normandy Invasion. Martha was livid. She complained to her confidante Eleanor Roosevelt, "I have been shoved back and back. It is quite a job being a woman isn't it; you cannot do your work and simply get on with it because that is selfish...Anyhow Ernest will get there (to Normandy) and he can always tell me about it." Her words dripped bitterness and resentment. She knew he had taken her press credential away merely from spite. Because of his name, he could have easily worked for any of the major magazines or newspapers.

Not one to be undermined, Gellhorn stowed away on a hospital ship in the D-Day fleet, disguised as a male stretcher bearer. She was able to witness the invasion firsthand after all. One of the reasons that she was such an intrepid reporter was, as she later explained, given the choice between boredom and death, she would prefer death. Or maybe she truly believed her husband's quote, "Nothing ever happens to the brave."

After the invasion, both Martha and Ernest made their way to England. However, angry at his wife, Ernest did not help her get a ticket on his flight. Unable to obtain one herself because of the crush of the war, Martha made her way to London via the Atlantic, on a Norwegian freighter that was transporting dynamite and amphibious personnel carriers. At the Dorchester Hotel in London, they finally met up, and it was there that they had their last showdown—a ferocious fight that resulted in Gellhorn walking out of Hemingway's hotel, and his life, for the last time.

She was the only one of Hemingway's four wives to leave him. As she later explained, "I wanted to escape from him and myself and from this personal life which feels like a strait jacket." Martha's leaving was an act he would never forgive. The end of the war coincided with the end of the Hemingway–Gellhorn marriage. A Hemingway biographer later wrote of the breakup, "His hatred of her was a terrible thing to see." Martha concurred with the comment, "Hell hath no fury like E. H. scorned." After she left she went to cover the liberation of the Dachau concentration camp and the Nuremberg Trials. Hemingway returned to Cuba with Mary Welsh, the woman who would later become the fourth Mrs. Hemingway.

Hemingway, in his novel *A Moveable Feast*, wrote, "If you are lucky enough to have lived in Paris as a young man, then wherever you go for the rest of your life, it stays with you, for Paris is a moveable feast." In a similar vein, when Martha Gellhorn married Ernest Hemingway she sealed her fate, forever to be associated with and forever overshadowed by the literary lion. For the rest of her life, whenever someone brought up his name, she would immediately exit the room. As she told a reporter many years after the divorce, "I was with him for eight years, and married for four. I've lived a lot of other lives."

Martha Gellhorn and Ernest Hemingway were initially drawn to one another because of their commonalities. At the close of their lives, they were to once more share another. Ernest Hemingway was forced from his home in Havana when Castro's forces took over. In despair, he returned to his birthplace, Idaho. Ill and unable to do the physical things he once loved, he committed suicide with a shotgun blast to his head. In London, elderly and nearly blind, Martha Gellhorn could no longer see the keys on her Remington typewriter, the one that had been her life's only constant companion. She committed suicide by taking poison.

The next day her obituary appeared in newspapers in London and the United States. Accordingly to them, Martha Gellhorn's claim to fame was that she had been the third wife of legendary writer Ernest Hemingway. Ironically, history did merely remember her as a "footnote in someone else's life." One can only imagine Martha looking down from heaven, reading her obituaries, her hand clenching into a fist.

19

The Heart Is a Lonely Hunter

CARSON MCCULLERS
(LULA CARSON SMITH)
1940

To Reeves McCullers and to
Marguerite and Lamar Smith

THE three people mentioned in the dedication to *The Heart Is a Lonely Hunter* are the ones who were able, as much as anyone could, to prevent Carson McCullers's heart from being "a lonely hunter." However, when all was said and done, the title of her novel could also have served as the title of her own autobiography.

The South is not so much a geographical location as a frame of mind, and the young Carson was raised on antebellum lore from her mother Marguerite, whose grandfather had been a plantation owner and Confederate war hero. Her mother, who was a gifted storyteller, regaled her daughter with tales of beautiful belles attending never-ending balls. However, at age fifteen, when her father, Lamar, bought her a typewriter, Carson wrote about life's outcasts, the emotional, psychological, and physical cripples who sought the acceptance of a society who shunned them. She later stated, "Writing, for me, is a search for God."

Much as Carson loved her parents, as a young teen she craved independence. Her first step was dropping her first name, Lula, for her middle name, Carson. At age eighteen, in a further quest for autonomy, she decided to move to New York City to attend the Juilliard School of Music. Her father agreed to finance her education by selling an heirloom diamond. However, arriving in New York, she left her tuition money, as well her roommate's, on the subway. As a result, she had to take menial jobs, but attended Columbia creative writing classes at night.

In 1935 Carson moved back to her hometown, where she met Reeves McCullers, a native of Alabama, who was stationed in the army at nearby Fort Benning. They discovered they had many commonalities: they were both aspiring writers, and both felt alienated and misunderstood by their Southern communities. In a move atypical of a small-town Southern girl, especially of her era, Carson decided to experiment with premarital sex. Even more unconventionally, she decided to inform Lamar and Marguerite of her decision. Later she said of the first Reeves/Carson encounter, "The sexual experience was not like D. H. Lawrence. No grand explosions or colored lights, but it gave me a chance to know Reeves better, and really learn to love him."

The new couple, if not in lust at least in love, decided to alternate working, to give one another time to write. Reeves went to work the first year, while Carson stayed home and worked on her first book. *The Heart Is a Lonely Hunter* is peopled by the dispossessed. The protagonist, John Singer, a deaf-mute, is paradoxically the confidant of the people of his small Southern town, who communicate to him about their loneliness and pain. At the end, bereft at the loss of his friend, he commits suicide, as he feels the only one left who truly understands him is gone. Carson based her title on a poem that, strangely enough, served as a premonition of her future with Reeves:

> Green wind from the green-gold branches, what is the
>   song you bring?
> What are all songs for me, now, who no more care to sing?
> Deep in the heart of Summer, sweet is life to me still,
> But my heart is a lonely hunter that hunts on a lonely hill.

The novel became a bestseller, and the shy twenty-three-year-old girl found herself the country's new literary light. There was never any further question as to who the writer was in the family. With Carson's new fame and wealth, the couple moved to New York City. However, while her book put her in the literary limelight, it also placed strains on the marriage. One of the tensions was caused by Reeves's envy of his wife's writing success. Other problems arose when they began to share other traits. Both had become alcoholic chain-smokers and both finally admitted, to each other and themselves, that they were bisexual.

After Carson caught Reeves forging her name on a large check, the couple separated. In response to the heartache caused by the breakup, Carson wrote another novel, *Reflections in a Golden Eye*, about the failure of love. A quotation from the novel, "The night was near at hand," was, in light of subsequent events, to become sorrowfully symbolic.

During this time, Carson moved into the house of her friend George Davis, the editor of *Harper's Bazaar*, where W. H. Auden was also living and where Gypsy Rose Lee and Richard Wright were frequent guests. In the spring of 1941, Carson and Reeves reconciled and began living together once more. However, the death knell of their marriage was soon to sound, when they both fell in love with the same man, the composer David Diamond. Who he ended up choosing (if either) is unknown, but the result of this love triangle was the McCullers's divorce in 1941. Although their marriage ended, McCullers would forever owe a debt to Reeves for his early encouragement and for bestowing upon her a surname that was far more in keeping with her eccentric personality than *Smith*.

The following year, Carson suffered a debilitating stroke that left the entire left side of her body paralyzed. Reeves came to nurse her through her illness. Grateful that he was there when she needed him, Carson remarried him in 1945. Unfortunately, her husband was not able to help her with her demons, and Carson attempted suicide in 1948. Hoping to get his wife and himself out of their depressions, Reeves moved himself and Carson to Paris, where they were befriended by Truman Capote and Tennessee Williams.

The trip did not turn out to be the romantic, therapeutic interlude they had planned. One night, while in their hotel, Reeves suggested that they commit double suicide. Carson, who was fighting for her own ever-elusive sanity, immediately packed her bags and flew back to the United States. Three days later, she was informed that Reeves had died of an intentional overdose of pills, washed down by alcohol. The night that "was near at hand" had come to pass. Carson was deeply affected by the news. Her relationship with Reeves McCullers had spanned twenty years, two divorces, countless separations and reconciliations. Her response to the tragedy was the bittersweet play *The Square Root of Wonderful*.

Depressed and ill, Carson moved into a home in Nyack, New York, which she shared with her mother until Marguerite passed away. In 1967, she was working on her biography, *Illumination and Night Glare*, when she suffered a final cerebral stroke. She was comatose for forty-seven days until she died. Perhaps in death, free from her body's tortured sexual ambiguity and chronic illnesses, she was united with Reeves, the only man she had ever loved and been loved by in return. Maybe in the next world, unlike this one, her heart no longer had to be "a lonely hunter."

20

Under the Volcano

MALCOLM LOWRY

(CLARENCE MALCOLM LOWRY)

1947

To Margerie, my wife

THE American writer Frances Mayes journeyed to Italy seeking emotional rehabilitation; she discovered it under the Tuscan sun. However, when Malcolm Lowry journeyed to Mexico for his spiritual salvation, it eluded him. Even the love of his life could not prevent an eventual eruption, one that petrified and left all in ashes.

Malcolm Lowry was born in Cheshire, the son of a wealthy cotton broker who owned plantations in Egypt, Peru, and Texas, and in leisure chased foxes. However, unlike his three older brothers, Malcolm rejected the family business for a life crammed with adventure, one which would provide material for his writing. More than anything he spurned the ordinary.

At age eighteen, Jack London's writings inspired Lowry to join the merchant marine. He drove to his ship in a Rolls-Royce limousine, which did nothing to endear him to the rest of the sailors. He set sail from Liverpool bound for Asia as a deckhand on the freighter S.S. *Pyrrhus*. When he returned, he graduated from Cambridge; along with his degree he carried the twin obsessions that would dominate his life: literature and liquor.

After college, Lowry lived briefly in London, existing on the fringes of the 1930s literary scene where he met fellow two-fisted drinker Dylan Thomas. Still in the grip of wanderlust, he began a sojourn through Europe, accompanied by his friend and mentor Conrad Aiken. In Spain, Malcolm met an American writer named Jan Gabrial; he believed their union was preordained as she shared the same name with the heroine of his newly published first novel, *Ultramarine*. They had a brief romance, followed by a wedding in Paris; however, from the onset it was far removed from the promise "to love and to honor."

After a period of estrangement, when Lowry took comfort in strumming his ukulele, he followed Jan to New York. Rather than the joyful reunion he had hoped for, he spent ten days in the psychiatric ward of Bellevue Hospital, following an alcohol-induced breakdown. Perhaps this disappointment led to his pronouncement that it's "rather a second-rate ambition to be an optimist." Upon his release, Lowry and his wife headed to Hollywood, where he planned to break into screenwriting.

As the West Coast provided neither lucrative connections nor domestic tranquility, the Lowrys traveled to Mexico in a last attempt to salvage their disintegrating marriage. They arrived on "El Día de los Muertos" (the Day of the Dead) and headed to Cuernavaca, ostensibly because there were many literary expatriates there. However, the more tangible attraction was its abundance of tequila and mescal, both of which Lowry imbibed in Herculean quantities. As Jan recounted in her biography, *Inside the Volcano*, "He would drink anything. I had thrown out the rubbing alcohol I'd use to massage his back, but he gulped the contents of a bottle he thought contained hair tonic but which Josefina had refilled with cooking oil." After two years, Jan left her husband for good.

Lowry, with tequila as his companion, explored the depths of hell. He translated his anguish into his masterpiece, the semiauto-biographical *Under the Volcano*, which concerns an alcoholic English diplomat in the rank Mexican town of Quauhnahuac. Shortly before his death the diplomat sees on a house an inscription that reads, "No se puede vivir sin amar" (One cannot live without love). Lowry described his novel as a "mescal-inspired phantasmagoria." However, before the manuscript could be completed (he once forgot it in a bar), the Mexican authorities arrested the drunken Englishman, and he was en route to deportation.

Lowry returned to Los Angeles, where he lived in the Hotel Normandie on Wiltshire. His only friend was Jack King, whom he had known from China during his stint on the high seas. King introduced Malcolm to Margerie Bonner, a former silent-film actress who entertained literary ambitions. Malcolm phoned Margerie and the two men agreed to meet her at the corner of Western Avenue and Hollywood Boulevard. Lowry took a bus to the rendezvous, and King was a few minutes late. By the time he arrived, Malcolm and Margerie were kissing, and still kissing several moments later. It was an embrace that was to last the rest of their lives.

Malcolm saw in Margerie an instrument to chase away the Furies; she saw in Malcolm a British aristocratic writer from a wealthy family. He described her as "a grand gal named Margerie;" they soon became lovers, though Malcolm had a lifelong fear of syphilis coupled with a sense of sexual inadequacy. However, Margerie gave him confidence in his virility, and he took to calling himself "El León" (the Lion) and gave her the pet name Miss Hartebeeste. Less than two months after they met, he wrote to her to declare his love: "The sensation of underground bleeding, of being torn up by the roots like a tree by a big wind—do you feel that? God, I do!"

Six weeks later, Lowry's American visa expired, and he moved to British Columbia. Dejected and lonely, he wrote Margerie, imploring her to follow, promising he would "unlock her from the prison of Los Angeles."

They married in 1940, one month after his divorce was finalized, and moved to a coastal village north of Vancouver called Dollarton, where they became squatters in a ramshackle cabin. (Lowry was rich only on paper, as a family trust just provided access to its interest, on the instructions of his less-than-impressed father). Built on city land, the structure could boast neither heat nor electricity nor running water.

After settling, the couple devoted themselves to revising *Under the Volcano*. Lowry's analysis of its earlier draft was "youth plus booze plus hysterical identifications plus vanity plus self-deception." Each morning, while Margerie typed out Malcolm's revisions, which he always wrote in longhand, he swam in the inlet, surrounded by seagulls. She also helped with suggestions; they referred to this process as "margerieversion." He wrote to Aiken of her guidance, "I'm more than glad I never got a chance to finish it without her." During this time, Margerie also worked on her own writing, completing a story titled "The Last Twist of the Knife," which Scribner's accepted for publication.

This was Malcolm's golden time, when he was able to work, swim, and play his ukulele in the company of his wife. However, accompanying this was the ever-present drinking, and Margerie could imbibe nearly as much gin as he. She later related how she had once found Malcolm passed out in a Vancouver whorehouse, having sold all his clothes for liquor except his underwear. She demanded the proprietor provide something for her husband to wear, and after he was dressed, she stood by him as he begged on the street for money for booze. At the cabin, there were violent fights, and Malcolm suffered from paranoid delusions. On one terrifying occasion, a fire engulfed their home; Margerie rushed in to rescue the almost completed *Under the Volcano*, though all his other material was consumed in the blaze.

Despite all the forces against him, Lowry finished his magnum opus, and in 1946, both English and American publishers accepted the book. Critics compared Lowry to James Joyce and Thomas Wolfe; his picture appeared on the cover of the *Saturday Review* and the novel made it onto 1947's bestseller list.

Lowry responded to fame much as he had to failure—he went on drinking. He wrote that his book's successful publication "[S]eemed to go off like a hundred skyrockets at once, and I am still trying to dodge the sparks and sticks."

To celebrate, the Lowrys went to New York City, where a friend said, "The city buzzes with your name." For many of the literati, these publication rounds were their first introduction to the second Mrs. Lowry, and though they applauded her effect on him, they found her pretentious and overly invested in her association with the British genius. Lowry's friend and fellow writer David Markson wrote, "She had a strange manner of speech. She was always saying things like, 'May I have a little more milk in my Scotch, duckie?'" Aiken stated he didn't want to be around Malcolm if Margerie was there.

With the novel's royalties, the Lowrys started traveling, stopping for a time in Sicily, where they stayed at a hotel in the shadow of Mt. Etna. Their time there was profoundly troubled and Malcolm tried to strangle Margerie on two occasions. Though she was a fraction of his size, she attacked him in turn. She wrote in her journal, "Is it conceivable that a man's weakness can be so strong, that such evil can overpower me & exhaust me to the point that I become evil too?"

They eventually returned to England to live in Sussex. While Malcolm's health began to falter, Margerie formed a romantic interest with a neighbor, Lord Peter Churchill. At the time, a psychiatrist told Malcolm that he believed Malcolm was either going to murder Margerie or she would murder him first. She considered having him lobotomized; however, some old friends of Malcolm's thwarted her plans.

One evening, the Lowrys started drinking, as usual, and started fighting, as usual. Margerie later told the police that to curtail her husband's drinking she smashed their gin bottle. When he threatened her with some broken shards, she fled to a neighbor. She claimed when she returned the next morning, she discovered her husband's body on their bedroom floor, amid the debris of broken glass, smashed furniture, and remains of food.

However, inconsistencies in her account began to arise. First, Margerie stated she had discovered a suicide note; when asked for it, she said she had destroyed it. Instead, she produced a bottle of sleeping pills, claiming he had taken an overdose. However, the cap was on the bottle, something a drunken, suicidal, tremor-ridden Malcolm would never have replaced. The coroner's verdict was an apt one: "death by misadventure;" specifically, Lowry had choked on his own vomit. Whatever the ultimate cause, it shadowed his alter ego's words in *Under the Volcano*: "Christ, this is a dingy way to die."

Lowry was laid to rest in a corner of a thirteenth-century churchyard. A dozen mourners accompanied his widow. She never had another husband, as she said, "I was married to Malcolm for eternity." Margerie hoped to be buried by his side, but by the time of her passing, the spot next to him had been taken. Her body was interred forty yards away, at the opposite end of the ancient burial ground. Inseparable in life, El León and Miss Hartebeeste lay apart in death.

21

The End of the Affair

GRAHAM GREENE
(HENRY GRAHAM GREENE)
1951

To C*

WHEN a writer commits words to the page, autobiographical elements seep in to varying degrees. Graham Greene admitted as much when he proclaimed, "I am my books." The main ingredients he borrowed from his life were his romantic attachments—one with a woman who gave him his god and the other with a woman who gave him his soul.

Upon graduating with a degree in history from Oxford University, Greene obtained a position as a reporter at the *Times*. He wrote a film review in which he discussed the Roman Catholics' worship of the Virgin Mary. He received a note from a young lady, rebuking him for his choice of a word. She told him that one did not "worship" the Virgin, rather one "venerated" her. Greene was "interested that anyone took these subtle distinctions of an unbelievable theology seriously." He wrote back with

*The American version is To Catherine

an apology and invited her out for tea, and when they met, he was immediately smitten with the innocence and beauty of the twenty-year-old Vivien Dayrell-Browning.

Vivien was not eager to reciprocate Graham's affections. However, after two thousand love letters—sometimes as many as three a day—over the next two and a half years, as well as Graham's promise of lifelong devotion, a chaste marriage (she was leery of sex), and his conversion to Roman Catholicism, she agreed, in 1927, to become his wife.

The couple rented a house where Vivien soon after had two children. During this time, Graham worked as a novelist. Sometimes his journalistic duties and his insatiable wanderlust led him to the ends of the earth. In his book of his travels, *Journey Without Maps*, he dedicated to Vivien: "To my wife: I carry you like a passport everywhere."

However, marriage and travel were not able to lift an ever-present shadow of depression, with which he had struggled from a young age. He soon turned to London prostitutes. Ever methodical, he compiled a list of forty-seven prostitutes he used during the 1920s and 1930s. Vivien, aware of her husband's Jekyll and Hyde lifestyle, stated, "Some of the people he picked up were quite frightful . . . I think all of his judgment of character went into his novels."

During the Blitz, Vivien and the children escaped to Oxford, while Graham remained in London. When the Luftwaffe bombed their house, Vivien was terrified for his safety. He was, however, unharmed as he had spent the night in the home of his mistress, Dorothy Glover. Of this Vivien would later remark, "Graham's life was saved by his infidelity." It was while he was married to

Vivien and having an affair with Dorothy that Graham was to meet his soul mate, his beloved "C."

After the war, Vivien entertained hopes that when she and the children returned to London, she could resume her marriage. As it turned out, she was the one who unwittingly severed it beyond repair. She was contacted by Catherine Walston, a woman who was anything but the "quiet American" and who was the wife of the aristocratic Henry Walston, one of the wealthiest men in England. Catherine told Vivien that Greene's books had persuaded her to convert to Catholicism, and she asked if Greene would be her godfather in her new faith. Happy to oblige, Vivien arranged for a priest to perform the ceremony, which she attended. When Graham finally met his new goddaughter, his feelings were anything but paternal. He was immediately enamored by both her great beauty and personality; her character was akin to his own. She was similarly attracted; part of her admiration stemmed from the fact he was the famous author of *The Power and the Glory*.

Shortly thereafter, Graham and Vivien were invited by the Walstons to spend a weekend at their magnificent estate, Thriplow, near Cambridge. When the Greenes went to catch the train back to Oxford, they were amazed that their hostess not only insisted to arrange for a flight back on her private plane but also wanted to accompany them. Greene later recalled that as he stood by Catherine on the snowy airfield, waiting to board, her long, dark hair brushed against his face. A year later he wrote Catherine about the memory, "The act of creation is awfully odd and inexplicable like falling in love—A lock of hair touches one's eyes in a plane with East Anglia under snow and one is in love."

The woman who was to become the inspiration for *The End of the Affair* was born in New York. As a nineteen-year-old student at Barnard College, while on a ski vacation in New Hampshire, she met Henry Walston. He was enraptured with her beauty; she with his power and prestige. When he proposed a few days afterward, she dropped out of school and followed him to England. There they settled into a life of fantastic wealth: a country house in Cambridgeshire; a flat in St. James's, Piccadilly; a cottage on the west coast of Ireland; and a banana plantation in St. Lucia. Together they had six children; apart they both embarked on numerous affairs.

Graham and Catherine had a great deal in common: both were passionate Catholic converts who had engaged in extramarital liaisons and were tormented over their serial adultery. However, as Graham wrote, "What would a novelist do without a sense of guilt?" With the full knowledge of their respective spouses, Catherine and Graham escaped to her private island, Achill, off the west coast of Ireland. On the journey she wore a red dressing gown. Later Greene was to tell Vivien that Catherine, so clad, "was the sexiest image of a woman he had ever seen." With Catherine, he found a woman who shared his insatiable appetite for sexual gratification.

The two of them then embarked on a trip to Italy. In a letter to Vivien, which was his mea culpa, he explained he was not willing to give up his mistress for his wife. "The fact has to be faced, my dear, I shall always & with anyone have been a bad husband. Unfortunately the disease is also one's material. Cure the disease and I doubt whether a writer would remain." Vivien was devastated by her husband's "disease;" however, as a committed Catholic, she could not divorce her philandering spouse. She bought a home in Oxford and turned her attention to restoring doll-houses, filling them with exquisite miniatures. These dollhouses were worlds that she could control. She became an authority on the subject, traveling the world to obtain furniture, and wrote respected books on her passion. She and Graham were never to live together again. Greene spent every possible occasion with his lover. When forced to be apart, he wrote her numerous letters, always declaring his love. In one he expressed his feelings, "I want you and nothing but you for the rest of my life." Despite his religion, he repeatedly implored her to leave her husband and marry him. However, this was something she was unwilling to do.

Sadly enough, Catherine, after a few years, began to back away. Part of the reason for her distancing herself from the man she loved was a deepening sense of guilt over her sexual lifestyle. The religion that had brought them together was now tearing them apart. Fearing her ultimate rejection, Graham added twenty-four aspirins to a half pint of whisky, but his suicide attempt failed. When she broke off their relationship, the devastated author wrote *The End of the Affair*, dedicated to her and based on their passionate and star-crossed story.

That Greene's love was reciprocated is evidenced by Catherine Walston's last letter to him before he embarked to Capri. "What happy times I had there with you and won't ever forget them from the day we walked through the gate for the first time with Bernardo . . . What a vast amount of pleasure you had given me playing Scrabble on the roof at Rosaio and teaching me to swim underwater at Ian Flemming's [sic] house; smoking opium at Ankor etc. . . . There has never been anyone in my life like you."

After Catherine there were other relationships, one with Anita

Björk, a Swedish actress, and a long-term one with Yvonne Cloetta; he moved to Antibes to be with her. However, the only time Graham was ever to experience "the power and the glory" was with his cherished "C."

22

Atlas Shrugged

AYN RAND

(ALISSA ZINOV'YEVNA ROSENBAUM)

1952

To Frank O'Connor and Nathaniel Branden

IT took a revolution that changed the face of twentieth-century history to bring Frank O'Connor and Ayn Rand to one another. And, once united, Ayn was faithful to Frank, in her fashion.

When she was twelve years old, Alissa Rosenbaum witnessed the first shots of the Russian Revolution from the balcony of her home in St. Petersburg. The communist regime confiscated her father's pharmacy, which reduced the once financially comfortable family to poverty. Thus was born Alissa's lifelong hatred of Stalin's USSR. From that time forth, she had a burning desire to escape the tyranny of the sickle and hammer.

At age twenty-one, under the guise of visiting relatives in Chicago, Alissa was able, although with great difficulty, to obtain a temporary visa. Once in the United States, she did not look back. She was never to see any member of her family again, with the exception of a brief visit from her sister Nora, who stayed with her for an unfulfilling time. Once in Chicago, she changed her name from Alissa to Ayn (after a Finnish author), and she changed her last name from Rosenbaum to Rand, after her Remington-Rand typewriter.

Always enamored with the American film industry, with a dream of becoming a screenwriter, Ayn borrowed fifty dollars and set out for Hollywood, where she rented a room in a YMCA. There she managed to meet the famed director Cecil B. DeMille, who was impressed by her and gave her the nickname "Caviar." He also gave her a job as an extra on his film *King of Kings*. On the set she became attracted to fellow actor Frank O'Connor, and, with her characteristic *chutzpah*, she purposely tripped him to make his acquaintance. With Uncle Sam holding the gun, their romance was forced into a shotgun marriage in order to prevent her deportation. However, their marriage was based on love, and it lasted for half a century. When Frank O'Connor took his wedding vows, he knew he was marrying a Jewish, penniless, friendless refugee from Russia who hardly spoke English; what he could never have fathomed was that his bride was going to undergo a radical metamorphosis to become one of the most eminent authors of the century.

Their lives changed dramatically with the publication of *The Fountainhead*, which was dedicated to Frank. The novel became an international bestseller, as well as a movie starring Gary Cooper. With the newfound fame and financial security, Ayn and Frank moved to New York City, where she felt at home in the capital of capitalism. However, *The Fountainhead* was to bring Ayn other, unimagined, results.

The novel especially aroused a chord in teenage intellectual circles, and became for them a rite of passage. This was especially true for fourteen-year-old Nathan Blumenthal in Brampton, Ontario, Canada, who was so smitten with *The Fountainhead* he wrote its author a letter, which went unanswered. A few years later the boy, now a young adult, became romantically involved with a fellow Rand devotee, Barbara Weidman. They ended up moving to California to study at UCLA, at which time the then eighteen-year-old Blumenthal wrote another letter to Rand, who was living in a huge glass and steel ranch house in the San Fernando Valley. She invited him to her home; he arrived at 8:00 p.m. and did not leave until 5:30 a.m. the following day. In a true meeting of minds, they stayed up talking until the dawn. Ultimately, Nathan and Barbara transferred to NYU, and became extremely close with both Ayn and Frank, who served as the matron of honor and the best man at their wedding.

Ayn used her New York apartment as a literary salon, which she presided over as the grande dame. Each week her protégés (which included the young, clarinet-playing future chairman of the Federal Reserve, Alan Greenspan, whose nickname in the group was "the Undertaker") would sit entranced as Ayn waved her omnipresent cigarette holder and expounded on her philosophy in her heavily accented voice. She was the equivalent of a Jewish, female Dostoevsky transported to Manhattan.

Nathan and Barbara were part of this charmed circle. (Nathan Blumenthal had changed his name to Nathaniel Branden.) Rand was especially drawn to Nathaniel, whom she referred to as her "intellectual heir." As such, she made him her official spokesman, and with that endorsement he was able to open the extremely lucrative Nathaniel Branden Institute in the Empire State Building, where it rented eight thousand square feet. She allowed him the privilege of answering her mail and gave him carte blanche ability to speak for her, as his thoughts were so closely aligned with her own.

Nathaniel soon took on another role, that of Ayn Rand's lover. Perhaps one of the reasons she was drawn to him, in addition to the physical attraction of a man much younger than her husband, was their commonalities. They had both been born Jewish, left their place of birth, undergone name changes to distance themselves from their pasts, and were intellectual titans. Their affair was undertaken despite their twenty-five-year age difference and the fact that they were both married and friends with one another's spouses. Barbara went along with their liaison, and soon indulged in ones of her own. Frank agreed to vacate their apartment for his wife's twice weekly sexual trysts and headed to a bar, where he would down one drink after another to try to ease his pain.

In 1957, Rand's epic novel, the one-thousand-plus-page *Atlas Shrugged*, was published. It had the unique distinction of being dedicated to both her husband and her lover. The former man had her love, the latter, her passion. Between her two men she had achieved the perfect male balance.

Her magnum opus had taken fourteen years to write, and, when it was completed, she fell into a variation of postpartum depression. During that time she told Nathaniel that she wanted a hiatus from their sexual relationship, as she was in an emotional and psychological slump. Her lover was secretly relieved, because although he was still in intellectual awe of his mentor, he no longer was sexually attracted to her. He took this opportunity to begin dating a married model, Patrecia Scott, who had attended one of his lectures. The entire situation imploded when Rand wanted to resume her sexual relationship with Nathaniel. Sensing his reluctance, she turned to his wife, Barbara, for clarification. While Atlas may have merely shrugged, Rand hit the proverbial roof when Barbara told her about the other woman. She also summoned Nathaniel to her apartment and slapped him hard in the face. Whatever else she hit him with, or what choice phrases she hurled at him in a mixture of Russian and English, is not known.

Ayn now looked upon Nathaniel as her Judas, who betrayed her for a younger and more beautiful woman. The result of his "sin" was excommunication from her inner circle and being fired from his position as her spokesperson. She told her disciples the reason for his banishment was financial mismanagement; her cowering followers never questioned the veracity of the breakup. Furthermore, she told her publisher that all future editions of *Atlas Shrugged* were to expurgate the dedication to the name that she could no longer bear mentioning. It was not mere happenstance that Nathaniel and Patrecia, who were subsequently married, moved to the West Coast. (They remained married until she was found dead in their backyard swimming pool.)

After Nathaniel's exodus, Ayn seemed to lose her passion. She became reclusive and never wrote another novel. Although she had once answered an interviewer who asked her where she got her ideas for her torrid love scenes by replying, "wishful thinking," the truth is her younger lover had been her sexual soul mate.

In 1974 Ayn was diagnosed with lung cancer and Frank was slowly slipping into dementia. When he died a few years later, she had him interred in Valhalla, New York. On his grave she placed a white marble headstone with the inscription: Frank O'Connor 1897–1979. With his passing, she was left without any family. She had always been steadfast in her desire not to have children, maintaining that the only posterity she wanted was her writings.

Eight years after the death of her husband, Rand died of heart failure in the place where she had lived most of her life, her New York City apartment.

Ayn Rand's funeral was attended by many of her followers, including Alan Greenspan, her former protégé and now a powerful politician. By her coffin someone placed a six-foot-high floral arrangement in the shape of a dollar sign. For Rand, capitalism was the most humane of all the economic systems. She was buried next to her husband, with an adjacent matching headstone. On it was engraved her third and final name: Ayn Rand O'Connor. Ayn had been faithful to Frank, in her fashion.

23

Lolita

VLADIMIR NABOKOV

(VLADIMIR VLADIMIROVICH NABOKOV)

1955

To Vera

Aʟʟ of Nabokov's novels bear the same dedication: To Vera. There is the old saying "opposites attract," but the Vladimir–Vera relationship proves that commonalities are the ties that bind. This literary couple shared a place of birth, a love of privacy, and an unswerving belief in the brilliance of Vladimir.

Vladimir and Vera were born in St. Petersburg, Russia, and both their families were forced into exile because of the Russian Revolution. The Nabokovs had to flee because they were extraordinarily rich and members of the Russian aristocracy. Their home was the size of one of the Romanov palaces, and Vladimir was chauffeured to school in a Rolls-Royce. In 1919, as the Red Army approached, the Nabokovs left behind their old, privileged world, and sailed away, forever, from Russia on a ship named *Hope*.

The Slonim family escaped because, as Jews, they felt that they were going to be a target of the new antireligion Soviet dictatorship. Because there was a large Russian émigré population in Germany, both families decided to make that country their adopted home.

At the age of twenty-four, at a charity masquerade ball, Vladimir met a woman wearing a black mask with a wolf's face: Vera. From that moment, for the next fifty-two years, they were inseparable. They married soon after and had their only child, Dmitri.

Life was financially difficult for the refugee couple, and Vera went to work to support the family while Vladimir stayed at home doing what he loved best, writing. In 1922, Vladimir's father, Vladimir Dmitrievich Nabokov, was murdered by Russian assassins, although their real target was Pavel Milyukov. The son was devastated by the murder, and, upon hearing the news, sought solace in Vera's arms.

The Nabokovs continued to live in Weimar Germany, but they did so with increasing alarm. SS thugs and swastikas began to dominate the city, and, as Vera and Dmitri were Jewish, the Nabokovs found themselves once more on the run from political persecution. Again in the role of refugees, they fled to France. In 1940, on the eve of the Nazi invasion of Paris, the Nabokovs escaped once more, this time to the United States.

Nabokov obtained a position as a Russian professor at Cornell University, and this provided him with both a comfortable income and free time in which to write. And wherever Vladimir was, Vera was his shadow. She attended every lecture he gave (he introduced her as his assistant), filled in for him when he was ill, and admonished any student who talked while her husband was speaking with the words, "Do you not realize that you are in the presence of a genius?" In addition, because Vladimir was extremely withdrawn (he once remarked, "Socially I am a cripple"), she protected him from students, faculty, and, when he attained notoriety, the press. The wolf mask that she had worn on their first meeting proved to be a symbolic one as well.

Outside of the university Vera was as indispensable to her husband as in it. She worked as his interpreter, editor, literary agent, chauffeur (he never learned to drive), and muse. She took the role of being Mrs. Vladimir Nabokov (as she always signed her name) very seriously. She once stated that she had a need to be needed, and her husband definitely qualified. She was also an avid partner in his lifelong pursuit of collecting butterflies, and would accompany him on his walks to study and capture rare species. In the Nabokov Museum in St. Petersburg (the building is housed in his former childhood mansion), there is a painting of butterflies drawn by Vladimir, with the inscription: To V. From V.

In 1945, after talking to a relative who had remained in Germany, Vladimir needed Vera almost more than ever. He was informed that his brother Sergei, who was homosexual, had been picked up by the Gestapo in Nazi-occupied Austria and sent to a concentration camp because of his sexual orientation. He died in the camp at Neuengamme, Germany. Once more, as with the assassination of his father, Vladimir sought solace in Vera's arms.

On a vacation from teaching in the 1950s, the Nabokovs set off across America to do research on a book her husband was writing, *Lolita*. She drove an Oldsmobile across America, with Vladimir in the backseat, writing a first draft. They stayed in motel rooms that would become models for the ones in which Humbert Humbert stayed. It was also Vera who rescued the manuscript of *Lolita* from flames when her husband attempted to destroy it, rightly dreading the storm of controversy the novel would surely raise. Vera later said that the reason she saved the papers was because she "feared that the memory of the unfinished work would haunt him forever."

With the financial success of *Lolita*, the Nabokovs never had to worry about money for the rest of their lives. Feeling that they were by temperament more European than American, the Nabokovs emigrated once more. They moved into the Montreux Hotel, overlooking Lake Geneva in Switzerland. After Vladimir had lost his beloved childhood home, where he had enjoyed, as he described it, "a perfect childhood," he had refused to ever own a house again. But in Switzerland, the Nabokovs, who had spent so many years in so many countries, finally had one to call their own. After a life of upheavals, they spent their days in tranquillity, often collecting butterflies that they found on their walks along Lake Geneva.

In 1977, Dmitri visited his parents in Switzerland, and kissed his father's forehead just before his departure. Upon doing so, Vladimir's eyes filled with tears. When his son asked him why, he replied that a certain butterfly was already on the wing, and that he did not think that he was ever to see it again. His premonition of death proved correct, for he passed away shortly afterward, a result of a viral infection. Mercifully, he was able to find solace in his transition from this world to the next in the arms of his ever-devoted Vera.

24

Long Day's Journey into Night

Eugene O'Neill
(Eugene Gladstone O'Neill)
1956

For Carlotta, on our 12th Wedding Anniversary

Dearest: I give you the original script of this play of old sorrow, written in tears and blood. A sadly inappropriate gift, it would seem, for a day celebrating happiness. But you will understand. I mean it as a tribute to your love and tenderness which gave me the faith in love that enabled me to face my dead at last and write this play-write it with deep pity and understanding and forgiveness for all the four haunted Tyrones.

These twelve years, Beloved One, have been a Journey into Light-into love. You know my gratitude. And my love!

Gene
Tao House
July 12, 1941

THE woman who became Carlotta O'Neill, more than any-one else, saved Eugene O'Neill from being one of the "haunted Tyrones" he referred to in his play *Long Day's Journey into Night*. However, she was ultimately unable to bring him salvation from the family curse that played itself out with the inevitability of a Greek tragedy.

Long Day's Journey into Night is O'Neill's autobiographical play detailing his tortured childhood, a nightmare landscape that cast its shadow over his subsequent life. The patriarch of the real-life Tyrones (the family featured in the play) was his Irish-born father (a product of potato famine parents), James, an actor who starred in the title role of a traveling production of *The Count of Monte Cristo*. Having grown up in poverty, he was as stingy with money as he was with his affection, with the result that his family's only home was a series of dreary hotel rooms. In fact, his last words to Eugene only reinforced his legacy of negativity: "Eugene—This sort of life—here—all froth—no good—rottenness!"

Eugene's mother, Ella Quinlan O'Neill, was a morphine addict (she had become one after her doctor prescribed the drug to help her with Eugene's difficult birth). Her addiction and a suicide attempt left emotional scars that her children would bear for the rest of their lives.

The last of the family was James, who, as a mentor to his younger brother, Eugene, "made sin easy for him." James was an alcoholic who drank himself to death at the age of forty-five.

Long Day's Journey into Night was O'Neill's entry into the confessional, "written in tears and blood," where, with the help of his last wife, Carlotta, he attempted to exorcise the "Tyrone" family demons.

Eugene met the woman who gave him "the faith in love" that enabled him to face his dead in 1926, when he told his literary agent, Richard Madden, that he needed a new port of call, a place where he could write, and, just as importantly, stay sober. He, his second wife, Agnes, and their two children, six-year-old Shane and two-year-old Oona, moved to Maine, on Belgrade Lakes, in a cottage named "Loon Lodge." He was to tell friends, "The above name of our camp is no horrible jest but a fact! After a winter spent at Bellevue, I'll say it looks as if God had taken to symbolism, what? However, I remain not only sane, but also sober."

Sanity and sobriety being two requisites for O'Neill to write, he embarked on his play *Strange Interlude*. After a month, boredom, always a deadly enemy to O'Neill, set in. However, Eugene soon met the woman that would end his boredom: Carlotta Monterey. Their "strange interlude" was to alter the course of their lives.

Carlotta Monterey was christened Hazel Neilson Tharsing. Her father, Christian, was an immigrant from Denmark who worked as a sailor until settling in California, where he married his second wife, Nellie Gotchett. However, when Hazel was four, Nellie, bored in her role as a poor farmer's wife, decided to pursue a more exciting life in San Francisco. She left her daughter in the care of her sister who lived in Oakland and already had her own children to care for. When she was a young woman, Hazel traveled to Europe to study theater. There, because of her dark beauty, her desire to distance herself from her pedestrian roots, and the pain of a childhood that involved abandonment by her parents and poverty, she changed her name to Carlotta Monterey. Upon her return she went to audition in New York, where she obtained a small role in a Eugene O'Neill play, *The Hairy Ape*. She was not impressed by the famous playwright and called him, "the rudest man I've ever met." She was not to see him again until four years later, and when she did, she was to play a very different offstage role.

At the time Eugene, Agnes, and their children were staying at Loon Lodge, Carlotta was staying at a nearby cabin, Long Pond, as the guest of a wealthy real estate mogul, Elisabeth Marbury. Her hostess was also the business partner of O'Neill's literary agent. One afternoon, when the O'Neills were visiting Elisabeth, Carlotta, wearing a revealing bathing suit, showed Eugene the bathhouse so that he could get ready for a swim. He was immediately attracted to the exotic-looking beauty. Later he was to comment that "Carlotta had the same eyes as his late mother."

Carlotta, for her part, was willing to reciprocate. She invited herself along on his daily canoe trips, although she could not swim and was afraid of water. Her "attraction" may have been motivated by the fact that she was now in her early forties and had just been divorced from her third husband. In any case, Carlotta and Eugene started meeting by arranged accidents at the large home of actress Florence Reed. Eugene confided in Carlotta that he needed her. She was later to state, "My maternal instinct came out. This man must be looked after, I thought. He broke my heart." At the end of the summer O'Neill, his wife, and children returned to their home in Connecticut. Although their relationship had remained platonic, Eugene left with Carlotta's Manhattan address.

During the winter, the O'Neills stayed in their home in Bermuda, while Eugene made frequent trips to New York to supervise the production of *Strange Interlude*, and to rendezvous with Carlotta, with whom he was now smitten. Realizing, most probably with Carlotta's insistence, that he wanted to be with his mistress more than his wife, he told Agnes he wanted a divorce. She was furious and told him that they should try to work it out, especially for Shane and Oona. He refused and, shortly after, feeling it expedient to put physical distance between his two bitter ex-wives (he was married once before Agnes) and his three children (he had a son from his first marriage), Carlotta and Eugene set sail for Europe. In Tours, France, they leased a palatial, forty-five room estate, the Chateau du Plessis, decorated with marble floors, tapestries, and a number of employees. It was a far cry from Hazel's impoverished childhood home in Oakland. When Eugene's divorce became final, he wed his third wife in a private ceremony in Paris in 1929. Carlotta later remarked about her wedding ceremony, "Our knees shook for an hour."

The years in France were to become golden ones. Carlotta became a wife like Vera Nabokov, her greatest good ensuring that Eugene had the tranquillity in which to work. While there, in 1931, he wrote *Mourning Becomes Electra*, which was based on an ancient Greek tragedy. Carlotta's role was what the Swedish playwright August Strindberg described as "the labor of keeping the filth of life at a distance." In gratitude and in love, Eugene also dedicated this play to Carlotta.

With the encroaching political storm clouds gathering over Europe, and needing to return to the States for the production of *Mourning Becomes Electra*, the O'Neills found themselves in New York City, which Eugene referred to as Sodom and Gomorrah. Longing for the permanent home that he had never had, Eugene and Carlotta purchased 158 acres of land in the San Ramon Valley in California, which Eugene hoped would be their "final harbor." There they lovingly erected Tao House, christened so because of Eugene's love of Chinese philosophy. Carlotta decorated their estate in an Asian style; indeed, Eugene's teak bed had the unique history of coming from China, where it had been used as an opium couch. Unfortunately, their dream house soon provided a backdrop for a waking nightmare.

Eugene, like his father before him, loved his children, although he had always had trouble expressing it. He was stricken with grief when his oldest son, Eugene Jr., a Yale classics professor who suffered from alcoholism, committed suicide at the age of forty. His second son, Shane (who was to also commit suicide later), was a heroin addict who constantly needed money for drugs and bail. His daughter, Oona, infuriated her father when, as an eighteen-year-old, she went to Hollywood and started dating a man whom her father disapproved of, as he was a well-known womanizer, was currently involved in an acrimonious paternity suit, and was three times older than Oona. When she married Charlie Chaplin, her father never spoke to her again and expunged her name from his will.

Alongside the heartache caused by his children, Eugene's health began to decline. His hands trembled so much—either as a result of Parkinson's disease or the toll of years of alcoholism—that he could no longer do what had been his lifelong reprieve, writing. To compound matters, his marriage to Carlotta began to unravel. Eugene's depression over his children and his declining health exacerbated her own fragile mental stability. The passion they once felt for each other was now used in their ever-accelerating fights.

Eugene's final home was the Shelton Hotel in Boston, where, weary of "The Great Sickness" (his epithet for life), he waited for the end. In the weeks before his death, he told Carlotta that he "wanted no priest or minister, or Salvation Army captain at his deathbed: He would confront God—if there was a God—man to man." His last words to his wife, who was at his deathbed, were, "Born in a hotel room, and God dammit, died in one!"

In respect of his final request, Eugene was not buried in the O'Neill family plot in St. Mary's Cemetery in Connecticut. This was partly because many years before he had traded in his childhood Roman Catholicism for the philosophy of Nietzsche. It was also his final attempt to do in death what he was never able to do in life, which was to at last distance himself from the "four haunted Tyrones."

25

Peyton Place

GRACE METALIOUS
(MARIE GRACE DE REPENTIGNY)
1956

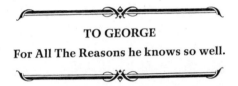

TO GEORGE

For All The Reasons he knows so well.

THE reasons that "George [knew] so well" become apparent when one examines the unique challenges it must have taken to be married to Grace Metalious, which George Metalious was—twice. However, despite these reasons, he never fell out of love with his "Pandora in blue jeans."

George and Grace first met when they were nine years old, in the working-class mill town of Manchester, New Hampshire. At the same time as she received her high school diploma, she received confirmation of her pregnancy and decided to go the conventional route and marry George, the baby's father. It was to be one of her last conventional acts. Both families, not knowing Grace was expecting, were against the marriage. The Metaliouses wanted a girl with a Greek heritage, who was a member of the Greek Orthodox Church. Grace's family, the de Repentignys, wanted a boy with a French Canadian heritage who was a member of the Roman Catholic Church. But because it was the 1940s, and she was pregnant, Grace became Mrs. Metalious.

The marriage was not just necessitated by circumstances, however, as Grace was attracted to George. She stated she fell in love with the kind of man who always attracted her: "tall, dark, handsome and massive. Protective, dominating, fatherly." The last trait was because her own father had abandoned her family when Grace was ten years old.

The new couple lived, along with their three children, in squalor. Partly as an escape from the drudgery of her daily life, partly in the dream of receiving financial remuneration, Grace spent these early years of marriage writing—something she had done from an early age. As a child, desperate for a quiet place to work, she used to lock herself in her aunt's bathroom, sit in the tub, put a washtub across her lap, and compose countless stories.

When World War II broke out, George was drafted into the army. When he was gone, for the first time Grace indulged in an adulterous affair; however, George did likewise in Germany. When they were reunited, Grace found herself in the role of P.H.T.—her acronym for Putting Hubby Through. What she was putting George through was the University of New Hampshire. When he graduated in 1954, he obtained a teaching position and then became a principal at an elementary school in a small town called Gilmanton, New Hampshire. They purchased a run-down house that Grace christened It'll Do.

George's new position as principal of a small-town school put strains on their marriage, because Grace refused to mold herself into the image of the proper principal's wife. She adamantly ignored her husband's pleas to exchange her customary garb of a man's lumber shirt, jeans, and running shoes for the expected stockings and pearls. Mrs. Cleaver she wasn't. She said, "I did not like belonging to Friendly Clubs and bridge clubs. I did not like being regarded as a freak because I spent time in front of a typewriter instead of a sink. And George did not like my not liking the things I was supposed to like." The more the women of the town censured her, the more Grace took refuge at her Remington. Indeed, so preoccupied was she with writing that she completely ignored her role as housewife. Once, when a guest was at their house, she made an attempt to clean the table. Unfortunately, what she took to be a Brillo pad turned out to be a dead mouse. George, although not thrilled with his domestic situation, accepted it. He later stated that while his wife was grinding out her libido-laden novel, "I cooked, fed the kids, ran the school and never once objected." Perhaps it was because he did all this that Grace would later dedicate her book to him: "To George—for all the reasons he knows so well."

One night, an event occurred that was to shake up not only the Metaliouses' marriage, but the country as well. George related the genesis: "At 3:00 a.m. she woke me up and she had the whole plot in her mind. She hadn't slept. She got up and she outlined what she thought was a good story." The story was the sensational *Peyton Place*. The debut novel revolutionized the publishing industry. It sent ripples of shock waves throughout the country, which was mired in the extreme conservative Christian mores of the 1950s, an era when TV had married couples sleeping in twin beds and one could not use the word *pregnant* on-air, a time when *Roe v. Wade* was not even on the horizon. It astounded people that a novel dealing with rape, incest, alcoholism, abortion, and female sexuality could have been written by a housewife from a small New England town.

The press instantly dubbed Grace "Pandora in blue jeans." Reporters from across the country descended on Gilmanton. Grace Metalious became an overnight international celebrity— and local pariah. When Hollywood decided to make a movie and TV miniseries based on her blockbuster debut, the frenzy of the press intensified. The residents of Gilmanton were furious; they felt that the novel was a magnifying glass that exposed their town. Although the novel brought fame and wealth, like Pandora's box, it opened up endless evil. George Metalious was fired from his job as principal because of the notoriety, and mothers refused to let their children play with the Metalious kids. George's reaction was to move, by himself, to Stowe, Massachusetts, where he had obtained a position as a teacher. His rationale for leaving his wife was that as she had created the storm, she should be the one to weather it.

Grace told a reporter, "New England towns are small and they are often pretty, but they are not just pictures on a Christmas card. To a tourist these towns look as peaceful as a postcard picture, but if you go beneath that picture it's like turning over a rock with your foot. All kinds of strange things crawl out." The slime that oozed out from under this rock spread its venom over the Metalious family, and in 1942, the marriage of childhood friends and high school sweethearts ended. Grace always felt that it was the charge that she had based the characters in her novel on the people of Gilmanton that had led to her husband's dismissal and the subsequent erosion of their marriage. When John Michael Hayes, the screenwriter for the book's adaptation, asked her if the novel was autobiographical, Grace responded by purposely spilling her drink on him.

Without the steadfast influence of George, and unable to handle celebrity status, Grace turned more and more to alcohol for solace. As she was later to say upon self-reflection, "I looked into that empty bottle and saw myself." Grace indulged in affairs and married a disc jockey, but these did not bring her any solace. Then, in 1960, she remarried George. She recalls, "After I had left my second husband I sat for a long time in my house in New Hampshire. Last spring, one day, George came to my house and said, 'Now are you ready to come home?' I said yes." However, their remarriage hit the skids and they divorced once again. In 1964, at age forty, Ms. Metallious fell from "grace" for the last time when she died from cirrhosis of the liver, brought on by years of alcoholism. Her companion in her last days was her British lover, to whom she willed what was left of her fortune. Her last words to him were "Be careful of what you want. You may get it." In the final analysis, the only man who had ever truly loved the Pandora in blue jeans was George, "for all the reasons he knows so well."

26

Dr. Zhivago

BORIS PASTERNAK
(BORIS LEONIDOVICH PASTERNAK)
1957

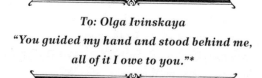

To: Olga Ivinskaya
"You guided my hand and stood behind me,
all of it I owe to you."*

THE lyrics for "Somewhere My Love" (also known as "Lara's Theme") in the 1965 motion picture *Dr. Zhivago* are haunting and tragic, detailing how snow "covers the hope of spring." Tragically, Lara and the woman on whom the character was based, Olga Ivinskaya, were never fortunate enough to experience the melting of the snow.

Olga Ivinskaya (her mother's name) was partly of German-Polish descent and was born in 1912, in the ancient town of Tambov. Her childhood was an ordinary one, although her adult life would be anything but. Her father was a provincial high school teacher, and when Olga was three, they relocated to Moscow. Since

---

*This dedication appears only on the original manuscript. Because Pasternak was married, he did not include it in the published version.

her adolescence she had been an ardent admirer of Pasternak, and attended literary gatherings to listen to his poetry. Her passion for Pasternak's writing influenced her decision to attend the Editorial Workers Institute. It was to influence her destiny as well.

Olga Ivinskaya's life was first afflicted with tragedy when her husband hung himself, either because of fear of arrest in Stalin's Great Purge, or because Olga had told him she was leaving him for another man, Alexander Vinogradov. She ended up marrying Vinogradov, but their union was beset with difficulties. Due to the economic deprivations under the new communist regime, housing was extremely scarce. Olga's home was a two-bedroom apartment, which she shared with her husband, two children, mother, and her mother's companion. In 1940 Olga's mother was arrested and sentenced to a prison camp for allegedly making slanderous remarks about Stalin. One can only imagine what Olga felt when, during the trial, she discovered that it was Alexander who had denounced her mother. This led to the beginning of the breakdown of her second marriage, which ended two years later when Alexander died in a sanatorium located next to a railroad station named, ironically, Recreation. In 1945, Olga's mother was released from prison, and returned to their apartment.

Although Olga had experienced the deaths of two husbands, the imprisonment of her mother, single parenthood, and economic privation, at thirty-five years old, when she began her position as an editor for the journal *Novy Mir*, she remained as beautiful as ever. As someone who loved novels and poetry, she adored her new position; from the window she could see the Pushkin memorial as well as eminent literary figures. When Pasternak, then fifty-six, brought in his poetry, the secretary, an older woman, greeted him by saying to the famous writer, "Now I will introduce you to a lady who is one of your most fervent admirers." When he met Olga, he gave her the customary kiss on the hand; however, they then indulged in the uncustomary activity of talking at length, mainly about his forthcoming novel, which he was later to name *Dr. Zhivago*. Little did either of them dream that the finished manuscript would include their relationship set across the backdrop of the Russian Revolution. Of her first impression of Boris, she was to recall of his exotic looks, "A curious African god in European dress." Similarly, after hearing Boris give a public reading she told her mother, "Leave me in peace; I have spoken with God today."

The next day, on Olga's desk were five autographed volumes of Pasternak's poetry, and at closing time he appeared, as he would each evening, to escort her home. In 1947 Pasternak declared his feelings for Olga in a letter, in which he wrote, "my life, my angel, I love you truly…This inscription is eternal and valid forever. And can only grow stronger." However, their romantic relationship could not be consummated. This was because Olga shared her flat with three other people, as did Boris, whose home included his two sons and Zinaida Nikolayevna, his wife. Needing someone to confide in about his situation, he turned to his friend Lyusya Popova. He told her, "A bright ray of sunlight has entered my life and it's so good, so good. I'm in love, Lyusya, you see." To which she responded, "What will happen to your life now, Boris Leonidovich?"

When Boris and Olga finally were able to be intimate, he first told her that he regretted his marriage; however, he added that he did not want to terminate it, as he was a man bound by duty. As time went on, the mistress, as so often happens, started pressuring to be the wife. Olga's mother also badgered him to legitimize her daughter, especially as the Soviet regime was strongly opposed to non-state-sponsored liaisons. Pasternak told his would-be mother-in-law,

"I love your daughter more than my life, but please do not expect our life to change outwardly at once." A tug-of-war ensued between Zinaida and Olga, with Boris the rope. Who the ultimate victor was is a matter of subjectivity. Olga tried to emotionally distance herself from her lover and would, on occasion, turn his photograph to the wall. At these times she hated that she loved him. Later, missing the face of her dear Boris, she would relent, and not only turn his picture once more toward her, but seek out his embrace. During a reconciliation he told her, "Olyushenka, let it be like this all our lives—we'll fly into each other's arms and there's nothing more important than for us to be able to be together. We mustn't predict anything or complicate things and we mustn't harm anybody." After one of her meltdowns at his refusal to leave his wife, he told her that her behavior was like "something out of a bad novel." Little did they realize that the bad novel was to turn into a tragic one.

In 1949, Olga discovered she was pregnant, which she hoped would convince Boris to make her Mrs. Pasternak. However, before she could present this new situation to her lover, her Moscow apartment was raided by the dreaded Soviet secret police, who sent her to Lubyanka labor camp. Her sentence was five years for the crime of "being close to persons suspected of espionage." When Judge Sernyonov told her that the reason why she associated with Pasternak was because she shared his unorthodox, bourgeois views, she answered that she was with him only for love. His response was, "I simply cannot believe that you as a Russian woman could love an old Jew like that."

The real reason for Olga's imprisonment was that the authorities wanted to get at Pasternak, whose writings did not follow official Party dogma. However, because Pasternak was born in Georgia, the same region as Stalin, and as the dictator liked his translation of

Hamlet, Boris bore the mark of Cain. Therefore, all the wrath of the authorities landed on the hapless Olga's head. Olga recalls that one day while in prison, she was told that Pasternak was also in the jail and that she was to be allowed to visit him. She was instead taken to the prison morgue and told to lift the lid on a coffin. She refused to do so and was taken back to her cell. The authorities orchestrated this scenario to get Olga to implicate Boris. They thought if she assumed him dead, she would be willing to implicate him, something that she previously had refused to do. From his end, Boris was in despair over his lover's imprisonment and the forthcoming birth of his baby. He asked his wife to adopt his child; incensed, she refused. The issue soon became moot when Olga miscarried in her fifth month. After five years, Olga was released from prison, and she and Boris resumed their love affair once more.

In 1958, Pasternak was named the winner of the Nobel Prize for his epic masterpiece, *Dr. Zhivago*. He had smuggled the manuscript to Italy for publication because the Soviet authorities had refused to allow its release, deeming it anticommunist propaganda. Upon hearing the news of the award, Boris sent a telegram to the Swedish Academy: "Immensely thankful, touched, proud, astonished, abashed." Four days later, he retracted, and told the Academy that he would not accept the prize. The government had informed him that if he were to travel to Stockholm to accept it, he would be considered a traitor and would not be allowed back into the Soviet Union. Boris was desperate not to be exiled, as he was still deeply in love with Olga, with whom he would maintain an intimate relationship until his death in 1960.

Although there was only a brief mention of his passing in the newspaper, thousands came to Boris's funeral, where mourners recited *Hamlet*: "Good night, sweet prince / And may bands of angels sing thee to thy rest." In his will, he left all the money from the foreign royalties from *Dr. Zhivago* to Olga.

After the passing of Boris, the KGB raided Olga's home once more, seizing all of Pasternak's love letters, as well as his manuscripts. The charge this time was for accepting money from abroad from the sale of the seditious *Dr. Zhivago*. Her arrest and eight-year sentence to a gulag in Siberia were echoed by Lara's fate in the novel, "One day Lara went out and did not come back. She must have been arrested in the street, as so often happened in those days, and she died or vanished somewhere, forgotten as a nameless number on a list which was afterwards mislaid."

The price Olga paid for loving Boris was surpassingly steep, involving as it did not just being the "other woman," but arrests by the KGB and imprisonments in Stalin's Siberian gulags. One can wonder whether Boris's love was worth the horrors Olga had to endure. The answer can be found in Olga's memoir, *A Prisoner of Time*, which she published abroad and dedicated to her departed lover, Boris Pasternak: "The greater part of my conscious life has been devoted to you—and what is left of it will also be devoted to you."

27

To Kill a Mockingbird

HARPER LEE
(NELLE HARPER LEE)
1960

Dedication
For Mr. Lee and Alice
in consideration of Love & Affection

O NE of the most beloved American authors is also one of its most reclusive. Harper Lee guards her privacy as fiercely as her memorable eccentric, Boo Radley. However, in her dedication to *To Kill a Mockingbird* she raises the curtain on her private life by revealing the two people who were the most important to her, Mr. Lee and Alice.

Perhaps one of the reasons why Nelle Lee has steadfastly refused to give interviews is that *To Kill a Mockingbird* is in many ways a mirror of her life, and that is all she is willing to share. The author grew up in Monroeville, a small town in Alabama, during the Great Depression. She was the last of four children and her parents named her Nelle, which was a reversal of her grand-mother's name, Ellen. In light of her future unconventionality, this backward spelling would prove symbolic. For example, while girls at this time dressed in pink frilly dresses, Nelle (as did her fictional counterpart Scout) refused this garb in favor of overalls.

The man who dominated her childhood was her father, Amasa Coleman Lee, who went by his initials A.C. Her mother, Frances Cunningham Finch, lived with her husband and four children, but only in a physical sense. She suffered from what would probably currently be diagnosed as bipolar disorder and agoraphobia; her husband referred to his wife's condition as her "nervous disorder." She spent her days endlessly working in her garden and her nights endlessly playing her piano. Her spouse and her children were mere shadows in her life. A.C. was a steadfast husband, however, and never strayed from his marital vows. Similarly, he was never heard to complain. His philosophy was that everyone had a cross to bear, and his perennially distraught wife was his. The neighbors' term for her condition was "second childhood." Fortunately, A.C. was able to provide enough nurturing to his children that they never suffered too much.

On the surface, A.C. appeared to be a very strict parent. He dressed in suits, was a devout Methodist, and frowned upon alcohol. He was also a pillar of Monroeville. He was a partner in the law firm of Bugg, Barnett & Lee; owned and edited the town's newspaper, the *Monroe Journal*; was a deacon in the church; and served in the Alabama State Legislature. However, within the confines of home, he was a loving and devoted father figure. In the evenings he would let Nelle sit on his lap, where they would do crossword puzzles and go over the articles in his newspaper. They also invented a game whereby Nelle increased her vocabulary. While doing so, she imitated his habit of endlessly playing with his gold pocket watch. Growing up under the tutelage of Mr. Lee, his daughter was light years ahead of her classmates.

The other main friend and role model in her life was her eldest sister, Alice, who, because of Frances's illness, served as both a sister and mother to her younger siblings. This was essential to the Harper household, as A.C. was extremely busy with his law firm and civic and religious duties. Alice's nickname in the family was "the Bear."

Growing up, Nelle's companion was her next-door neighbor, Truman Streckfus Persons, who appeared in *To Kill a Mockingbird* as the character Dill. He, too, would later achieve fame as the writer Truman Capote. To amuse the precocious children, and to help keep them from trouble, A.C. brought home a marvel of 1930s technology: a black Underwood typewriter. Little did he realize that the two children who poured endlessly over the keys would become two of the best-known authors of the twentieth century.

A.C. also gave Nelle a gift, one that would prove far more enduring then the black typewriter: lessons on how to live a moral life. He taught her that the popular thing was not always the right thing, and to stand against injustice even if one's stance brought wrath upon one's own head.

A.C. did not teach through mere words. In August of 1934, one hundred members of the local branch of the Ku Klux Klan assembled at the Monroeville Elementary School parking lot, and then proceeded to march along South Alabama Avenue toward the courthouse. Along the way, they passed the Lee home, where the family watched the white-hooded figures stand out in sharp relief against the night sky. A.C. went up to the Grand Dragon and told him that he was going to write a scathing indictment of them unless they dispersed. They did so. The scene where Atticus Finch stands vigil over the courthouse where Tom Robinson is imprisoned, thereby protecting him from a lynch mob, was born.

One of the few times that Nelle defied both Alice and A.C. was when she dropped out of law school in order to move to New York City to pursue her dream of becoming a writer. Alice was upset with the decision because she felt by leaving Alabama Nelle would not be sharing in the care of their mother. A.C. was disappointed because he had hoped that Nelle would join him and Alice in their law firm. Moreover, the ever-practical A.C. felt that she was just being unrealistic and that her quest of becoming a writer was a mere dream. He believed that she was just trying to imitate what Truman had already accomplished. Nelle was not to be dissuaded. Accordingly, A.C. refused to finance her. However, he did load his daughter's possessions into his black Chevy and drove her down South Alabama Avenue, droppping his prodigal daughter off at the railroad station. Alice was left, in her words, to "keep the home fires burning."

In New York City Nelle, with the objectivity of distance, was able to write her fictionalized memoir of coming of age in the South in the 1930s. Her first draft of the novel was named *Atticus*, after the lawyer and father of Scout Finch. Nelle had chosen the name after Cicero's best friend, Titus Pomponius Atticus, whom Cicero described as a "wise, learned and humane man."

The success of *To Kill a Mockingbird* surpassed everyone's expectations, especially Nelle's, whose greatest hope for her debut novel was that it "would die a quick and merciful death." Her father was thrilled, though astounded, that his daughter's gamble had paid off. Truman, characteristically, was envious that his old friend's fame had eclipsed his own. And Monroeville, that "tired old town," was shocked that one of its own daughters had become so famous that it became a mecca for newspaper reporters.

This was especially true when Hollywood decided to turn the

novel into a feature film. Gregory Peck, in order to research his role, made his way to Monroeville to analyze firsthand the man upon whom his role was based, A. C. Lee. Harper, fearful for Peck's privacy, did all she could to keep Monroeville's citizens, especially its female ones, from stampeding a path to his hotel door. One of the characteristics that Peck picked up on in his observations of A.C. was his habit of playing with his gold pocket watch when he was thinking, or in times of stress. The same idiosyncrasy would hold true of the onscreen Atticus Finch.

In 1963, the film version of *To Kill a Mockingbird* was nominated for eight Academy Awards. On the night of the ceremony, Nelle went to a friend's house to watch the show because she did not own a TV; this was because she felt it would disturb her writing. She did not want to attend the awards ceremony, as she had developed a huge distaste for the red carpet. However, when Gregory Peck had received a nomination for Best Actor, she sent him A.C.'s gold watch (he had recently passed away). On it she had inscribed "To Gregory from Harper." As Peck awaited the announcement of who would be chosen as Best Actor, in true A.C./Atticus fashion, he endlessly played with the watch. In his acceptance speech, one of the first people he thanked was Harper Lee.

Currently, Nelle divides her time between her apartment in New York City and her sister's home in Alabama. "The Bear," now in her nineties, continues to "keep the home fires burning." When in Monroeville, the two sisters often go to Dave's Catfish Cabin for lunch. When reporters are in town, through prearranged signals, the residents of Monroeville warn the two reclusive sisters, so they can quietly make their getaway. The fictional Maycomb County, Monroeville, ultimately learned to protect its mockingbird.

28

The Bell Jar

SYLVIA PLATH

1963

For *ELIZABETH* and *DAVID*

WHEN Sylvia Plath received the most staggering blow of her life, the place she sought refuge was a cottage in Devon. In gratitude, she dedicated *The Bell Jar* to the two friends who opened their door and hearts to her when she had no place else to turn.

The path that led to the door in Devon began when the brilliant young American poet Sylvia Plath won a Fulbright scholarship to study at Cambridge University. At a party, she met another poet, Ted Hughes. She was immediately smitten. She strode up to him and began reciting his poetry. The girlfriend he had arrived with became an instant footnote. The two poets danced and drank. At one point, their physical attraction was so great that Plath bit his cheek so hard that blood poured down his face. He confiscated her hair band to ensure a future meeting. They were married four months later.

The two moved into a London flat, but soon longed for a place in the country in which they could write and raise children in a tranquil setting. They rented their London home to a Canadian poet and his wife and moved to Court Green in Devon. The years that followed were wonderful ones. Sylvia was madly in love with Ted, had two children, wrote poetry, and felt content in her country home and its flower-filled garden. It was in Devon that Sylvia became good friends with her neighbors David and Elizabeth Sigmund. Elizabeth explained that the friendship between the two couples was founded on "the basis of a shared love of literature and love of the country and the wish that our children should grow up in a healthy and beautiful environment." Elizabeth and David were thrust in the role of a Greek chorus, watching with horror but unable to intercede in the tragedy that was to be enacted before them. The tragedy began when a snake entered Ted and Sylvia's Eden.

One weekend, Ted and Sylvia invited the poet to whom they had rented their London flat to Devon for the weekend. He brought along his wife, Assia, a striking Elizabeth Taylor–like beauty. Over dinner she explained she had grown up in the 1930s in Berlin, the daughter of a Jewish doctor and a German Christian mother. Because of the growing anti-Semitism, the family had fled to Palestine, where the mother was looked upon with suspicion because she was German. When the fighting broke out between the Jews and the British, Assia had fled the country. Sylvia was endeared by her; Ted was enamored. As he later wrote in a poem, Assia was "slightly filthy with erotic mystery." Soon after, he went to the London advertising agency where she worked and left her a note with the firm's receptionist: "I have come to see you, despite all marriages." Ted was tall, with an imposing physique and a beautiful face; moreover, he had a British accent and he was a poet. Assia's response was to pluck a blade of grass, drench it in Christian Dior perfume, and mail it to Ted. Three days later she opened an envelope. In it was a blade of grass from Devon, lying beside the first one.

They rendezvoused in a London hotel. Afterward, Assia, not one to be shy about her sexual exploits, told people at her agency about Ted's "violent and animal lovemaking." She also added that the sex was so ferocious that "in bed he smells like a butcher." Shortly after their first tryst, Assia called Ted at home in Court Green. When Sylvia answered, she pretended to be a man. The voice was obviously a female's; moreover, it had a unique accent. Sylvia flew into a rage and ripped the phone out of the wall. After exchanging what must have been some very unpoetic words with Ted, she grabbed her baby, Nicholas, and fled to the home of Elizabeth and David. In tears she told them, "My milk has dried up. Ted lies to me all the time. He has become a little man." She stayed the night with the Sigmund family and later said, "I have given my heart away and I can't take it back—it is like living without a heart." Sylvia ordered Ted to leave the house.

Elizabeth recalls that after Ted left Sylvia and their two children and moved in with Assia, Sylvia, in a downward spiral, continued to visit the Sigmunds. When she announced her decision to leave Court Green and move back to London in order to get a fresh start, Elizabeth was concerned that she was also leaving behind friends who cared about her. Sylvia ended up leasing a flat in London that had once been occupied by the Irish poet W. B. Yeats. Plath considered this a good omen. Her last letter to David and Elizabeth was upbeat. She wrote that she planned to come back for a visit to Devon and would return "in time for my daffodils. Thank God you will be there." She also added, "Ted comes to visit, and I can't help longing for lost Edens."

That winter was the coldest one that London had experienced

in a hundred years, and the water pipes froze. Sylvia and the two children, whom she was caring for on her own, all came down with the flu. To compound this, she may have learned that Assia was now pregnant. Always psychologically fragile, Sylvia found that her small flat had become her very own bell jar, claustrophobic and locking her in a world of depression. Unable to cope, and feeling smothered by depression, she left milk and bread on her children's night tables, carefully sealed the doors of the kitchen with towels, and placed her head in the oven.

A week after Sylvia's suicide at age thirty, Elizabeth went to visit Ted and his children, who were all living in Sylvia's apartment, as it was the environment the children were accustomed to. Assia was upstairs, in Sylvia's bed, where she was recovering from an abortion. Ted handed Elizabeth a copy of *The Bell Jar* and showed her the dedication. Then he started to boil water for a hot water bottle for Assia. He turned to Elizabeth and said, "It doesn't fall to many men to murder a genius." When Elizabeth protested that he hadn't, he continued, "Just as well. I might just as well have." Obviously in great emotional pain, he continued, "At night I hear the wolves howling in Regent's Park, it seems appropriate." Elizabeth recalls that Hughes was "semi-conscious with grief. I think he was absolutely heart-broken and horrified about Sylvia's death. He looked absolutely destroyed."

Once Assia had asked Elizabeth, "Do you think Ted and I can be happy?" to which Elizabeth replied she thought not because "Sylvia will always be there between you." Elizabeth's words proved prophetic. Six years later, in a horrific reenactment of her rival's death, Assia dragged some quilts into her kitchen. She gave Shura (her four-year-old daughter with Ted) some sleeping pills dissolved in a drink and then took some herself, washed down with whisky. Then, holding Shura, she turned on the gas of the kitchen stove.

One can only imagine the anguish Ted Hughes had to endure when his two wives' suicides and his daughter's murder were now laid at the door of his conscience. The triple tragedy haunted him for the rest of his life. After it he confided to Elizabeth, "My creativity presented me with a demon. If I get close to people, I destroy them."

Elizabeth Sigmund (now divorced from David) currently lives in a stone cottage in Cornwall. In her home is evidence of Sylvia Plath, who she says she always felt "was my utterly brilliant younger sister." On the coffee table sits the original edition of *The Bell Jar* that Ted gave her almost a half century ago. There is also a faded newspaper, folded at the page that recounts the tragedy that befell the two poets, once merely her next-door neighbors. Recently, when Elizabeth was asked to be a consultant on the movie *Sylvia*, starring Gwyneth Paltrow, she stated of the woman who had impacted her life, "I have never ceased to miss her, and mourn the absence of a dear and brilliant friend."

29

The Graduate

CHARLES WEBB

1963

TO EVE

IN the theme song of the film adaptation of *The Graduate*, "Mrs. Robinson," Simon & Garfunkel sing, "We'd like to know a little bit about you for our files." However, the information in the file of the real-life Benjamin and Elaine, whom the author based upon himself and his wife, Eve, could make a novel of its own.

Charles Webb met Eve Rudd in the 1960s while attending an all-male college in Massachusetts, Williams, and Eve was attending an all-female college, Bennington, in Vermont. Prior to becoming acquainted, Charles had seen a drawing entitled "Nuns in the Cold" and had immediately stated of its artist, "I have to meet this person." He had an opportunity to do so at a Halloween party. They were both on the fringe of the get-together, but when they saw one another, they immediately gravitated toward each other. When Charles learned she was the creator of the picture that had intrigued him, he was instantly smitten. For her part, Eve asked her stock question for determining whether she could be interested in a member of the opposite sex. She wanted to know if Charles had ever heard of Ring Lardner. She asked this because she felt that Lardner was the funniest author she had ever read. When Charles responded that he had, she knew that she "loved him totally at that point."

Their first date was at a local cemetery. Charles chose the unique dating locale because he was a connoisseur of gravestones. Soon Eve was Charles's Morticia Addams. They became inseparable in what Charles called a mutual protection society. One of the links that bound them was their shared sense of alienation. As Charles states, "Neither of us felt very at home at home." Eve said that they were "oddbods."

Webb has stated that the fictional Benjamin Braddock was based on himself and the fictional Elaine Robinson was based on Eve. It was this latter fact that made Eve dissatisfied with the book. Charles explains this by saying, "To be honest, [Eve's] never worried about the Mrs. Robinson thing; the thing that's bothered her most is that the character of Elaine is wimpy. And conventional. That chafed. There's not been a lot that is conventional about our relationship." Perhaps it was to emphasize this point that Eve appeared nude in *Newsweek*.

Unlike the story in the book, Eve's mother never tried to seduce Charles, as the infamous Mrs. Robinson had done to Benjamin. What she did try to do, however, was break up their relationship. She felt that the Webb's nouveaux riche money (Charles's father was a heart surgeon) was not equivalent to her East Coast old money. She did not succeed, and Charles and Eve married—the last conventional act they were ever to do.

Shortly after their wedding, the couple decided to sell back their presents to their guests, as they felt that their booty was too bourgeoisee. They spread the gifts out on their lawn and had a garage sale. Similarly, the house that they had purchased with the money from the film version of *The Graduate* was given to their realtor as a present. They also gave away art by Warhol, Rauschenberg, and Lichtenstein. The recipients of their largesse were causes such as Friends of the Earth and the Anti-Defamation League.

In the early 1970s, they divorced for two reasons. The first was that Eve wanted to protest the American government's ban on same-sex marriages. The second was because Eve had unsuccessfully campaigned for New York to repeal one of its archaic laws that still proclaimed women were their husbands' chattel. She became Charles's ex-wife, though in fact continuing to live with him and continuing their marital relations.

Another transition Eve was to make in her life was to change her name from Eve to Fred. (As with Cher and Madonna, she now has no surname.) She did this in solidarity with a California men's support group called Fred, whose members all bear that name and share the common denominator of low self-esteem. Fred also shaves her head because she wants to free herself from the tyranny of female stereotypes that society tries to pressure women to conform to.

Charles and Fred have been guided by their aversion to materialism and convention. In addition to the above changes, they also went on the lam to avoid enrolling their sons in the California school system, preferring instead to homeschool them, a system that wasn't approved. To repudiate their middle-class values, they took jobs as dishwashers, cleaners, cooks, fruitpickers, clerks at Kmart, and managers of a nudist camp. Their dwellings have included a VW van and cheap motels, as well as a series of shacks and an apartment above a pet food store. Of his repudiation of wealth, Charles explains, "I've never felt quite comfortable about money. I got $20,000 for *The Graduate*, and I've now signed the copyright over to the Anti-Defamation League." The film has earned over $100 million since its 1967 release.

In 2000, the Webbs decided to immigrate to Britain. Not surprisingly, in Brighton, they are also considered "oddbods." Charles has a long, gray ponytail, and Fred's bald head is swathed in a turban. In their postgraduate lifestyle, they live in a run-down hotel in a room paid for by social services. Glancing around at the shabby hotel lobby, with its stopped clock (in reminiscence of Miss Havisham) and threadbare button-backed armchairs, whose ambience is reinforced with the smell of disinfectant, an interviewer asked Charles if he regretted the road he chose to walk. Webb replied, "We have led the most chaotic, illogical, irrational lives, although the more I look at it, the more I can see there is a bizarre order to it all."

In 2001 Fred had what Charles describes as "a really severe breakdown." He attributes this to the eating disorders that had plagued her for most of her life. For the first two years of her mental collapse, all she mainly did was sleep. When she came out of the pattern, it left her with two distinct personalities. Charles says that "one day she will be perfectly normal, and the next she'll be this five-year-old child." He admits that at first he found it disturbing to live with two people inhabiting the same body, but that he has learned to adapt. He elaborates by explaining his unique living situation: "Actually, I've become more and more fond of the five-year-old. To begin with she was really horrible to be around: violent, uncooperative, seeking attention all the time. But now we can have conversations and I hope we're going to start playing dominoes soon."

The refrain in the Simon and Garfunkel song "Mrs. Robinson" is "Heaven holds a place for those who pray." However, if heaven also holds a place for those who live their lives exactly the way they choose, without caring an iota what the world thinks of them, then Charles and Fred will be assured a prime place. And, when that happens, even the angels will not be immune from shock at the "oddbods" in their midst.

30

After the Fall

ARTHUR MILLER
(ARTHUR ASHER MILLER)
1964

For my wife, **Ingeborg Morath**

WHEN one thinks of the spouse of playwright Arthur Miller, an iconoclastic photograph of a woman in a white dress on a subway vent immediately comes to mind. However, although *After the Fall* was based on Marilyn Monroe's life, it was not dedicated to her. That tribute was reserved for Ingeborg Morath.

Shakespeare wrote, "Some men are born great, some achieve greatness, and some have greatness thrust upon them." The second and third part of the quotation applies to Arthur Miller. The writer was born in New York City, the son of Jewish, Polish German parents, Isidore and Augusta (Gussie). The family's comfortable lifestyle disappeared when their clothing and coat manufacturing business was a casualty of the Wall Street Crash of 1929. The Millers were forced to abandon their spacious uptown Manhattan apartment and relocate to cramped quarters in the Gravesend section of Brooklyn, similar to the house lived in by the Lomans in *Death of a Salesman*. Similarly, the theme of the play, the American Dream, was born in the fallout of the collapse of Isidore's business.

In Brooklyn, young Arthur engaged in nonintellectual pursuits. As he recalled, "If I had any ideology at all it was what I had learned from Hearst magazines." However, his life changed when he uncharacteristically read Dostoevsky's *The Brothers Karamazov*. Reading the novel motivated him to enroll in the University of Michigan.

After graduation, Arthur married his college sweetheart, girl-next-door Mary Slattery, the Catholic daughter of an insurance salesman. The couple had two children, Jane and Robert. His first attempt at writing for the stage was *The Man Who Had All the Luck*. He almost abandoned his career when the Broadway production closed after four performances. In 1948, he built a home in Roxbury, Connecticut. It was there, in a mere six weeks, that Miller penned his masterpiece, *Death of a Salesman*. The play won the Pulitzer Prize and premiered on Broadway; it was directed by Elia Kazan and starred Lee J. Cobb as Willy Loman. Arthur Miller had achieved greatness.

In 1952, Elia Kazan, who had shared in the production of Miller's play, was summoned to appear before the House Un-American Activities Committee. To save himself from being blacklisted in Hollywood, he named eight people from the theater as communists. Greatly disturbed by his friend's testimony, Miller traveled to Salem, Massachusetts, to research the witch trials of the past because he felt they were being reenacted in the present. The result of this was *The Crucible*, wherein Miller likened the witch trials of Salem to the McCarthy witch hunts of communists. The author denounced the mass hysteria of the 1950s, which "accepted the notion that conscience was no longer a private matter but one of state administration." For his liberal views, he was to be branded with the red letter *C*.

In 1955, Miller's marriage to Mary ended, a result of his affair with Marilyn Monroe, whose own marriage to Joe DiMaggio had recently terminated as well. The press had a field day, and dubbed them the Hourglass and the Egghead. A year later, "the man who had all the luck" married the screen goddess. Miller had greatness thrust upon him.

However, soon after, the wheel of fortune started turning. First, the House Un-American Activities Committee, furious at his denunciation of them in *The Crucible*, refused to issue him a passport when he wanted to travel to London for *The Crucible*'s opening performance. Then, deciding to capitalize on Miller's newfound notoriety because of his association with Monroe, they called him to appear before the Committee. Marilyn accompanied Miller to the hearing, jeopardizing her own career in the process. When they asked Miller to name names, his response was, "I could not use the name of another person and bring trouble on him." As a result of his failure to comply, Miller was found guilty of contempt of Congress. He was fined $500, sentenced to thirty days in prison, and blacklisted. His conviction was later overturned when it was proven the chairman of the HUAC had lied to him by promising him in advance that he was not going to be asked to provide names.

When he was allowed to resume work, Miller began production of his play *The Misfits*, which was to be Clarke Gable's last role; Miller dedicated his work: "Dedicated to Clark Gable, who did not know how to hate." However, the same sentiment did not apply to Marilyn, who starred alongside Gable in what was also to be her last role. Miller later admitted that this time was one of the worst of his life. Although he had ostensibly married the quintessential sex symbol, Marilyn Monroe, in reality he was married to the ever-fragile orphan Norma Jean Baker. He later told a French newspaper, "All my energy and attention were devoted to trying to help her solve her problems. Unfortunately, I didn't have much success." It was during the making of *The Misfits* (whose title sadly described his wife) that Miller fell out of love with the woman in front of the camera and in love with the woman behind it.

While Arthur Miller had to grow up feeling the deprivations of the Depression, Ingeborg Morath had to live under the tyranny of the Third Reich after it annexed her native Austria. When she was fourteen, the Nazi Party organized an exhibition of *entartete Kunst*—what they determined was "degenerate art." The purpose of the show was to inflame public opinion against modern art. However, it had an opposite effect on Ingeborg. She said, "I found a number of these paintings exciting and fell in love with Franz Marc's Blue Horse. Only negative comments were allowed, and thus began a long period of keeping silent and concealing thoughts."

After World War II broke out, Ingeborg was compelled to complete six months of service for the Reichsarbeitsdienst (Reich Labor Service) before she was permitted to enroll in Berlin University, where she studied Romance languages, ultimately becoming fluent in French, English, Romanian, Spanish, Russian, and Chinese. There she ran afoul of authorities when she refused to join the Nationalist Socialist student organization. As a result, her educational privileges were withdrawn and she was forced to work assembling airplane parts at Tempelhof Airport in Berlin. The factory was being bombed daily, and her fellow workers were Ukrainian women, whose deaths would not cause any uproar. During an attack by Russian bombers, the factory gate was blown open, and with the Red Army fast approaching, Ingeborg fled back to Austria on foot. As a talisman against harm, she ran through the rubble of Berlin holding a bouquet of lilacs over her head.

After the war, Ingeborg discovered her life's calling. Having been repressed under the Nazi regime, she found her voice in photography. She said, "Photography is a strange phenomenon...You trust your eye but bare your soul." Throughout her long career, she photographed many subjects: celebrities such as Marilyn Monroe, Bedouin women dancing in the desert, soldiers of the People's Republic of China climbing over a statue of a Buddha, and a llama's head protruding from a car window in Times Square. However, one thing that she would never take a picture of was war or its aftermath, because of her personal experiences. "Everyone was dead or half dead. I walked by dead horses, women with dead babies in their arms. I can't photograph war for this reason." In 1949 her work caught the attention of Robert Capa, and he invited her to join the newly founded Magnum Photos in Paris. While there, she met and married the British journalist Lionel Birch and moved with him to London. However, the marriage was short-lived, and she returned to Paris and her first love: the camera. During the 1950s Magnum sent Morath on assignments all over Europe, the Middle East, Africa, the United States, and South America, where her work appeared in publications such as *Paris Match* and *Vogue*.

Like many Magnum members, Morath worked as a still photographer for motion pictures. In this capacity, she was sent to the Nevada desert to work with director John Huston, who was filming *The Misfits*. The off-the-set drama rivaled the onset one. John Huston was often intoxicated, and at times fell asleep while filming. Marilyn was sinking further into a haze of alcohol and prescription drugs. At one point, she was so addicted that Huston had to shut down production to send her to the hospital for detox. She often arrived late to the set or didn't show up at all. The main tension, however, was caused by the breakdown of the Miller–Monroe marriage. It was also at this time that Arthur met Ingeborg. After his divorce to Monroe later that year, he married Morath.

As unhappy as their prior relationships were, their marriage was happy. The couple traveled extensively, often collaborating on books in which Ingeborg supplied the photographs and Arthur the accompanying text. Their first book was on Russia, and another was on China. In *Chinese Encounters* they were able to take advantage of the fact that for the first time in more than thirty years the Chinese people were allowed to talk to foreigners. In the States, they lived in Connecticut, where, after seven months of marriage, their daughter, Rebecca, was born. The couple doted on their beautiful baby and took her with them wherever they went. This included dinners at the homes of their famous neighbors, such as artist Alexander Calder and novelist William Styron. She also accompanied them on their trips around the world. However, misfortune struck four years later.

When Ingeborg gave birth to a boy, Arthur was overjoyed, and called a friend to say he was going to name his son Eugene, after the playwright who had won the Pulitzer Prize for *Long Day's Journey into Night*. However, Inge and Arthur were devastated when the doctor delivered the news that the baby had Down syndrome. Arthur told his friend Robert Whitehead that the baby was a "mongoloid" and he was "going to have to put the baby away." Ingeborg was shattered at Arthur's decision, but he was adamant. Daniel ended up at the Southbury Training School, where his mother came to visit almost every Sunday, without Arthur. She described the institution by saying, "You know, I go in there and it's like a Hieronymus Bosch painting." Apparently, the bouquet of lilacs did not prove a strong enough talisman against evil. In *Death of a Salesman*, Miller wrote, "Attention, attention must be finally paid to such a person." Ironically, the playwright's humaneness was not as strong off the stage as on. With his abandonment of his son, Miller tarnished his greatness.

Although Arthur excised Daniel out of his life, he remained devoted to Rebecca. While she was visiting her parent's home in Connecticut, she met Daniel Day Lewis, who was acting in her father's screen version of *The Crucible*. They fell in love and were married two weeks before the film's release. They gave Ingeborg and Arthur grandsons Ronan and Cashel.

In 2002, Morath fulfilled her goal of revisiting the land of her birth, and returned to Austria. She documented her travel in the book *Last Journey*. The title proved prophetic; later that year she succumbed to cancer. Arthur Miller wrote of the years he spent with her as "the best" of his life. He also dedicated his only autobiography, *Timebends*, to Inge.

The woman born in Graf, Austria, found her real home in Roxbury, Connecticut. The house was filled with books, and she loved to work in her garden or swim in its pond. Although the Millers often traveled, they were always content to return home, where they often entertained family and friends. However, for Ingeborg, the absent Daniel was always present, and his shadow was one that never fully disappeared. A quotation from *The Crucible* mirrors her pain: "I have not moved from there to there without I think to please you, and still an everlasting funeral marches round your heart." Tragically, it is never the fate of mere mortals to ever know complete happiness "after the fall."

31

In Cold Blood

TRUMAN CAPOTE
(TRUMAN STRECKFUS PERSONS)
1965

**FOR *Jack Dunphy* AND *Harper Lee*
WITH MY LOVE AND GRATITUDE**

CAPOTE dedicated *In Cold Blood* to the two people with whom he had a lengthy on-again, off-again relationship. One was his longtime companion Jack Dunphy, and the other was his childhood friend Nelle Harper Lee. These two people, as much as they were able, provided an anchor for the restless man, who was always seeking a port of contentment, one that forever eluded him.

Nelle first met Truman Streckfus Persons when his mother left him in the care of three maiden cousins who lived next door to the Lee family in her hometown of Monroeville, Alabama. His mother, the former Lillie Mae Faulk, had given birth to him when she was sixteen; his father, Archulus Julius Parsons, was a con man whose main swindle had been to convince the Alabama beauty queen that he was wealthy and to become her husband. He evaded jail long enough to father a son. With the breakdown of her marriage, Lillie went to New York City to try to pursue the high life. At night, she would lock her little boy in a hotel room, with instructions to the staff to ignore the high-pitched screams coming from her room. Finally, unable to cope, she left him permanently in Monroeville.

When Nelle befriended him, Truman was a pariah to the other children. He did not live with his parents, carried a dictionary instead of a baseball bat (one that Mr. Lee had given him), was a Yankee in the South, and was extremely effeminate. He might as well have gone to Monroeville Elementary with a "Kick Me" sign on his back. However, his tomboy neighbor, who genuinely liked him and was a champion of the underdog, beat up anyone who made fun of Truman. Later, Nelle was to immortalize her friend as the character Dill in *To Kill a Mockingbird*. She wrote of him in her novel, "We came to know him as a pocket Merlin, whose head teemed with eccentric plans, strange longings, and quaint fancies."

When Nelle was not in the role of Truman's white knight, they were busy writing stories on the typewriter Mr. Lee had given his daughter. They wrote about the characters they knew, and therefore the denizens of Monroeville became their unwitting dramatis personae. Although he enjoyed the company of Nelle and his maiden cousins, Truman dreamt of a more exciting world than his small southern town, and his constant prayer was to get out of Monroeville and become a rich and famous New York writer.

His first big break came with the publication of *Other Voices, Other Rooms*. The controversy over this book was as much responsible for catapulting the young author to fame as its story, which dealt with a young man coming to terms with his homosexuality. The dust jacket for the novel depicted a young, angelic-looking

Truman reclining on a sofa, with a nonsubtle come-hither expression. Jack Dunphy was one of those on whom the come-hither worked its magic, though the adjective *black* should rightfully be inserted before the word *magic*.

Truman and Jack met in 1948, when both men were on the romantic rebound. Capote had just broken up with his first serious lover, Smith College professor Newton Arvin, who had won the National Book Award for his biography of Herman Melville. Dunphy had just ended his marriage to fellow dancer Joan McCracken (who later married Bob Fosse). The affair with Truman was Jack's first sexual liaison with a man. He later recalled of Capote, whom he had met at writer Leo Lerman's apartment, "He was cute, adorable looking. We sat on the couch and talked about trains. I had a mad desire to go somewhere." Where they ended up going was Taormina, Sicily, to a house where D. H. Lawrence had once lived. Once back in the States, a newspaper article in the *New York Times* would lead to Capote's next novel, which would carry him to heights of wealth and fame that even surpassed his boyhood dreams.

The news event that riveted him dealt with the grisly murders of the Clutter family in rural Holcomb, Kansas. He sensed he could turn the article into a new literary genre, a nonfiction novel. Sensing that he would need assistance, he was successful in persuading Nelle to travel to Kansas with him to help him with research. Although eager to begin work on her next novel, as she had just sent the final draft of *To Kill a Mockingbird* to her publisher, she decided to accompany him.

Nelle's help proved invaluable. Although the murderers cooperated with Truman, the small-town residents did not feel comfortable with his highly affected mannerisms, eccentric clothing, and unnaturally high-pitched voice. They were more than willing to open up to Nelle, whose homespun ways mirrored their own. Although Jack had not accompanied Truman, the two kept in touch. When Capote hired a lawyer for the murderers, his motivation for doing so was partially to delay their execution long enough to get their stories. Dunphy cautioned his lover with the admonition, "Be careful of what you do to get what you want."

After two months filled with the intensity of the investigation, Truman and Nelle took the train back to New York City. When Nelle first opened the novel that Truman had named *In Cold Blood*, she was livid. Nowhere in the book did Capote acknowledge her role. The dedication that she shared with Jack Dunphy, who had not contributed one iota to the work, was infuriating. She felt that Truman should have given credit where credit was due, rather than taking all the glory as his own.

The year following the publication of *In Cold Blood* was Capote's glory days. He partied with the rich and famous and became the luncheon confidante of many high-placed female celebrities. Nights found him on the talk-show circuit, mostly on *The Johnny Carson Show*, or partying in Studio 54 with Andy Warhol. During this time, he tried to reconcile with his mother, who, he felt, would accept him now that he was a member of the rich and famous whom she idolized. However, she held him at arm's length, as she could not get over her aversion to her son's homosexuality.

Despite Truman's contention that people "lost an IQ point for every year spent on the West Coast," he purchased a home there with Jack. The author soon began, on a religious basis, to over-indulge in alcohol and drugs. This caused him to fight with the conservative Dunphy, which led Capote to frequent bathhouses, where he picked up boys half his age. Nelle and Jack tried to intervene, but their efforts proved fruitless. Intoxicated and high on drugs, he now became the joke of the talk-show circuit. His good looks had dissipated: he was balding, pasty-faced, and heavy, a far cry from the angelic boy whose photograph had caused an uproar. Jack started to live a separate life from Truman, in the Swiss condominium and home in the United Nations Plaza in New York City, both of which had been purchased by Capote.

In his final years, barely able to write, Capote finally produced an article for *Esquire* titled "Answered Prayers." The title is an allusion to Saint Teresa of Avila, who said answered prayers cause more tears than unanswered ones. In it he revealed the confessions that his jet-set friends had entrusted to him. Although portrayed as fiction, readers knew to whom he referred. Victims of his poison pen were the Duchess of Windsor, Montgomery Clift, Tallulah Bankhead, and others from the upper echelons. En masse, the jet set closed their doors to the Tiny Terror, as he was dubbed.

In 1984, Truman Capote died of liver disease complicated by drug intoxication. He passed away at the home of his one remaining friend, Johnny Carson's ex-wife, Joanne. His last words were for his mother. Nelle flew to Los Angeles to attend his memorial service. Three years later, Jack Dunphy published his memoirs of his life with Truman in his book *Dear Genius*. In it he revealed what it was like to live under the giant shadow cast by his diminutive lover.

Considering their decades-long relationship, it was fitting that when Jack Dunphy died eight years later, both his and Truman's ashes were scattered at Crooked Pond on Long Island, where the two men had owned a property and where they had kept their own individual homes.

In his last book, *Music for Chameleons*, Truman said that his epitaph should state: "I tried to get out of it, but I couldn't." That succinct phrase could easily apply to most aspects of his life. In retrospect, the happiest time for Truman was when he was living with his maiden aunts, making up stories with his protector and friend, Nelle. Saint Teresa was prophetic in regard to Capote's "Answered Prayers."

32

Valley of the Dolls

Jacqueline Susann
1966

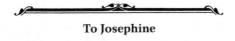

To Josephine
who sat at my feet, positive I was writing a sequel*

* but most of all to Irving

The first part of the dedication to *Valley of the Dolls* only makes sense when one learns that Josephine was Jacqueline's poodle and that the author's first book was about her dog. Jacqueline acquired Josephine in the 1950s, and it was love at first sight. She took her puppy everywhere, most usually dressed in outfits matching her own. When Susann was a model hawking embroidery on nighttime TV, she was often shown with Josephine, both of them wearing matching embroidered outfits. Her experiences with her dog became the subject of her first book, *Good Night, Josephine*.

The second part of the dedication refers to the author's husband, Irving Mansfield. In life, as in the dedication, he often had to play second fiddle to Josephine, who more than him, was the recipient of his wife's affection. Josephine's dish was always filled with choice meats, but Jacqueline never cooked for her husband. When it was time for dinner, Irving would obediently head for the car.

From the beginning, Mansfield, a press agent, was the pursuer and Susann the pursued. Knowing that the object of his affection was desirous of obtaining celebrity status for her acting career, in any way she could, instead of courting her with wine and roses, he wooed her by placing photos of her in theaters and in New York City newspapers. Although not sexually attracted to him or madly in love, she decided to marry Irving in 1939. She did so because she thought he would devote himself to promoting her, thereby giving her the fame she so desperately sought. A second reason she may have married him is that she felt he was the only one who would be able to put up with her flamboyant, outrageous personality and childlike desperation for attention.

Once married, Jacqueline became extremely promiscuous with people other than Irving. In this regard, she was following in the footsteps of her father, Bob. A serial adulterer, he'd pretend to his wife that he was taking their daughter to a movie and would leave her there while he had a sexual rendezvous. On the way home, he would grill Jacqueline about the movie, in case his wife asked questions about it. Despite this, Jacqueline sided with her father. In an interview the author gave when she was forty-three, she described her mother as "the rock against which I've been banging and bloodying my head all my goddamned life."

Perhaps in an effort to distance herself from her unhappy childhood, she preferred that the men she cheated with were stand-up comedians. Methodically she went through Borscht Belt celebrities such as Eddie Cantor and George Jessel, to name but a few. As a "friend" was later to remark, "Whoever the local comedian was, that's who she was having an affair with." Apparently, Susann was an equal opportunity adulteress, for she also indulged in extramarital lesbian affairs, including ones with Coco Chanel and Ethel Merman.

In 1940, Susann began two new careers: one as a playwright and the other as a mother. Her play *Lovely Me* took its title from her remark as she looked in despair at her pregnant belly in a mirror and sighed, "How could this have happened to lovely me?" While in Philadelphia for its opening, her water broke and she hopped on a train back to New York City for the delivery. She derived the baby's name, Guy, because, seeing it was a boy and not her long-prayed-for girl, she remarked with disappointment, "Oh, it's just some guy." Not surprisingly, the child's first three words were "Mommy," "Daddy," and "dammit." Irving and Jacqueline received some of the most traumatic news of their lives when they were informed that Guy was severely autistic. They placed him in an institution and explained his disappearance by saying he was extremely asthmatic and had to be sent, permanently, to Arizona, because of its climate.

In 1943, Irving was drafted, and Jacqueline decided it was time for her to become AWOL from the marriage. She wrote Irving a Dear John letter, one which she proceeded to read aloud in front of the cast of *Lovely Me*. "Irving, when we were at the Essex House and I had room service and I could buy all my Florence Lusting dresses, I found that I loved you very much, but now that you're in the Army and getting $56 a month, I feel that my love has waned." Perhaps she did this just for shock appeal, because when Irving returned, they reconciled in 1945. This was a positive move for her, because, in light of subsequent events, she was going to need Irving "most of all."

It was Irving who suggested Jacqueline turn to novel writing. He had the revelation after noticing a woman on a park bench engrossed in *The Carpetbaggers*. He came home with a typewriter, which he sprayed pink, his wife's signature color. Right away she latched on to the idea, and decided to write about what she knew best: woman's lust for wealth, fame, power, and sex, as well as pills—both uppers and downers—which she herself had been addicted to for most of her life. Susann euphemistically called these tablets "dolls," and based her characters on the actual lives of three addicted rich and famous women. The character Neely O'Hara was based on Judy Garland, Helen Lawson was based on Ethel Merman, and Jennifer North was based on Carole Landis.

During the writing, however, Jacqueline developed breast cancer and had to undergo a radical mastectomy. At one point, she became so suicidal that she attempted to leap off her terrace to her death. Irving handcuffed himself to her until her depression abated. Rallying, with characteristic *chutzpah*, she made a Faustian pact with God that if He gave her one more decade in which to finish a bestseller, she would go without a fight.

When *Valley of the Dolls* was released, Jacqueline and Irving went on a marketing blitz. They rented a truck and literally filled it with copies of the novel, helping it on its way up the bestseller list. They drove cross-country, stopping in at the major book chains. Jacqueline snapped up any chance to go on promotional tours, and every time she did so, she would appear in her trademark look: huge earrings, teased hair, spiky false eyelashes, bagel-sized sunglasses, and skintight pink and purple Gucci. In her arms was Josephine, wearing an outfit color-coordinated with her own. Off to the side was the ever-present Irving, tirelessly promoting his number one client, his wife.

In an interview at this time he said that "*Valley of the Dolls* was the same as *Gone with the Wind*—only dirty." The book went on to sell 29 million copies, outsold only by the Bible. The result of this publishing phenomenon was that Jacqueline Susann became fabulously wealthy and extremely famous. Her two most sought-after dreams had come true; she had attained both fame and wealth. Because of this she became the darling of the talk-show circuit and secure enough to feel justified in throwing a drink at Johnny Carson when he aggravated her. (Her preferred projectile when her husband aggravated her was an ashtray.) However, now it was her time to uphold her end of the bargain.

In 1974, Jacqueline's cancer returned, and this time there was to be no more divine bargaining. God had kept His end by allowing her the time to finish not only *Valley of the Dolls* but also her next novel, *Once Is Not Enough*. She instructed Irving that he was to have her cremated, and that her urn be in the shape of a hardcover book with the inscription: Jacqueline Susann 1918–1974. Her last words were, in true Jacqueline fashion, to Irving: "Let's get the hell outta here, doll." After a lifetime of pain—an unhappy childhood, recurring cancer, chemotherapy, a suicide attempt, and an institutionalized child—death might have presented a welcome alternative. Unlike the title of her last book, once was probably enough.

When she envisioned heaven, she surely imagined reuniting with her beloved Josephine, where they could spend eternity in matching Gucci outfits, Irving standing by.

33

I Know Why the Caged Bird Sings

MAYA ANGELOU
(MARGUERITE JOHNSON)
1969

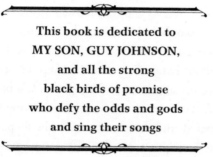

**This book is dedicated to
MY SON, GUY JOHNSON,
and all the strong
black birds of promise
who defy the odds and gods
and sing their songs**

WHILE there are many adjectives that Guy could use to describe life as the only son of Maya Angelou, *ordinary* would never be one of them. Not by the longest of shots. It could not possibly have been ordinary when Maya and Guy lived in the States, Egypt, and Africa. It could not possibly have been ordinary when Guy was raised in the company of Dr. Martin Luther King Jr., Malcolm X, Muhammad Ali, and Timothy Leary, to name but a few of the historic figures Maya counted as her friends. It could not possibly have been ordinary during Maya's marriages to a Greek sailor, a South African revolutionary, and Germaine

Greer's ex-husband. It could not possibly have been ordinary to have been the only child of such a "phenomenal woman."

In 1945, when Maya was a seventeen-year-old student at Madison High in San Francisco, after a brief sexual relationship she became pregnant by a boy in her neighborhood. When she confided in her mother, Vivian Johnson asked Maya if she loved the boy, to which Maya replied that she didn't and that the boy didn't love her either. Vivian's response was, "Well, there's no point in ruining three lives. We're going to have us a baby." She never pressured Maya into having a shotgun wedding, or any other kind of wedding. Bowing to convention was not something that the Johnson women ever subscribed to. When Maya and Vivian went to the hospital for the birth, because it was a Jewish holiday Maya's doctor was not there. Undaunted, Vivian, who was a nurse, washed up and took her daughter into the delivery room. There she kneeled on a table and took Maya's hand in her own. Every time a pain came, to distract her daughter from the agony she would tell a joke. Maya recalls the birth. "And she said, 'Here he comes, here he comes.' And she put her hand on him first, my son."

Although thrilled to be a mother, the specter of poverty hung over her head, and, determined to somehow be self-sufficient, Maya refused welfare as an option. Nevertheless, her economic prospects were grim. Not only was she hampered with the lack of a college diploma, the 1940s did not offer promising prospects for black, poor, single mothers. Some of the jobs that she took were as a Creole cook, Calypso singer, cocktail waitress, and exotic dancer in the Garden of Allah. In addition, she ran a lesbian escort service and managed a San Diego brothel that employed two prostitutes. Finally, in a bid at respectability, Maya left Guy in the care of her mother and toured Europe and Africa with a U.S. Department of State production of *Porgy and Bess*. After a year, she felt derelict in regard to her duties as a mother and returned to be with her son.

Back in the States, Maya and Guy settled into a beatnik lifestyle by joining a commune that lived on a houseboat in Sausalito, San Francisco. There the two of them went barefoot, wore jeans, and embraced a free-spirited bohemian lifestyle. However, after a year, Maya began to yearn for a more bourgeois way of life. Accordingly, with the help of some friends, she was able to rent a home in the white enclave of Laurel Canyon, where she enrolled Guy in the local school.

They moved again, however, when the principal and two counselors called home to say that Guy would not be welcome on the school bus the following semester. When Maya went in for a meeting she was told, "We do not allow Negro boys to use foul language in front of our girls." When Guy was in the car, he explained that he had not used profanity on the bus, but rather had explained the facts of life to some of the girls, who had begun to cry when he outlined that their fathers had done it with their mothers. In response to Guy's query as to whether he had been right, she told him, "Sometimes it's wiser to be right in silence, you know?" It was this incident that prompted Maya to look for a new neighborhood, one where "black skin was not regarded as one of nature's more unsightly mistakes."

Although Maya and Guy moved to a more racially diverse New York neighborhood, trouble unfortunately shadowed them. When Guy was in high school, Maya accepted a two-week job as a singer in a Chicago club, the Gate of Horn. In a Brooklyn newspaper she found an older black woman, Mrs. Tolman, who would come over and cook and clean for her son for three hours a day. In Chicago, Maya received a phone call from her friend John Killens, who delivered the words that every mother most dreads: "There had been some trouble." John said that he would explain everything when he saw her and then the phone went dead. When Maya arrived, heart in mouth, John explained that Guy had been threatened by a local gang, the Savages, when a girlfriend of a gang member accused Guy of hitting her (in actuality, he spurned her advances, saying he was faithful to his girlfriend, prompting her to complain to her boyfriend Jerry).

That night, while nursing a bottle of Scotch and water, Maya may have recalled a night in 1959 when she and her mother, Vivian, visited San Francisco, and had stayed at the Desert Hotel, which had just lifted its ban on black guests. Sensing the hostility, Vivian gave her daughter a speech about masking fear. She told her daughter that if the whites "mess with either of us, they'd better start looking for some new asses, 'cause I'll blow away what their mamas gave them." She then showed what was hidden in her purse, a Luger.

The next morning, Maya decided on a plan of attack to protect her son. She found Jerry, pulled a pistol out of her purse, and then, in a calm voice that masked her fear, said if her son was harmed she would "find your house and kill everything that moves, including the rats and cockroaches." Jerry looked at all six feet of Maya and replied, "OK. I understand. But for a mother, I must say you're a mean motherfucker." Jerry had fallen for her bluff. However, given how deeply Maya loved Guy, if tested, it probably would not have proved a bluff after all.

The romantic episodes in Maya's life prove that even phenomenal women can make phenomenally bad choices. In 1960, in John Killens's home, Maya met Vusumzi Make, a South African dedicated to destroying Apartheid. After hearing his speech, she wrote in *The Heart of a Woman*, "Intelligence always had a pornographic effect on me." At the end of the evening, Vusumzi asked Guy's permission to escort his mother home. When Guy declined the offer, Maya felt like pinching her son until he screamed. A mere week later, Maya had broken up with her Brooklyn bail bondsman fiancé, and had agreed to marry Vus and move with Guy to Cairo, where Vus was stationed. The "honeymoon" started to unravel when Maya noticed lipstick smudges that weren't made by her and the scent of perfume that did not come from her bottles. Further problems occurred when people came to repossess their furniture.

With Vus's serial adultery, money mismanagement, and controlling ways, Maya came to the realization that she no longer loved her husband. She had no friends in Cairo and did not have enough money for her and Guy to fly back to the States. Guy and Maya left Egypt for a new life in Ghana. When Maya first started living with Vus, she received a call saying that her son had been involved in a terrible accident and was in critical condition in the hospital. That turned out to be a cruel trick to try to get her to convince Vus to terminate his anti-Apartheid activities. However, in Ghana, the cruel ruse became a reality.

In Africa, Guy and a married couple, Richard and Ellen, had gone on a road trip for a picnic. Several hours later, Ellen came to Maya's door; she was covered in blood and when she saw Guy's mother she screamed. In answer to Maya's look of terror, Ellen wailed that when she had left Korle Bu Hospital, "I swear he was still breathing." When Maya arrived at the hospital, she saw Guy stretched on a gurney; his face was gray, his eyes were closed, his head was splayed in an unnatural position. In anguish she gazed at her son, whom she had always referred to as "her monument in the world." Guy's arm, leg, and neck were broken in the car accident.

When Guy came back home, they celebrated with their favorite dinner, roast chicken. Shortly thereafter, he moved into the dormitory of the University of Ghana. Guy was ecstatic; Maya, bereft. The cornerstone of her life was leaving the nest. His parting words to his mother were "Mom, I know I'm your only child and you love me. But there's something for you to remember. It is my neck and my life. I will live it whole or not at all." Maya went home, secure in the knowledge that like dust, she would rise.

Guy Johnson completed college in Ghana. After graduation, he managed a bar in Costa del Sol, Spain, ran a safari service from London through Morocco and Algeria to the Spanish Sahara, and worked on oil rigs in Kuwait. He currently resides in Oakland, California, with his wife, son, and grandchildren.

Although life with Maya involved eighteen different schools, several countries, and Maya's many relationships, he says that the one constant was his mother's love. Following in her giant footsteps, Guy is also a poet and novelist. He says that he is often asked the question of what it is like to stand in Maya's shadow. To that he has replied, "The truth is I have never been in her shadow. When you are around someone who has genius and all they want is the best for you, you are standing in the light."

Because for most of their lives all Guy and Maya had was each other, when asked about growing up as her only child he answered, "I would say I had the great fortune of living with one of the most inspiring creative people, and she was my mother." Maya Angelou has accolades from some of the most acclaimed people of the twentieth century; however, the tribute from her son, Guy Johnson, must be the greatest one of all.

34

Carrie

STEPHEN KING
(STEPHEN EDWIN KING)
1976

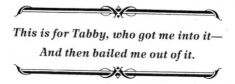

This is for Tabby, who got me into it—
And then bailed me out of it.

STEPHEN King is master of the horror genre; however, the person who did the most to save him from falling prey to horror in his own life is his wife, Tabitha (Tabby) King.

Stephen King met his emotional life jacket in 1967 at the University of Maine, where he received his BA in English. Tabitha Jane Spruce first saw Stephen when a friend of hers pointed him out as he was walking across the campus. He was wearing jeans and cut-down green rubber boots. He sported a bushy black beard and hair that hadn't been acquainted with a barber for over two years. In a celebrity look-alike contest he could easily have passed for Charles Manson. Turning to her friend, in a voice dripping with sarcasm, Tabitha said, "I think I'm in love."

However, their paths were to cross once more when they both had a job shelving books in the school's Raymond Folger Library. Serendipitously, they both simultaneously reached for *The Joy of*

Sex. That act broke the ice, and they subsequently got to know each other and started to accompany one another to poetry workshops where they discovered their shared love for words and writing. King gave her a short story he had written entitled "I Am the Doorway," and her response was that it was one of the best science fiction stories she had ever read. King later said her comment "Flattered me out of my socks."

What with the flattery and the shedding of the apparel, the Kings' first son was born. Stephen and Tabitha married in 1971 and soon had their second child. The Kings were in love and thrilled with their children, but their problem was poverty. Penury was something that King had grown up with; when he was a child, his father, Donald, said he was stepping out for some cigarettes one evening and was never heard from again. Now it pained him to see his own children and wife without money and living in a trailer. He recalls that their old Buick was kept going with the assistance of duct tape and bailing wire. He called this period the "hard dark years."

During this time Tabitha worked at Dunkin' Donuts and, unable to obtain a teaching job, Stephen worked at an industrial Laundromat washing table linen from Maine's lobster restaurants. Stephen believed that he could write, and this was a belief his wife shared. Because of this, Tabitha created a writing area in the trailer's cramped laundry room by placing a small desk between the washer and the dryer. She put her Olivetti portable typewriter on the desk. During King's acceptance speech for the National Book Award he said of his wife, "She still tells people that I married her for that typewriter but that's only partly true. I married her because I loved her and because we got on as well out of bed as in it. The typewriter was a factor though."

Stephen later recalled that most wives living under these conditions would have given their husbands the "you can't buy a loaf of bread or a tube of toothpaste with rejection slips" speech and then told them in no uncertain terms to get real jobs to help them dig their family out of their financial hole. However, Tabitha never did this. Had she done so, the world would have been deprived of literature's Hitchcock.

Finally, Stephen was able to obtain a teaching position, but his annual salary was merely $6,400. When the head of the English department asked Stephen to take on additional duties as a debate club advisor for an extra stipend, Tabitha discouraged him from accepting, explaining it was not worth it, as it would take too much time away from what was truly important to her husband, writing. It was then that King decided to try to use his Olivetti to supplement his income and began selling short stories, mainly to men's magazines. Finding the extra cash extremely helpful, if one of the children got ill and they needed to buy medicine, Tabitha would jokingly say to her husband, "Come on, Steve, think of a monster."

King did think of a monster, at least one whose persecution turned her into one. King began writing a short story based on the tragic tale of two girls from his own high school. He blended the two girls into one and gave the character kinetic powers. However, dissatisfied with the story, he threw the pages into the garbage can. Later on, Tabitha retrieved them, shaking off the cigarette ashes, and read her husband's discarded work. She told him it was good and he should continue. When he replied that he didn't know how, she gave him insight that provided the necessary background about girls' locker rooms. As a result, *Carrie* was born and the concept of prom night was never the same. (Incidentally, Carrie White was not based on King's own prom date; to that he went solo.)

After *Carrie* was sold, Stephen was able to tell Tabitha that with the check of $400,000 she could stop pushing sugared dough at Dunkin' Donuts, he could quit teaching, and they could move out of the trailer. Upon hearing the news, Tabitha, who was sitting on a sofa that she had salvaged from a yard sale, put her head in her hands and wept. Tabby had got Stephen "into it," by encouraging her husband's writing when he most needed it.

Unfortunately, some of the horror from King's writing crept into his personal life as well. In the early 1970s Stephen became an alcoholic. In *On Writing* he admits that he was even drunk while delivering his mother's eulogy and was so intoxicated that after completing *Cujo* he did not have any memory of writing it. Tabitha, who realized the seriousness of her husband's alcoholism, called family and friends to stage an intervention. They emptied his trash bin in order to make him confront its contents. Out poured beer cans, cigarette butts, marijuana, cocaine in gram bottles and plastic Baggies, coke spoons caked in snot and blood, Xanax, Valium, NyQuil, tranquilizers, Robitussin cough syrup, and bottles of mouthwash. Tabitha gave him an ultimatum: either become sober or move out. It was the horror of losing Tabitha and his children that forced him down the road of sobriety.

The ensuing years were wonderful to the Kings. Stephen became one of the most prolific American writers (three hundred million copies of his novels have been published), and a number of his novels have had film adaptations. The erstwhile trailer dwellers purchased a waterfront mansion on the Gulf of Mexico in Sarasota, Florida, from which the "King of Horror" writes. Sales from his books and film adaptations have made his net worth exceed two hundred million dollars. However, horror was to visit King once more.

In June 1999, as the author was taking his customary four-mile walk, a blue 1985 Dodge Caravan struck him. The driver, Bryan Smith, had become distracted from the wheel by his Rottweiler, who was trying to get into a food cooler. King was left with severe injuries that included a collapsed right lung, multiple right leg fractures, and a broken hip, and had to spend the next three weeks in a hospital where he underwent five operations. When he finally came home, Tabitha knew the best psychological therapy for her husband would be to resume writing, and to this end she set up a makeshift desk in their Victorian-style home. There he tried to write, with his crutches at his side, propped up by foam pillows to ease the ever-present pain that consumed his now-emaciated body (the recovery had caused him to drop fifty pounds). Somehow King managed to overcome his bitterness. Anxious that the minivan that hit him not go on sale on eBay because of King's celebrity, Tabitha bought it for $1,500. King said that he wanted to destroy it with a baseball bat, but he put that fantasy to rest when Tabitha said that what they should just do is "get past this whole thing." In a twist reminiscent of a King novel, the driver, Smith, died from an overdose of pain medication on September 21—Stephen's birthday.

Stephen King's style of writing has evolved during his three-decades-long career. However, one thing in his life has remained constant, as can be seen in one of his latest novels, *Lisey's Story*, which is dedicated to the same person his first novel was: Tabitha.

35

The Professor of Desire

PHILIP ROTH

(PHILIP MILTON ROTH)

1977

For Claire Bloom

IT was a wedding seemingly made, to borrow the cliché, in heaven. Claire Bloom was the famous Jewish queen of London's stage, and Philip Roth was the famous Jewish king of American letters. However, a mere four years later, their acrimonious divorce resembled the clash of the Titans.

Claire Bloom's father, who had started life with the name Blumenthal and later changed it to Blume, was called Eddie by his daughter. He was one of those men who always had a get-rich-quick scheme up his sleeve that never materialized. He deserted his family when Claire was sixteen, planning to go to South Africa, marry a rich woman, and then send money back to his ex-wife and children in London. His dream became a casualty of the best-laid plans of mice and men. No money was ever forthcoming, which is not surprising in light of the fact that he was a compulsive gambler. The family didn't hear from him for three years until he reappeared, accompanied by a new wife. He showed up at the Old Vic, where Claire was performing in the role of Juliet. She snubbed him. When he died three days later, Claire, filled with guilt, felt that it was her rejection that had killed her father.

Claire's feelings of abandonment at her father's desertion would strongly influence her romantic destiny. For her twelfth birthday present, her mother took her to see a production of Anton Chekhov's play *The Three Sisters*, where she related to the women who desperately needed a male to replace their lost father. They were willing to enter into abusive or dead-end relationships in order to satisfy their childhood emotional deprivation.

When the Luftwaffe bombed their home during the Blitz, Claire, her mother, and her younger brother escaped to a relative's home in Florida. Forced to leave her country and home further increased Claire's feelings of abandonment and loss. Claire's emotional reprieve was the theater—a world which she dreamed of entering. With her ethereal beauty and prodigious talent, her dreams were soon to be realized.

Claire's proverbial break came in 1949 when she landed a role in Christopher Frye's play *The Lady's Not for Burning*, performed at the Globe Theatre. She starred with another unknown young actor, one who had penetrating green eyes, a pockmarked face, and an unforgettable Welsh accent. His presence on stage was hypnotic; his presence offstage, even more so. At a future date, Claire was to surrender both her heart and her virginity to the man—Richard Burton.

The impediment to their romance was that Richard was, inconveniently, married to his wife Sybil. In her memoir, *Leaving a Doll's House*, Claire wrote, "I felt absolutely no guilt about anything, because I knew that to make love to Richard was something that *had* to happen." They would rendezvous at the home

Claire shared with her beloved mother, who, not wanting to be in the way of the lovers, moved to her own flat. When Richard left for California, he wrote to Claire, "I love you with an awful intensity sometimes when I just sit in a trance staring at a piece of paper, pen poised and immovable, longing for you and remembering you and imaging you. I love you horribly and beautifully."

While Claire later had a fling with Laurence Olivier, the grand passion she felt for Richard was not dampened by that dalliance. The Burton–Bloom romance lasted five years. After that time, she realized that Richard would never leave his wife. What ultimately terminated their relationship was her walking into Burton's dressing room without knocking and seeing him in a passionate embrace with Susan Strasberg. In anger she said, "F*** off, the pair of you!" and that, as the expression goes, was that. To put distance between herself and Richard, she moved to Hollywood, and had a brief relationship with Yul Brynner.

In 1958, Claire acted on Broadway and costarred with Rod Steiger. This was the first time that she would have a husband, quite literally, of her own. The couple married when Claire became pregnant and had their daughter, Anna Justine. Their marriage ended when Claire began an affair with Hillard Elkins, the producer of Oh! Calcutta, a man she made her second husband. Their marriage ended when he had an affair soon after, and for Claire, Hillard would forever more be referred to as "the Unmentionable."

One afternoon in the mid-1970s, Claire was walking up Madison Avenue on her way to have tea with her yoga teacher, and Philip Roth was walking down the street on his way to his psychoanalyst. Having previously met, they started a conversation that led to an eighteen-year relationship. Claire ended up leaving London to live with Philip in his remote, eighteenth-century Connecticut farmhouse. Not enamored of the teenaged Anna, Roth told Claire that he would not live under the same roof as her daughter. Anna moved out. Later Claire decided that Philip had been adamant against Anna not so much because he disliked her (which he did), but because he wanted to assert control over Claire.

Claire and Philip had lived together for fifteen years when Claire decided that it was time for husband number three. Claire's friend Gore Vidal warned her against marrying fellow writer Philip Roth. He told her that she had already experienced Portnoy's complaint (her marriage to Elkins), and therefore "Do not involve yourself with Portnoy." However, as the proverb states, women do not ask for advice until after they have bought their wedding dress, and the Bloom–Roth nuptials (after Roth made her sign a grossly unfair prenuptial agreement) took place.

In the first two years things were fine, and Roth dedicated not only *The Professor of Desire* to Claire but *Operation Shylock* as well. However, what followed was a waking nightmare. Philip began to spiral into deep depression, coupled with paranoia, and even accused his wife of trying to poison him. Finally, exhibiting suicidal feelings, Philip checked into a psychiatric hospital. So distraught was Claire from the stress that she checked in as well.

However, what floored Claire was when she was served with divorce papers shortly afterward, in 1993, which accused her of "cruel and inhuman treatment of her husband, Philip Roth." Claire found herself excluded from both the couple's home in Connecticut and their New York City apartment. When she tried to contest the agreement, which left her with nothing, Philip responded that he would rather lose $200,000 in lawyer's fees than give her a penny. This was followed by a flurry of faxes, one saying he was suing her for $62 billion. Ironically, the day the divorce was finalized, Claire was onstage performing the role of Medea. Later on, Claire was to discover that what had taken the "bloom" off their marriage was that "the professor of desire" now desired another. Erda, a woman who had been a friend of the couple for years, was involved in an affair with Philip.

Claire's revenge was her 1996 tell-all memoir, *Leaving a Doll's House* (though the word *doll* should have been substituted with the word *mad*). Roth was enraged at its publication, which detailed all the good, bad, and ugly of their years together.

When Philip first initiated the separation from Claire, she was devastated to be deserted after an eighteen-year relationship, when she was sixty-two years old. She said that for a long time afterward she was lonely and full of regrets. Claire used this time for self-reflection, wondering if she were destined to be a spider, forever doomed to weave the same disastrous, romantic relationships. Why had she always spurned the good boys for the bad? She turned to her past for answers. She concluded that, as a fatherless girl, she was subconsciously re-creating the lack of certainty of her early childhood. Philip had once observed the coincidence that all his loves had been fatherless. Claire, with the clarity of hindsight, realized that it had not been coincidental at all. She said that she finally understood that "fatherless women gravitate toward emotionally unavailable men." Philip's attraction for her was that "he was the fleeting shadow of the one who had disappeared. That was Eddie's legacy to me." However, in true Nora fashion, armed with her new insights, Claire has learned to see the positive in the slamming of the door of "the doll's house."

Claire's final words in her memoir are "Now begins the rest of my life." One closes the book believing that there will be many future curtain calls "for Claire."

36

Schindler's List

THOMAS KENEALLY

1982

TO THE MEMORY OF OSKAR SCHINDLER,
AND TO LEOPOLD PFEFFERBERG,
WHO BY ZEAL AND PERSISTENCE
CAUSED THIS BOOK TO BE WRITTEN

SERENDIPITY seems a strange word to use in association with the Holocaust, but a happy coincidence is what occurred on an August morning in 1980. It was then that the lives of an Australian Catholic, a German Nazi, and a Polish Jew converged. One result of the occurrence was conceivably the most important film of the twentieth century. Another result was that the name of one of the Righteous Gentiles was exhumed from the dustbin of history. And both of these events came about because of the "zeal and persistence" of Leopold "Poldek" Pfefferberg.

The summer day started out as an ordinary one, giving no hint that it was to be one of the most pivotal of Thomas Keneally's life. He was in Los Angeles and searching for a replacement briefcase and, under financial constraints, eschewed the astronomical prices of Rodeo Drive. As he hesitated before a shop called the Handbag

Studio, the proprietor approached him, asking why he didn't come into the air-conditioned store to escape the 105-degree temperature, and that he wouldn't eat him if he did. Once inside, the owner asked a question that would set off a chain reaction that was to impact both men's destinies. "So then, how did a gentleman like you bust your hinge?" Tom explained that he had just returned from Italy, where he had stuffed too many papers in his briefcase and now was on a layover in the States on a book tour. As soon as the proprietor, Leopold, heard "book tour," he felt compelled to tell his tale in true mariner fashion.

While Sol, a partner and fellow Holocaust survivor, worked on processing Keneally's Australian credit card for the briefcase, Leopold introduced his wife, Misia, and their son, Freddy. He then took Thomas past a curtain at the back of his store and began his litany. "I know a wonderful story. It is not a story for Jews but for everyone. A story of humanity, man to man. I tell all the writers I get through here.... But it's a story for you, Thomas. It's a story for you, I swear." Of course, every writer has heard that line umpteen times; however, Thomas was held captive because of the business transaction. Leopold continued, "I was saved, and my wife was saved, by a Nazi. I was a Jew imprisoned with Jews. So a Nazi saves me and, more important, saves Misia, my young wife. So although he's a Nazi, to me he's Jesus Christ. Not that he was a saint. He was all-drinking, all-black-marketeering, all-screwing, okay? But he got Misia out of Auschwitz, so to me he is God."

Later that day, Thomas, with the background noise from the television's Notre Dame game in the background, found himself reading the photocopied testimonies of the Schindlerjuden (Schindler's Jews). However, equally engrossing was the portrait that was emerging of Oskar Schindler. Keneally was intrigued by the man, who was a serial adulterer, hard-core drinker, and opportunist, and, at the end, relinquished his fortune and jeopardized his life to save his Jewish workers. Thomas had spent six years in a Sydney seminary studying to be a priest, but had left when he suffered a nervous breakdown. As a former theologian, he was intrigued by the interplay of good and evil that had composed the soul of Oskar Schindler. In addition, his writer's interest was piqued when he heard about the irony inherent in the Schindler story. During the war, his workers had depended on him for survival. After the war, destitute, Oskar had depended on them.

The next morning, Thomas met Leopold for breakfast but was overcome with doubts that he was the one to tell the tale. As is so often the case, what is exhilarating in the romance of the evening is less than thrilling in the glare of the morning. He told Leopold that he was not the one to write the book, as he and Misia were the first Holocaust survivors that he had met, and that he had no personal experience with anti-Semitism. Leopold was undeterred. After every objection, Leopold answered, "This is not a book for Jews, this is a book for Gentiles. This is a great story of humanity, man to man." Leopold accompanied him to the plane, and his last words were beseeching ones: "Thomas, who will do it if not for you? You think I have them queued up?"

Through the Pfefferbergs, Thomas had discovered firsthand accounts of the horrors of the Holocaust: of Misia rubbing beets into her face so that she would appear healthy, thereby sidestepping the selection for death; of how, even four decades after the war, some survivors never left home without a hidden crust of bread. Thomas returned home "a sadder and a wiser man."

Upon arrival in Sydney, Thomas took his wife, Judith, and teenaged daughters, Margaret and Jane, out for coffee. He told them about Leopold and the list that meant life; he told them about the enigma of Oskar. When his family was captivated over the project, Thomas decided that he would undertake writing Leopold's book. Every life deserves one grand passion, and professionally, Thomas had found his. More precisely, it had found him.

Anxious for his friend's enthusiasm not to wane, Leopold kept phoning from California and claimed that when the book was published Thomas would win "the Novell Prize—I've already booked my seat to Oslo!" The dream of the book took a turn to reality when Thomas's friend Nan Talese, of Simon & Schuster, championed the project. Nan came through with a $60,000 advance, which was a very sizable amount in the 1980s. Thomas used a portion of it to finance a research trip for him and Leopold, to interview the Schinderjuden who had emigrated all over the world.

Thomas and Leopold ended up traveling to the States, Argentina, Germany, Poland, Austria, and Israel to flesh out all recollections of Oskar Schindler. The two men worked in tandem: Thomas had the publishing connections and writing ability; Leopold provided the key to unlock the reluctance of the survivors who would have resisted revisiting their anguish-filled pasts with a younger, non-Jewish stranger. With his trademark zeal and persistence, Leopold would not countenance any of his fellow survivors' refusals to be interviewed. He only had to ask how they could refuse to give Oskar immortality when Oskar had given them life. After liberation, in Munich, during a card game, Leopold had made a vow that his life's mission would be for the name Oskar Schindler to be remembered, and revered. He said that it was his sacred task to tell the world what had happened, how "even on the days when the air was black with the ashes from bodies on fire, there was hope in Crakow because Oskar Schindler was there."

In 1981, thirty years after Leopold had begun trying to get a book published about Oskar, the novel was sent off, with the title *Schindler's Ark*. Thomas chose this name because Noah was the savior of the Jews, and because of Oscar's covenant with his workers. The title had been suggested to him by Leopold. However, David Green, the head of Simon & Schuster, wanted the title *Schindler's List*. Surprisingly, Leopold did not weigh in on the debate. All he said was whatever the final choice, the subtitle should be *A Great Story of Humanity, Man to Man*.

The sales of *Schindler's List* exceeded both Thomas's and Leopold's wildest dreams, but the latter was still not content. He wanted Oskar's story to be turned into a movie so that it would reach an even greater audience. The two men's delight knew no bounds when Steven Spielberg (the "wonder boychickel" as Leopold called him) arranged a meeting to discuss that possibility. They met at the palatial Bel Air estate of Sid Sheinberg, the head of Universal Studios. During their luncheon, Leopold assured Spielberg, "I tell you, Steven, you make this film of humanity, man to man, it will win you an Academy Award! Guaranteed! You'll get an Oscar for Oskar!" Much to Leopold's chagrin, although the director was interested, he would not commit to the undertaking. Leopold phoned the director every week for eleven years, always asking him "when he was going to get beyond making movies about dinosaurs and little furry things."

Almost a decade later, Steven Spielberg was ready to turn his long-term interest in the project into a commitment. He said that he had arrived at an age in which his ancestry and heritage meant more to him than when the book had first appeared. He stated that it would be in Crakow where he would "make his truest film." Leopold and Thomas flew with Spielberg and his cast to Poland, where they were hired as film advisors.

In 1993 *Schindler's List* premiered in Washington, and in attendance were President Clinton and First Lady Hillary. In Thomas's memoir, *Searching for Schindler*, he writes, "at the end of the screening, people did not know whether to clap or gasp. Once the applause began it became a frenzy." Misia turned to her husband and Thomas and paid tribute: "You two did it. Before the actors, before Steven, you two were there."

Leopold had, from the beginning, assured Spielberg that he would get an Oscar for Oskar, and he did, seven in fact. Leopold and Misia were Spielberg's guests on the night he won his first Academy Award for best director. In his acceptance speech he thanked "a survivor named Poldek Pfefferberg. I owe him such a debt. He has carried the story of Oskar Schindler to all of us." Leopold had traversed the road from Auschwitz to the Academy.

SS Obergruppenfuhrer Hans Frank, before he was hung for war crimes, declared, "A thousand years will pass and the guilt of Germany will not be erased." Because of the "zeal and persistence" of Leopold Pfefferberg, the memory of Oskar Schindler will likewise not be erased. His life was truly "a story of humanity, man to man."

37

Love in the Time of Cholera

GABRIEL GARCÍA MÁRQUEZ

1985

For Mercedes, of course

MERCEDES Barcha Pardo was thirteen years old when she vowed to be forever faithful to Gabriel García Márquez. Although she was very young when she made her pledge, and though oceans, politics, poverty, and dictators forced them apart, it was a vow from which she never wavered.

Gabriel García Márquez was born, the oldest of twelve children, on a banana plantation in Aracataca, Colombia. Because there was not enough food, his parents sent him to live with his maternal grandparents. It was his grandmother whose voice was to form the basis of his two greatest works: *Love in the Time of Cholera* and *One Hundred Years of Solitude*. Tranquilina Iguarán Cotes told him stories of the surreal, of ghosts, omens, and spirits, and talked about them as if they were real. From his grandfather, Nicolás Ricardo Márquez Mejía, he developed a social conscience. Once he told Gabriel that the greatest burden a man can carry was to have killed another man. Later Gabriel would state,

"I feel that all my writing has been about the experiences of the time I spent with my grandparents."

At age eight, with the passing of his grandfather and the onset of blindness in his grandmother, Gabriel rejoined his parents. After high school, under the prodding of his father, he began to study law at the National University of Colombia. It was during this time he had an experience that was to alter his destiny. While on vacation from school, he was introduced to a thirteen-year-old girl, Mercedes Barcha Pardo. She had the looks of her Egyptian ancestry and was, he said, quiet and mysterious as a sphinx. After meeting her, the smitten Gabriel declared that Mercedes was "the most interesting person" he had ever met. A short time later, he proposed. She gave her assent, but said that he would have to wait until she had finished school. They never shared with others the secret of their pact.

In the ensuing years, García Márquez switched from law to journalism, and began living in a brothel because of its cheap rent. He found a job writing a column for *El Heraldo* and also began dabbling in fiction. It was at this time that he reconnected with Mercedes, who was now in her early twenties. She would accompany him and her father, Demetrio, to a tavern. In his autobiography, *Living to Tell the Tale*, García Márquez writes that the reason Demetrio did not know of his passion for his daughter was because "it was the best-kept secret of the first twenty centuries of Christianity." It was at this tavern, El Tercer Hombre, that Demetrio remarked that "the prince who will marry my daughter hasn't been born yet." Gabriel was elated when she finally agreed to go with him to a dance at a hotel, the El Prado. He was even more thrilled when she showed up without her ever-present escort, Demetrio. However, despite her pledge when she was thirteen, at this time she refused to take his proposals seriously.

In 1955, García Márquez wrote a story that was obviously an indictment of Colombia's then reigning dictator, Rojas Pinilla. Concerned about his safety, the editors of his newspaper spirited him out of the country. On the taxi ride to the airport, he drove down Avenida Veinte de Julio, the street where Mercedes lived. In his autobiography he wrote that she was sitting on the steps of her home "with the intense stillness of someone waiting for a person who will not arrive." For a fleeting moment he thought of stopping the cab to say a final farewell, but, with the feeling that he was catching his last glimpse of the woman he had loved for so long, he continued on his way.

Once on the plane, he deeply regretted leaving without saying good-bye. To compensate for this, he took out the paper that was in the back pocket of the seat in front of him, compliments of the airline. On earlier occasions, he had used the paper to write poems, and then upon arrival would make them into paper airplanes, which he would send off. However, this time he used the paper in a far different fashion. On a blue sheet he wrote the things that he had left unsaid by not stopping at Mercedes's home. He explained that he was leaving for Europe; he had been compelled to leave so quickly that he had not even been able to tell her what had happened and why he was forced into exile. In the postscript he added that if he did not receive an answer to his letter within a period of a month, and if she did not agree to become his wife, he would remain forever abroad and never see her again. He received her response within a week.

With her acceptance of his proposal, while alone in Europe he had the comfort that Mercedes was waiting for him back in Colombia. Overjoyed, he wrote her a letter every week. In 1958 he managed to slip back into the country, and fourteen years after his first proposal, he married Mercedes.

Immediately after the marriage the newlyweds fled to Caracas, but soon were once more on the move because of Gabriel's commitment to left-wing politics. Their next stop was Havana, in order to report on Fidel Castro's revolution. There Gabriel began a friendship with the Cuban dictator, which has lasted until today. The following year Mercedes gave birth to their first son, Rodrigo, and the family moved to New York City. Gabriel was to run the North American branch of Castro's news agency, *Prensa Latina*. Anticommunist forces, angered by the leftist newspaper in their midst, began to send death threats to García Márquez. Fearful for his life, they moved to Mexico City and were subsequently informed that he would no longer be welcome in the United States. In Mexico City, their second son, Gonzalo, was born.

The next few years Gabriel was happy in his personal life, but wretched in his professional one. He was working writing subtitles for films and collaborating with others on screenplays. His lifelong dream of being a novelist was becoming more and more distant. Then, on a vacation to Acapulco with his family, he abruptly stopped his car. He had an epiphany for a novel that had been struggling to be born for the past twenty years. He later recalled, "All of a sudden—I don't know why—I had this illumination on how to write the book—I had it so completely formed, that right there I could have dictated the first chapter word by word to a typist." And the tone of the voice was one that had been long silenced, that of his beloved grandmother.

The Márquezes headed back to Mexico City. Once there, Gabriel immediately began to write, something he did obsessively for the next eighteen months. Pounding away at his typewriter, he would consume six packs of cigarettes a day. His wife and friends began to call the smoke-filled room where he had holed up "the Cave of the Mafia." So intent was he on pursuing his novel that he stopped working at his job. Therefore, though the bills kept coming in, the money did not. Mercedes first sold her jewels and when that money was depleted, they sold their car and later on their household appliances. When everything they owned was gone, they borrowed from friends, which left them ten thousand dollars in debt. During this period of penury, García Márquez never lost belief in his book, and Mercedes never lost her belief in her husband.

At last, Gabriel emerged from his smoke-filled cave. When he did so, he was holding thirteen hundred pages in his nicotine-stained fingers. Mercedes and Gabriel rushed to the post office to mail the novel to his editor in Buenos Aires. Once there, they discovered that the price of the postage was 160 pesos, and Mercedes only had 80 pesos left. They mailed the first half off and then they pawned Mercedes's Mixmaster and hair dryer. With that money they mailed off the second half.

Within one week, all eight thousand copies of *One Hundred Years of Solitude* were sold. Fame and fortune had finally come to the erstwhile poverty-stricken couple. As a final crowning glory, Mercedes and Gabriel, in 1982, journeyed to Stockholm to receive the Nobel Prize for literature. A few years later he published *Love in the Time of Cholera*, which was based on his parents' courtship and dedicated to his beloved Mercedes.

The following year, after a quarter of a century, Gabriel returned to his hometown of Aracataca, which he had immortalized as the fictional town of Macondo in *One Hundred Years of Solitude*. Mercedes and Gabriel were greeted by hundreds of fans shouting "Long live Gabo!" in a train painted with yellow butterflies.

They toured the town in a horse and carriage and were treated to a dance by local schoolgirls dressed as butterflies. When they drove past the home where he had grown up with his grandparents, it must have made for an extremely emotion-laden homecoming.

Gabriel and Mercedes spend most of their time in Mexico City and the rest in their other homes in Cuernavaca, Paris, Barcelona, Havana, Cartagena, and Barranquilla. Observing the interactions between husband and wife, even after forty-one years of marriage, one can observe that Gabriel is still very much in love. In the course of a conversation, he refers constantly to his wife, and with the greatest of affection. A friend said of the couple, "She is his link to the earth. She's the practical one, the one who looks after their properties, the Eon at his side. He would be totally lost without her." Mercedes's father, Demetrio, had been wrong when he had declared that "the prince who will marry my daughter hasn't been born yet."

Tragically, in 1999, Gabriel was diagnosed with lymphatic cancer. Mercedes and he are fighting this new enemy by traveling to clinics in Mexico City and Los Angeles. However, when the inevitable comes, and they lose each other, every day will surely seem like "a hundred years of solitude." And when Gabriel makes the transition from this world to the next, his last thought will be "For Mercedes, of course."

38

The Satanic Verses

SALMAN RUSHDIE

1988

For Marianne

I N 1988, a unique name was emblazoned in the media: Salman Rushdie. His novel *The Satanic Verses* unleashed a chain reaction of events not commonly associated with a book. Rushdie became a symbol of blasphemy in one part of the world, a martyr in the other. However, lost amid the scandal was a forgotten figure, his wife, Marianne Wiggins.

Marianne's childhood gave no indication of the extraordinary road she would walk. She was raised in Lancaster, Pennsylvania, in a community that was influenced by its strong Amish neighborhood. Her mother, Mary Klonis Wiggins, was the daughter of Greek immigrants who had settled in Virginia. Her father, John Wiggins, was a farmer by occupation and a preacher by vocation. John preached in a conservative Christian church that had been founded by Marianne's grandfather. The most traumatic event of her childhood was her father's suicide.

When she was nine, she was baptized into her mother's sect. She later recalled of her conversion, "I left those wooden pews for

rooms full of icons and incense and men in robes." Her formative years were strongly impacted by diverse religious influences:
the fundamentalist Christianity of John, the ritual-filled Greek
Orthodox practices of her mother, and the neighboring Amish
community's endeavors to create a utopian God-centered society. She later recounted her childhood religious upbringing as
"a Bible-beating, reactionary kind of church, the first Church of
Christ Salvation or some long thing like that." Marianne would
later revisit, and attack, organized religion as the great evil in her
novel *John Dollar*.

Upon graduation from Manheim Township High School, at
age seventeen, she married Brian Porzak, a film distributor, on
June 6, 1965. In Rome, four years later, Marianne gave birth to her
only child, daughter Lara. The marriage foundered, and five years
later the couple divorced. Marianne raised Lara single-handedly,
mainly in Martha's Vineyard. She supported herself and Lara
by working in a stockbroker's office until her first novel, *Babe*,
was published, which enabled her to pursue a full-time writing
career.

Marianne later lived abroad for many years, mainly in Paris,
Brussels, and Rome, before she finally settled in London, where
she lived for sixteen years. It was in Britain where she was to meet
her next husband.

Salman Rushdie was born worlds away from Marianne's Amish
community, in Bombay, India. His parents were devout Muslims
and members of the upper middle class. As such, Salman and his
three sisters were sheltered from the misery of the thousands of
homeless people who slept on the streets of Bombay. Instead, his
childhood was filled with tales of Aladdin and his magic flying
carpet.

Reality came calling on his privileged world when he was sent to the private British boarding school Rugby. There, "the little prince" (as his parents called him) had a rude awakening, as his skin color made him an outsider, and he was called a "wog" by fellow students. Teachers also treated him with hostility, and he was often excluded from social activities. Salman found writing therapeutic, and he wrote a short autobiographical novel called *Terminal Report*. This made him want to choose writing as a profession.

After graduation, he rejoined his family, who were now living in Pakistan. However, there, too, he felt like an outsider. His years in England had left him with an upper-crust British accent, and people associated him with the hated former colonial officials. Feeling as alienated at home as abroad, he decided to accept the scholarship he had won to Cambridge. He described his return in 1965 as "one of the most disorientating moments of my life." He graduated with a masters in history with honors, and in 1970 married a proper English woman, Clarissa Luard, thereby becoming a British subject. Their son, Zafir, was born in 1979. With the publication of his novel *Midnight's Children*, he was able to devote himself to writing full-time. Nine years later, the couple divorced, and a mere three months after, he married his second wife, Marianne Wiggins.

Marianne and Salman were initially drawn to one another because of their commonalities. They both were born in 1947, brought up in religious environments, expatriates living in London, novelists, and divorced with one child. They were married in January 1988, and during their first years together they enjoyed London's literary milieu and culture. However, life as they knew it radically changed with the publication of Salman's *Satanic Verses*.

The novel was immediately banned in Rushdie's native India and in Singapore, as well as every Muslim nation, because it was viewed as an irreverent depiction of the Prophet Muhammad. The controversy hit even closer to home when the book was burned on the streets of Bradford, in Yorkshire. Shop owners in Britain's Muslim communities were told that if they failed to stick anti-Rushdie posters in their windows, their shops would be damaged. However, Rushdie was not overly concerned by this display of intellectual terrorism. He had always viewed his purpose as an author as being an antagonist to the state, in the hope his satirical works would improve it. He thought that he was free to write what he felt, that in a democratic society, freedom, like mercy, should not be strained. It was at this time that Salman and Marianne left England for the United States in order to go on a book tour.

On Valentine's Day most wives expect red roses, chocolates, and even jewels if their husbands are feeling amorous or are affluent. Marianne, however, got something far different. On February 14, 1989, on Radio Tehran, Ayatollah Ruhollah Khomeini, then supreme leader of Iran, condemned Salman Rushdie to death for *The Satanic Verses*, which he denounced as "exactly what it is called—verses inspired by Satan himself." Ironically, the novel, just as most of Rushdie's writings, was meant to be funny. Apparently, the Iranian spiritual ruler did not share Rushdie's sense of humor. He called on all faithful Muslims to execute the writer, as well as the publishers and translators of the book, in a fatwa (religious edict). Khomeini called "on all zealous Muslims to execute them quickly, whenever they may find them, so that no one will dare to insult the Islamic sanctions. Whoever is killed on this path will be regarded as a martyr, God willing."

As further inducement to murdering Rushdie, an aide to the

Ayatollah offered a million-dollar reward for the person who carried out the execution. The bounty was eventually upped to $5 million. The Japanese translator of the book was stabbed to death; the Italian translator was knifed, but survived. The Norwegian publisher escaped assassination after an attempt on his life in Oslo.

Marianne, who initially was flattered at her husband's dedicating *The Satanic Verses* to her, became far less enamored of the tribute, as it put her life in jeopardy as well. Fearing the wrath of the Muslim faithful and avaricious bounty hunters, Salman and Marianne immediately went into hiding in Britain. They lived in safe houses, under the protection of Scotland Yard. For security reasons, they had to move fifty-six times within the period of a year. They missed the loss of their home, personal possessions, and liberty. Salman was devastated at not being able to visit with Zafir. To help compensate for this, he wrote a children's book, *Haroun and the Sea of Stories*. For the beleaguered couple, *The Satanic Verses* had become *The Satanic Curses*.

Although worldwide attention was drawn to Salman's plight, little regard was paid to that of the Ayatollah's other victim, Marianne Wiggins. Before *The Satanic Verses* had caused a political eruption, Harper & Row had planned a campaign to promote Marianne's novel *John Dollar*, beginning with a seven-city tour. Marianne, an avowed feminist, had made certain not to capitalize on her famous spouse's name. Indeed, the only indication to show that they were husband and wife were their novels' respective dedications: *The Satanic Verses*: "for Marianne" and *John Dollar*: "for beloved Salman." When American writers had a reading to support Rushdie, Ms. Wiggins sent a written statement, via her literary agent, Andrew Wylie, which was read by Susan Sontag,

It stated, in part, that writers "are a dangerous breed and always have been, because words outlive their authors, words can emanate from silence, words can find their way from hidden places." Marianne's present project was put on hold, along with her forthcoming one. The latter was to have been a nonfiction book about bullfighting. To that end, she had planned to visit Spain in the spring and Latin America in the winter in order to follow and interview matadors. Metaphorically, *The Satanic Verses* had become the red flag, the inflamed bulls his impassioned critics.

After five months in hiding, Marianne decided that this was not what she had signed up for. She rented a flat in London under an assumed name. In 1993, Wiggins and Rushdie divorced. There are few who would cast aspersions. The jump from an Amish-influenced childhood to being a target of a fatwa was, as the cliché goes, a bit much.

Although Marianne has led a far-from-conventional life, she engaged in the customary pursuit of ex-husband bashing. One acerbic quote was "All of those who love him wish that the man had been as great as the event." She told the *London Times* that she had finally broken out of what she called "a straitjacket of loyalty and public devotion" and faulted him for "focusing attention on himself rather than aligning himself with other persecuted writers." She also criticized him for going on television, whereby he publicly embraced Islam. Ms. Wiggins continued, "The very fact that he would go on television and announce a personal conversion shows how far his personality has been broken down." Even with this reaffirmation, the fatwa was not lifted.

In 1998, Marianne left for the States in order to go on a book tour to promote her latest novel, *Almost Heaven*. She stayed in New York City for a few days, visiting the home of her friend

Claire Bloom. The two women have a lot in common, including contempt for their respective writer ex-husbands Philip Roth and Salman Rushdie. However, while Claire dished the dirt in *Leaving a Doll's House*, Marianne had no desire to do a "hide and speak," although the public was clamoring for her to lift the curtain.

Salman, for his part, is equally unfond of Marianne. When a reporter asked him how he felt about his ex-wife, who publicly accused him of being a self-obsessed coward, he replied, "Do not start me on Marianne Wiggins." However, he was then generous enough to add that she is a good writer. It is true that one does not thoroughly know one's spouse until after the divorce proceedings.

Salman, for his part, moved on with his life. In 1997, while in hiding, he managed to meet a literary assistant with the British publisher Bloomsbury, Elizabeth West, with whom he had a son, Milan Rushdie. She stayed with him through the dark days of the fatwa, which led him to say of her fidelity, "In a time of bad luck, she was my good luck." The next year, when Iran lifted the fatwa, he emerged from hiding, making his first public appearance at a U2 concert in Wembley, in front of fifty thousand people. Bono was wearing a devil's costume on stage, which caused Rushdie to state, "I am not afraid of men who wear horns: I know who the real devils are."

In 2000, male lust superseded male loyalty. While in Italy, Salman's publicist gave him a magazine that had an article and photograph of stunning twenty-nine-year-old Indian actress and Ford model Padma Lakshmi. She had once hosted an Italian talk show wearing a bikini, speaks five languages, and wrote a cookbook, *Easy Exotic: A Model's Low-Fat Recipes from Around the World*. He admitted to his publicist, "If I ever meet this girl, my goose is cooked." They ended up meeting at a party by the Statue of Liberty, and his goose was indeed cooked, tandoori style.

At his lavish Manhattan wedding, the author remarked that each of his new wife's three names was shared by powerful Hindu deities. "Three goddesses in one. How could I pass this up, even if I am an atheist?" The ceremony took place in an enormous room overlooking the Hudson River. Rose petals were scattered on the floor, sitars played classical Indian music. The bride wore a two-piece purple sari that left her model's torso bared south of her navel. Her appearance was greeted with wolf whistles. The couple, in an Indian custom, exchanged toe rings. The 250 wedding guests, including Jay McInerney and Diane von Furstenberg, feasted on delicacies such as seafood curry, one of the bride's own creations.

In 2007 Salman Rushdie was appointed Knight Bachelor for "services to literature." Salman's response to the news was that he was "thrilled and humbled." Many did not share his sentiment. Mass demonstrations against the knighthood erupted in Pakistan and Malaysia. Al-Qaeda also condemned the honor, and calls for his death were issued. Al-Qaeda deputy Ayman al-Zawahiri stated the knighthood was "an insult to Islam," and it was planning "a very precise response." Later that year, Padma decided to obtain a divorce.

Marianne, safely ensconced in Los Angeles where she is a professor of English at the University of Southern California, has distanced herself from all things Rushdie. She is close with her daughter, Lara, who is an L.A. photographer to whom Marianne's novel *Dream Catcher* is dedicated. Moreover, she has a new romantic relationship with a man she describes as a professional explorer. "He built a leather boat and sailed across the Atlantic.

Then he built a bamboo raft and sailed across the Pacific." The couple sailed down the Amazon River together and then took a trip to Tonga. She shuns publicity and refuses interviews about her time with Rushdie. When a reporter asked her if her recluse status would send Salinger knocking at her door, she replied, "I think he's probably pretty busy. And quite frankly, I've had it with psychotics." The title of one of her novels aptly sums up her present life, *Almost Heaven*.

39

The Joy Luck Club

AMY TAN
(ENMEI TAN)
1989

To my mother
and the memory of her mother

You asked me once
what I would remember.

This, and much more.

AMY Tan dedicated *The Joy Luck Club* to her mother, Daisy, because the mother–daughter relationships at the heart of the novel have always been at the very heart of the author's life.

Daisy and John Tan were Chinese immigrants who settled in Oakland, California. Their daughter's Chinese name was Enmei, which means "blessing from America." Their other two children were boys, Peter and John. John Tan was an assistant Baptist minister, and his main priority was that his children were raised as members of his church. Daisy had extremely high academic expectations for her bright daughter. She determined that Amy would have a career as a neurosurgeon, and a hobby as a concert pianist.

Growing up in a predominantly white enclave, Amy wanted to be like the American girls. She was so ashamed of her wide nose that she began sleeping with a clothespin, in the hope it would become narrower. At the same time, her mother's differences from the American mothers were a constant source of humiliation for a girl who desperately wanted to fit in with her peers. For example, Daisy's Shanghai accent and broken English served as a source of cruel teasing by her classmates. While other mothers cautioned their children not to run into the streets, a Daisyism was, "You don't look, you get smash flat like sand crab."

Language was a source of alienation for Daisy in America, and the theme of miscommunication runs throughout the author's novels. Mostly, her parents talked to her in Chinese, but she would answer in English. Many years later, when Tan was asked to speak on a Voice of America radio program broadcast in China after the Tiananmen Square Massacre, she was asked to say something inspiring to the students in Chinese. However, the only words she knew how to say in Chinese were: "Turn off the light. Don't make trouble. Go to sleep."

Amy wanted to assimilate into American culture while her mother wanted her to retain her Chinese heritage. A further source of the depression that would shadow Amy's life and dissuade her from having children was Daisy's suicidal tendencies. Amy later wrote that her mother threatened to kill herself "sometimes weekly, sometimes daily, whenever she was displeased with me or my father or my brothers, whenever she felt slighted by her friends, whenever the milk spilled or the rice burned." All these factors

played into the mother–daughter conflicts that would character-
ize their relationship.

When Amy was fifteen, a dual tragedy occurred in the Tan
family, one that was to alter her life forever. Her father and eldest
brother both died of brain tumors within a year. One of the effects
of the catastrophes was that Daisy reverted to the Chinese super-
stitions she had repressed as the wife of a Baptist minister. Daisy
consulted a Ouija board on the best way to raise the now fatherless Amy and her younger brother. Feeling that her husband's and
child's deaths were caused by evil spirits in the home, she decided
to leave to escape further misfortune. She packed up her two children and moved to Europe. As Amy later recalled, "We thought
she was crazy, but at least she was crazy with a good idea."

After a Volkswagen odyssey through the Netherlands and
Germany looking for a furnished house, an American school,
and a place free from evil spirits, the family settled in Montreux,
Switzerland. Amy felt alienated in her new high school. As she
explained, it was difficult "graduating from a private school in
Switzerland among rich people and not being rich."

It was also in Switzerland that Amy's teen rebellion against her
exacting mother reached its zenith. Now that her daughter was at
an age when she might meet a boy at school, her mother warned her
about the perils of dating. Daisy cautioned Amy, "Don't ever let boy
kiss you. You do, you can't stop. Then you have baby. You put baby in
garbage can. Police find you, put you in jail, then you life over, better
just kill yourself." Despite her mother's dating mantra, she became
romantically involved with a man who even exceeded a mother's
worst nightmare. He was not only a drug dealer, but an escapee from
a German army mental hospital. Apparently, Daisy did not travel

far enough to escape the evil spirits. Her reaction was swift. She had the man arrested for drug possession and got her daughter dragged before the authorities. It also resulted in the most violent standoff that the mother and daughter had ever experienced. As Amy recounts in her new book *The Opposite of Fate*, "My mother slammed the door shut, latched it, then locked it with a key. I saw the flash of a meat cleaver just before she pushed me to the wall and brought the blade's edge to within an inch of my throat." Amy explained that she stayed pinned against the wall for twenty minutes, the blade never leaving her throat. She kept pleading with her mother, "I want to live. I want to live." Amy ended the romantic relationship.

However, from this clash of wills came an understanding between mother and daughter. Daisy felt that in order to bridge the distance between her and Amy, she had to unravel the enigma of her past life in China. The stories that Daisy recounted helped Amy begin to both understand and forgive her mother. The first and main story involved "the memory of her mother." Daisy explained that the tragedy began to unfold when her grandfather died in Shanghai. After that, her grandmother was raped by a rich man who then forced her to be his concubine. When she gave birth to a son, the baby was snatched from her and given to her rapist's high-ranking wife. Unable to cope with the horror of her reality, she committed suicide in front of her nine-year-old daughter Daisy by swallowing raw opium wrapped in rice cakes. As soon as Daisy Tu Ching was old enough, her relatives arranged a traditional marriage. Unfortunately, her husband was extremely abusive. Unable to endure his cruelty any longer, she divorced him. However, by doing so, she was forced to give up her three daughters. In 1949, as the Communist Revolution was taking over China, she left on the last boat before the new government would forbid future emigration. Joy Luck indeed.

The family eventually returned to California, and Amy attended a Baptist college in Oregon her mother had selected for her. However, when Amy met an Italian American boyfriend, Louis DeMattei, she left it to join him at San Jose City College. She further angered her mother by switching her major from pre-med to English. Daisy refused to talk to her for six months.

In 1987, Daisy became very ill. She asked her daughter, "If I die, what will you remember?" Amy made a promise that when her mother recovered, she would take her on a trip to China, where she could see her two surviving daughters, the babies she had relinquished forty years before. The trip to China, coupled with her mother's reminiscences, provided the seed from which *The Joy Luck Club* would grow.

In Daisy's later years she began to exhibit signs of encroaching Alzheimer's. Before the disease had obscured the past, Amy brought up the incident with the meat cleaver, which neither had mentioned since it had happened twenty years before. Daisy merely laughed and shrugged it off, claiming that it had never happened, that Amy had always been the good, obedient daughter, and they had never fought. Tan writes, "How wonderful to hear her say what was never true, yet now would be forever so."

In one of her last phone calls to her daughter, she asked Amy, with desperation in her voice, "I know I did something to hurt you...I did terrible things. But now I can't remember what...And I just want to tell you...I hope you can forget, just as I've forgotten." These words dredged up her mother's earlier question of many years ago, the first time that she was seriously ill. "If I die, what will you remember?" The inscription in *The Joy Luck Club* provides Amy's answer to Daisy:

> *You asked me once*
> *What I would remember.*
> *This, and much more.*

40

In the Time of the Butterflies

JULIA ALVAREZ

1994

For Dedé

JULIA Alvarez dedicated *In the Time of the Butterflies* to Bélgica Adela Mirabal (Dedé), a woman who has vigilantly kept the flame—so heroically lit by her sisters—alive for the past forty-five years.

Dedé's story is inextricably tied to the history of her country, the Dominican Republic, which suffered under tyranny's yoke from 1930 to 1961. Rafael Leonidas Trujillo, "El Jefe," suppressed all constitutional rights and exploited the country's wealth to aggrandize his own personal fortune. Anyone who opposed him received a "visit" from his secret police, who drove to their victims' homes in black Volkswagen Beetles. This was usually enough to silence Trujillo's enemies, but there were those who refused to be silenced. And it is those who refused to be silenced whose voices can be forever heard in *In the Time of the Butterflies*.

As members of the Dominican upper class, the Mirabal family moved in Trujillo's inner circle. At a dance he became attracted to the eldest of the four sisters, Minerva. His sexual invitations were more in the manner of a command, and he became infuriated when she publicly repulsed him. In retaliation, her father was jailed for two years. He died shortly after being released as a result of the prison beatings and malnutrition. Minerva was also briefly arrested, and she was not permitted to receive her law degree when she graduated.

Trujillo's actions, as well as his violation of his people's rights, spurred Dedé's sisters Minerva, Patria, and María Teresa, as well as their respective spouses, into action, and they joined an underground movement called the "Movement of the Fourteenth of June." The code name in the resistance movement for the three women was "Las Mariposas," the Butterflies. Their goal was the ousting of El Jefe, thereby ridding their beloved Dominican Republic from the noose that was strangling it. So powerful was the opposition from the three sisters that the dictator declared, "The only problems my government has are the Catholic Church and those Mirabal sisters."

Retaliation was swift. Minerva, María Teresa, and Patria's husbands were all arrested and placed in the remote La Victoria Penitentiary in Santo Domingo. On November 25, 1960, on the way home from visiting their spouses, the sisters' Jeep was forced into a sugarcane field on the outskirts of Puerto Plata by black Volkswagens. Members of the dreaded SIM beat and then strangled all three women, as well as their driver, Rufino de la Cruz. Their bodies were then stuffed back into their car, which was thrown off a cliff known as La Cumbre. The newspaper the next morning reported coverage of the tragic "accident."

It is staggering to imagine Dedé's despair when the coffins of her three sisters were delivered to a funeral home, with the dictatorial command that they were not to be opened. However, Dedé defied the order and received confirmation of the brutal manner in which her three beloved sisters had met their deaths. Before saying her last farewell, Dedé cut off the braid of her younger sister María Teresa, which was filled with slivers of glass, twigs, and dirt.

Ironically, Trujillo's plan of ridding himself of the Mirabal sisters backfired. Their murders sparked outrage in the Dominican Republic; they became martyrs to which their country rallied. Six months later, El Jefe was himself ambushed and assassinated on a country road on his way to visit his mistress. Dominicans claim that his death was not a murder but rather an *ajusticiamiento*, a bringing to justice. The anniversary of his death is now a national holiday in the Dominican Republic. Although the wings of the butterflies had been destroyed, their power still brought down a tyrannical regime.

Dedé's first task after the loss of her sisters was to be not just a mother to her own three sons, but to her now-motherless six nieces and nephews as well. Her now-grown niece says that her aunt had to survive in order to take care of them. Julia Alvarez says of Dedé, "I can truly say that although the heroism of her sisters was what led me to their story, it was the triumphant example and empowering story of Dedé Mirabal which inspired me to write *In the Time of the Butterflies,* which is why the novel is dedicated to Dedé."

Another important contribution Dedé made was opening and operating the Museo Hermanas Mirabal in Salcedo in the Dominican Republic. On the grounds, buried together, are the three courageous sisters, as well as Minerva's husband, Manolo. Across the street, in a park, there is a monument to the Mariposas; on its top are three butterflies. Not far away is the shell of the doomed Jeep with its mangled front from the orchestrated crash. Visitors to the museum are able to view photographs celebrating the Mirabals' lives, as well as objects that were precious to them: there is Patria's teacup collection and María Teresa's embroidery. One of the shrines is María Teresa's glass-filled braid, a metaphor for the Dominican Republic's twisted and tragic past.

Alvarez feels a personal connection to her novel as she is also one of four sisters born in the Dominican Republic. However, while the Mirabal sisters stayed and died for their cause, the Alvarez family fled to the United States when a black Volkswagen began blocking the family's doorway. Alvarez wrote, "They were the other sisters, the ones who stayed behind and paid for our freedom with their lives." Julia questioned her mother about their abrupt abandonment of their country, and why she had not told her children that they were leaving the Dominican Republic forever. Her mother replied, "Ay sí, and get ourselves killed! You had the biggest mouth back then."

In New York City, Julia missed her native country and her large extended family. Further contributing to her feelings of alienation was her classmates' reaction to the newcomer with the accent. Julia knew enough English to pick up on the fact that her classmates yelled "Spic!" at her. Her *mami*, however, assured Julia that the children were telling her to "speak!" Perhaps her mother's words gave birth to Julia's voice, which she ultimately expressed in her writing.

Dedé's sisters are now Dominican folk heroes, and the United Nations General Assembly has declared November twenty-fifth, the anniversary of the Mirabal murders, as the annual date of the International Day for the Elimination of Violence against Women. The mission of the museum is not just to honor the three women to whom it is dedicated. Dedé's other purpose for her museum is to educate its visitors to the horrors of dictatorship and the preciousness, and precariousness, of democracy. As Minou, Dedé's niece, says,

> She is at the museum every day. She goes there, she talks to students, to the researchers, to people who come and visit the place. She sees this as her duty. She repeats and repeats the story and never tires. She thinks it her duty to keep this story alive; the principles, the values that are involved in this whole story—she thinks she has to survive and that that's the way her sisters will survive, too.

Julia Alvarez concurs with Minou's sentiments about Dedé: "She had suffered her own martyrdom; the one left behind to tell the story of the other three." Oftentimes the true test of courage is not to die, but to endure.

Alvarez's novel *In the Time of the Butterflies* does in book form what Dedé's museum does. It expresses the truth that individuals can make a difference. Julia's "big mouth" has served to spread the heroism, and martyrdom, of the Mirabal sisters beyond their Dominican Republic homeland. As a survivor, Julia felt it incumbent upon herself to bear witness.

41

Under the Tuscan Sun

FRANCES MAYES

1996

For Ann Cornelisen

FRANCIS Mayes's memoir is dedicated to the woman who, more than anyone else, paved the way for fellow expatriates to bask under the Tuscan sun. Frances Mayes's journey from the peaches of Georgia to the grapes of Italy teaches us that it sometimes takes a villa to achieve la dolce vita.

Frances Mayes was a creative writing professor at San Francisco State University when she decided that although her twenty-year marriage had unraveled, she would not do likewise. With her new boyfriend, Ed Kleinschmidt, a poet and professor at Santa Clarita University, she decided to embark on her lifelong dream to travel to Italy. In *Under the Tuscan Sun* she wrote of her search to find an Italian home: "Because I had ended a long marriage that was not supposed to end and was establishing a new relationship, this house quest felt tied to whatever new identity I would manage to forge."

In the summer of 1990 Frances and Ed found, in Tuscany, a three-hundred-year-old villa that had been abandoned (except for the scorpions) and unoccupied for thirty years. Its name was Bramasole, which translates to "yearning for the sun." Its crumbling walls, nonflushing toilets, and the aforementioned arachnids didn't kill the couple's ardor—they were married in 1998. Nor did it kill their love for the villa—Mayes's memoir of their time rebuilding and making Bramasole a home is detailed in her bestselling memoir *Under the Tuscan Sun*.

Although she had long admired her work from afar, Mayes, while in Italy, finally met the woman to whom she would one day dedicate her book. Invited to a neighbor's lunch party, Frances and Ed were introduced to a number of successful authors from various countries who had made their new homes in Tuscany. Frances was eager to meet Ann Cornelisen in particular. Ann was an American woman who had spent twenty years in the poverty-stricken mountainous area of Basilicata, and had chronicled her experiences in *Torregreca: Life, Death and Miracles in a Southern Italian Village*.

Frances had first read the book in the 1970s and decided that it was one that she would reread many times, and share with both her students and her friends. When she moved to Tuscany, she was given Ann's phone number by mutual acquaintances in Georgia, where Frances was born and where Ann's parents were living. Although in awe of *Torregreca*, Frances had always dreaded making cold calls to strangers, and therefore was thrilled serendipity brought them together instead. Frances impulsively invited her to dinner, although her home did not yet have furniture, dishes, linens, or adequate kitchen supplies.

When Ann arrived for dinner, Ed moved an old, rickety table that had come with the crumbling house onto the terrace; its leg and top promptly fell off. Such an occurrence had the potential of proving to be an icebreaker or a disaster, depending on the nature of the guest. It proved the former.

That evening, Ed and Frances gave a tour of their home, and Ann shared her own renovating experiences, recounting how when a wall had come down on her first day there, she had discovered an angry pig, which had been left behind by the local workers. Over dinner, it quickly became apparent that from her twenty years in Italy, where she had dedicated her time to building nurseries for children living below the poverty level, she had her doctorate in knowledge about her adopted homeland. This fact ushered in what Ed and Frances would refer to as their ten thousand questions, and a typical conversation between them would be Frances turning to Ed and asking, "How long does it take to get to Urbino? When is the right time to fertilize olives? Where does the accent fall in 'Maritima'? How long was a Roman mile?"

"I don't know," he'd answer. "Ask Ann."

Later, Ed would turn to Frances and ask, "Will we need to buy a chain saw? Do you think the shutters must be oiled every year? Poliminia was the muse of what? Where will we get the well tested?"

To which she would answer, "Ask Ann."

That evening, under the Tuscan moon, with Frances wedging her knee against the table to prevent it from toppling, the friendship was sealed when she and Ann laughed at the same places, a key ingredient to friendship.

After that initial dinner, Frances and Ann saw a great deal of one another; however, as open as Ann was with her knowledge of Italy she was as private in regard to her own life. Even in her two travel memoirs, *Torregreca* and *Women of the Shadows*, she volunteered very little about herself. Of this reticence, Frances would write, "As much as I probed, I was secretly happy to find that she remains mysterious to me. Her private life remains so as well. She is humorous, superbly intelligent, methodical, acerbic, generous and—this must be an inheritance from her Southern-belle mother, she refuses to acknowledge that she is remarkable or complex, while everything she says or writes reveals, of course, that she is." Perhaps Ann's reluctance to reveal her past can best be summed up by the title of her 1971 novel, *Vendetta of Silence*.

Ann was born in Cleveland, Ohio, in 1926 and studied at Vassar College from 1944 to 1946. The school has a scholarship in her name; the funds go to students interested in studying abroad. After making her debut into Chicago society, she first married Gordon Carpenter O'Hara and then wed Charles Walker Cammack III. When her second marriage dissolved, the twenty-seven-year-old arrived in Florence, her trunk filled with what her genteel mother considered the essentials: several evening dresses with matching silk shoes, silk dresses, and other trappings of an affluent girl from Chicago. Her purpose in Europe was to study archaeology before she returned to the States. She had also come with a letter of introduction to Giovanna Guzzeloni Thompson, daughter of a Milanese aristocrat. She was a young widow who had lived in England during the Fascist regime, and then had moved to Rome. Their meeting was to irrevocably change the road that Ann would take. Giovanna, sensing a woman who she felt was far more suited to working with children than studying relics from the past, enlisted her in working for her organization: the British-based Save the Children Fund. This was the genesis of how, in 1959, a Vassar-educated, American woman from Chicago found herself driving a Jeep down a bluff along the Adriatic coast into the medieval-like village of Ortona, which she later was to fictionalize as Torregreca. The town and the woman would never be the same, as each indelibly left their mark on the other.

In Ortona, Ann encountered a world divorced from the twentieth century, far removed from her former life. In the village, she observed families living in homes with walls that had been blown off during World War II, men in the town square whose goal it was to be hit by a passing car in order to collect insurance, orphans living in an abandoned mill, women holding buckets crowding around fountains in order to have water for their families. In *Women of the Shadows*, Ann described them as "people born knowing they have no expectations." In her personal encounters with the town's inhabitants, she learned that they were deeply superstitious. They hid amulets in their mattresses and sprinkled salt on their bedsprings to ward off evil spirits. Similarly, the women, after close observation, asked Ann if shaving under her arms cost a woman her sexual powers. Ann, in her ambition of organizing nurseries, realized that her first task was going to be to overcome the people's deep-seated suspicions of someone so vastly different from anyone they had yet encountered. The things that they found most alarming were that she was a woman traveling alone, smoked, drove a car, dressed in Western-style clothing, drank rum punches at a public bar, and was not a Catholic.

In order to help rid them of these concerns, Ann had to adopt a code of *serietà*. This concept is more external than a moral code, outwardly proclaimed by dressing in clothing that was the antithesis of provocative and always acting in a very upright fashion. Ann wrote in *Torregreca*, "I worked on my *serietà* until men lounging in piazzas no longer considered me a loose woman.

Indeed, I doubt they considered me a woman at all." Ann rented an apartment where chickens and piglets roamed the stairways. In her bathtub she stored water that she used to fill her toilet, sponge herself, and boil pasta.

Ann successfully set up nurseries for the children, where they were nourished in body, mind, and spirit, and their mothers, the women of the shadows, were, with Ann's help, able to step out into the light as well. Other philanthropic projects, such as hospitals and housing followed, until, after thirty-five years, Ann decided to return to Rome, specifically, Rome, Georgia, although at that point she was probably more Italian than American. She wrote in the epilogue, "But always a part of me remains in Torregreca. I know it always will. Every woman has one love affair that remains unfinished." When it was time for her to bid farewell to the people to whom she had dedicated her life, she realized that though she would be gone she would be forever part of her Italian village's folklore. She writes in the conclusion of *Torregreca*, "They tell me of things I said or did, things which only I know I never said, I never did. I can imagine them with the wind rattling the windows and driving the smoke back down the stovepipe, saying, 'Once there was a woman…'" At the end, she was anything but the *serietà*.

The woman of the legend died of undisclosed causes at age seventy-seven, in 2003. Her obituary stated that she was not survived by any heirs; obviously the reporter did not understand the scores of children she had nurtured in Torregreca. And, if anyone were ever to philosophize to Frances or Ed what heaven must be like, husband and wife would surely turn to one another and respond in unison, "Ask Ann."

42

Harry Potter and the Philosopher's Stone*

J. K. ROWLING
(JOANNE KATHLEEN ROWLING)

1997

**FOR JESSICA, WHO LOVES STORIES,
FOR ANNE, WHO LOVED THEM TOO;
AND FOR DI, WHO HEARD THIS ONE FIRST.**

THE story of the dedication for the first Harry Potter book begins in Britain in 1964, when two eighteen-year-old strangers met on a train. The woman, Anne Volant (in a ruse as old as time), told Peter Rowling that she was cold. He gallantly offered her half his coat. This was followed by a lengthy conversation, which culminated with kisses. By the time they reached Scotland, they had forged a bond that would last for the rest of their lives. Their daughter Joanne was a result of this chance encounter, followed by her sister Dianne (Di) two years later.

* In the United States, this book was published as *Harry Potter and the Sorcerer's Stone*.

The two sisters experienced a fair share of sibling rivalry aris-
ing over the fact that Joanne was considered the bright one and
Dianne the pretty one. Rowling recalled, "We spent nearly three
quarters of our childhood fighting like a pair of wildcats imprisoned together in a very small cage." To this day, Dianne bears a
small scar over her eyebrow, a souvenir from when Joanne threw a
battery at her. However, during the quieter times, they were best
friends. One of their favorite games involved the stairs; the two
girls used them to enact a cliff-top drama. Joanne would dangle
from the top stair, holding Dianne's hand, while imploring her not
to let go. This would invariably end with her falling to her death.

As a child, Joanne loved to write and would often sit on her
younger sister to compel her to listen. An offshoot of Joanne's stories
was to turn them into make-believe. They would raid their mother's
closet and enlist the acting abilities of neighborhood children. One
of these was a young boy, with the surname Potter. He once threw a
rock at Dianne, and Joanne, the protective older sister, retaliated by
hitting him hard on the head with her plastic sword. Her justification
was that she was the only one allowed to throw rocks at Dianne.

The Rowling childhood home was a happy one. Peter Rowling
was able to earn a comfortable living at a nearby Rolls-Royce factory, which allowed Anne to be a stay-at-home mother. However,
when Joanne was twelve she entered a new school, Wyedean Com-
prehensive, and her mother joined her, as she had obtained a job as
a lab technician in the science lab. John Nettleship was both Anne's
boss and Joanne's science teacher. He recalls, "I did teach her about
the philosopher's stone, the alchemist's stone, and explained how it
turned things to gold. It seems to have worked for her."

In *Desert Island Discs* Rowling wrote, "Home was a difficult
place to be," and that began in 1978. The tragedy started when

Anne started dropping beakers at work and couldn't pour tea at home. The diagnosis was multiple sclerosis. Her loved ones could only stand helplessly by as the once-vital woman was reduced to crawling up the stairs.

In 1990, Joanne was staying with a boyfriend's family in what was the first time she had been away for Christmas. She was working on her manuscript (of *Harry Potter*) when she received a phone call from her father at seven o'clock in the morning. She instantly realized that the only reason for him to call at that hour was because he had terrible news. Anne Rowling died on December 30, at age forty-five. "The pain from her death is still raw. I miss my mother almost daily, and I feel desperately sad for all she missed. She died before either of her daughters got married, died before Di gave up nursing and became a lawyer; she never met her granddaughter, and I never told her about Harry Potter." It was Anne's passing that inspired the image of the Mirror of Erised. Erised read backward is "Desire," and when Harry looked into it, he saw his deceased mum and dad. Similarly, she stated she "would give almost anything for another five minutes with my mother which, of course, would never be enough."

Immediately after the funeral, Rowling's life went into a tailspin. She ended her current romantic relationship and found herself unable to cope with her grief. Perhaps feeling that physical distance would provide an antidote to pain, she accepted a position to teach English in Porto, Portugal. It was there, at a bar, that she met Jorge Arantes. They began to talk, and when he said that Jane Austen was his favorite author, kisses and phone numbers were exchanged. When they married in Porto's registry office, Joanne's only guests were Dianne and her sister's boyfriend. Her father was not invited. His daughters were upset with him for moving in and marrying his secretary right after Anne's death.

The couple had one daughter, Jessica, whom Joanne named after Jessica Mitford, the British writer she greatly admired. Indeed, at Jessica's christening she gave her a copy of Mitford's book, *Hons and Rebels*. The marriage lasted thirteen months and one day. In *Harry Potter and the Prisoner of Azkaban*, Professor Trelawney tells a student that the thing he was most afraid of would happen on October 16, which was the date of her wedding. The death knell was when her husband slapped her hard across the face and locked her out of the house, without Jessica. The next day Rowling came to the house, accompanied by a policeman, and escaped with her daughter. Terrified of the fury of her husband, she went into hiding with her baby. As soon as she could she boarded a flight back to Britain; in her arms she had Jessica, in her bag, her manuscript of *Harry Potter*.

Joanne and Jessica headed to Edinburgh, to the home of Dianne and the man whom she had recently married, Roger Moore. Dianne welcomed her sister, who was in a very bad state. Joanne was now a single mother, with no money and no job, and no home of her own. Dianne must have thought back to the stairs of their childhood home, with Joanne clutching her hand, begging her to save her. Dianne, as in the past, did her best to do so. One of the things that she did was to be the first person to read *Harry Potter*. This time Joanne did not have to sit on her sister to make her listen. Rather, Dianne laughed and lauded, which gave Joanne just the encouragement and hope she needed.

After a few weeks, feeling she could not impose on her sister's new marriage with two extra guests, Joanne went on welfare and obtained a small apartment for herself and Jessica. One of the worst parts of her new life was she felt that she had made a bad environment for her daughter in not providing her with a father, a nice home, or many toys. She said that her daughter's toys "could comfortably fit in a shoebox."

Rowling did not obtain another teaching job at this time because she wanted to finish *Harry Potter*, and she realized that with a baby and a full-time position she would never complete her manuscript. During the day, as a respite from the gloom of her apartment, she would take Jessica to her brother-in-law's restaurant, Nicolson's. Finally, in August 1996, she received a call that would be a turning point in her life. It was from her agent, Christopher Little, who told her that Bloomsbury Publishing was offering her a book deal. With this act, he set off a phenomenon unprecedented in publishing history. Rowling, because of *Harry Potter*, added as many new words and images to childhood as Walt Disney. After she hung up, she screamed so loud that she startled Jessica, who was drinking tea in her high chair.

Harry Potter, in true wizard fashion, was able to turn the penniless, single mother into a worldwide phenomenon known to millions. She became the first person to make a billion dollars from writing, and her novels have been made into blockbuster movies. Not only has her wealth surpassed that of the queen, Elizabeth II honored her with the title Officer of the Order of the British Empire. Moreover, she has found happiness with her new husband, Dr. Neil Murray, and two additional children. Her wedding to him included two bridesmaids: her sister, Dianne, and her daughter, Jessica. Anne, who loved stories, would have loved her daughter's most of all.

43

The Constant Gardener

JOHN LE CARRÉ
(DAVID JOHN MOORE CORNWELL)
2001

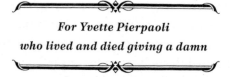

For Yvette Pierpaoli
who lived and died giving a damn

WHEN John le Carré wrote *The Constant Gardener*, he made his character Tessa Quayle a humanitarian who devoted her life to helping those who needed it the most. However, rather than draw her from an imagined ideal, he patterned her after a real woman, one whom he had met in Phnom Penh twenty years before he began his novel. Yvette Pierpaoli was a heroine who acted as society's conscience. Although Tessa and Yvette were diverse in terms of age, nationality, wealth, marital status, and occupation, they shared the commonality of "giving a damn."

Yvette Pierpaoli was a Frenchwoman of Italian descent who was born in Metz, Alsace-Lorraine in 1939. When she was ten years old, her teacher showed her class a map of France's colonies, and from that moment on, Yvette felt a strong connection to Cambodia. When the call of motherhood came, she fell in love with a Cambodian man living in Paris who fathered her child.

He ended up deserting them, which left her and the infant in dire financial straits.

When she was twenty-five and her daughter, Emanuel, was five, after years of saving, she bought them one-way tickets and they were off for an adventure, something she had always craved. Because of the cost of the trip, she arrived in Phnom Penh penniless. With characteristic nerve, she went to a small hotel and told the owner that although she could not pay rent, she was going to begin a successful business and that she would recompense him then. He agreed. Sure enough, Yvette began a lucrative import–export business. Not only did she make good on her promise of back rent, she used the bulk of her profits to buy food and medicine for Cambodia's destitute. The social activism that was to mark her life had been born.

In the Cambodian capital Yvette met another foreigner, a writer from Britain, David John Moore Cornwell, who wrote under the pseudonym John le Carré. He had come to Southeast Asia after telling a friend who was a painter, "Stop painting landscapes for a while and go live in one." That is what brought about the encounter between Cornwell and Yvette, which took place in a German diplomat's home in Phnom Penh and was accompanied by the sound of gunfire caused by Cambodia's political situation. The author says of this memorable meeting with the small woman with the large eyes:

> She could tip you with a smile to melt your heart, cajole, flatter, and win you in any way you needed to be won. But it was all for a cause. And the cause, you quickly learned, was an absolutely non-negotiable, visceral requirement in her to get food and money to the starving, medicines to the

sick, shelter for the homeless, papers for the stateless, and, just generally, in the most secular, muscular, businesslike, down-to-earth way you can imagine, perform miracles.

The author was right when he said that Yvette would try any means to achieve her ends—which were always humanitarian ones, which is illustrated in the following vignette. A wealthy, married Scandinavian businessman became attracted to Yvette and invited her to his private island off the coast of Sweden for an amorous interlude. She accepted, not out of mutual lust, but because she desperately wanted to secure his financial obligation to purchase hundreds of thousands of dollars of rice in order to give it to starving Cambodian refugees on the Thai border. Once there, on a stroll along the beach, she proposed the game where he places his hands on her eyes and asks her any question. Not surprisingly, his was about her sexual desire. She answered seductively that hers concerned "a certain handsome virile Scandinavian making love to her in a perfumed bedroom on a lonely island in the midst of a turbulent sea." When the position was reversed, she asked him if she could have the rice contract for the Cambodians. It is unknown whether he complied, or if it ruined the moment.

Not content to merely give money to the destitute, Yvette became the director of an orphanage. One day a three-year-old boy was brought in. He had been discovered under a pile of dead bodies in a village that had been bombed. He was the only survivor. Because of his trauma, he was antisocial and jealously hoarded his food. Since Yvette's role in the orphanage was not just a managerial one, she took an active role in bonding with the children under her care. One day the boy, whom she called Oliver, threw his thin arms around her neck and called her "Mama." From that moment on, where Yvette went the child was her ever-present shadow. In 1975, when the American troops withdrew from Cambodia, the Khmer Rouge overran her beloved Phnom Penh. Preparing to flee, she arranged for exit papers for Oliver, and flew with him and Emanuel back to France. There she later adopted the child who had initially adopted her.

After Cambodia, Yvette traveled where the winds of war carried her; she felt it her mission to aid those who had become refugees because of governmental conflicts. She spent time in Guatemala, Nicaragua, Bolivia, Colombia, Africa, and Albania. In between, she purchased a home in the south of France, in Avignon, where she visited with her now-grown children and where she hoped to retire one day.

When war broke out in Kosovo, refugees poured into neighboring Albania, and because there was great need, that is where Yvette migrated. In Albania, she stayed with a local family. Her first night there was punctuated with the sound of gunshots, a sound with which Yvette was all too familiar. However, this time, the shots were followed by the sound of the front door being forced open and then by screams from her hosts. Moments later, Yvette's own bedroom door was kicked open, and a man fired two shots into the ceiling. Yvette remembered thinking, at this point, "This is it." However, the man then merely yelled, "Albania 2, Yugoslavia 1!" and departed as suddenly as he had come. He was merely celebrating his country's victory in a soccer match.

Six months later, in 1999, two days after David Cornwell had arrived in Kenya in order to work on *The Constant Gardener*, he received a phone call telling him that his friend Yvette Pierpaoli had been killed in an accident. The car in which she was riding, due to rain and hazardous road conditions, had plunged hundreds of feet down a cliff. The Albanian driver, two Americans, and Yvette had all been on their way to secure radio satellite receivers for the Kosovo refugees, so that they could receive news and music and communicate with their relatives back home.

Yvette's children, as well as friends from Cambodia, the United States, and Thailand, convened in her home in Avignon to pay their final respects. In her garden her ashes were laid to rest with both Christian and Buddhist rites. David and his wife stated that it was the most moving funeral they had ever attended.

The Constant Gardener was given that title because gardening was the chief passion of the protagonist Justin Quayle; his hobby was to rid his garden of weeds in order to make it a more beautiful place. This is an apt metaphor for the character's wife, Tessa, and her real-life counterpart, Yvette Pierpaoli, whose mission was to leave humanity better than when she first found it. It is because of this that David Cornwell dedicated *The Constant Gardener* to his old friend, who "lived and died giving a damn."

44

Seabiscuit: An American Legend

LAURA HILLENBRAND

2001

For Borden

Laura Hillenbrand's dedication in *Seabiscuit* is to the man who has steadfastly proven to be her trusted companion for twenty years that have shown them more than their fair share of heartache. The only thing that has helped them weather their storm is their steadfast love for one another.

Laura, who was an English/history major, first met Brandon ("Borden") Flanagan at a deli in Kenyon College in Ohio on September 6, 1986. It was an afternoon dominated by the color yellow. The sun was shining; Craig, who ran the restaurant, was wearing his trademark fluorescent yellow sunglasses; and Laura was wearing a yellow dress (which she sentimentally has kept). She was drinking coffee, her face buried in a book, when all of a sudden she had an overpowering urge to look up. When she did so, she saw Borden, who was a twenty-year-old senior from Seattle.

Laura used his T-shirt, which read "The Smiths," as an excuse to start up a conversation. She did so by saying that she was also a fan of the 1980s British rock band, words spoken in honesty.

However, as she admits, even if he had been wearing a Monkees shirt, she would still have thought of a way of meeting the handsome student with the dark, wavy hair. She recalls of their initial conversation that he was both charming and articulate. His perspective of their first meeting was that he must have come off as a bore. In his nervousness at being approached by the beautiful girl with the great tan and athlete's body, he went on and on about what he was currently studying: Karl Marx. Afterward, Laura invited him to a party the next weekend. From that moment to this, as much as circumstances have allowed, Laura and Borden have remained inseparable.

Their waking nightmare began in March 1987, when Borden, Laura, and their friend Linc (Lincoln) were on their way back to Kenyon College after spring break. Laura was in the front seat, a rose from Borden on her lap, a 1940s taffeta gown slung over her arm, a twenty-dollar purchase from a thrift store. The conversation had drifted off, and Laura was happily daydreaming of her forthcoming year at the University of Edinburgh. Suddenly, Laura gripped her stomach, trying to stop the spasms of pain and nausea that were rushing over her in uncontrollable waves. Immediately upon returning to the campus, Borden contacted paramedics. They declared that it was food poisoning, and, indeed, the initial culprit was some tainted chicken that she had eaten on her road trip. That night, leaning against Borden's arms, she fell asleep sitting up.

However, her condition continued to deteriorate to such an extent that three weeks later she had to drop out of college and return to her family home in Maryland. Borden and Linc were the only two people, outside her family, who stayed in touch.

Borden and Laura found the separation excruciating. To help

lessen the pain of loneliness, Borden sent Laura offbeat postcards; she in turn sent him dirty limericks. When school let out in June, Borden came to stay with Laura and her mother. They made plans for the future, when Laura would be cured. However, as the months dragged on and so did her symptoms, Borden's friends began to tell him that he should not stay with someone who was a bedridden invalid. He didn't leave. He explained his reasons by saying that a number of things kept him from leaving, "the first being love. And I didn't want to leave her alone."

After a few months, Laura understandably fell into a deep depression. She had gone from an athletic, straight-A student, about to embark on a dream year abroad, to someone whose world was encompassed by the walls of her bedroom for months on end. She could no longer sleep on her side because she had lost so much weight that her bones dug into her; her hair fell out in clumps; her skin peeled off in layers. It was at this juncture that she considered suicide the only escape from her chronic agony. Digging through her mother's drawers, she pulled out a bottle of Valium that had been prescribed for back spasms. She emptied them on her quilt and played with them for approximately one hour. However, what prevented her from swallowing them was Borden. As long as he was part of her world, a shred of hope remained. As Laura was to repeat numerous times throughout the years, "Without Borden, I'd be dead."

In 1988, feeling somewhat stronger, Laura accompanied Borden to the University of Chicago, where he was studying political philosophy as a graduate student. They rented a room that could have been dubbed the Roach Motel. The former tenants had left the bathtub filled with kitty litter. Because the one-room apartment was on the fourth floor and there was no elevator, the house-ridden Laura spent her days reading and listening to a neighbor throw various objects at her husband.

As a break from their living environment and desperately needing some fun, Laura and Borden risked a ten-hour drive to see the Saratoga racetrack. This was something that Laura really wanted to do, as she had been fascinated from childhood with horses, even going so far as to have worn riding boots to her elementary school. However, the trip had been predicated more on wishful thinking than medical soundness. By the time they had reached the New Jersey farmhouse of their friends Bill and Sarah, Laura became more ill than ever. When she slid into a delirious state, Borden lay beside her and held her, as if both their lives depended on it. With her still-rational mind, she repeated her endless litany to Borden, "I love you. I love you. I love you."

When they returned to her mother's home, Borden, to help keep Laura's mind focused, would compose various lists with her: candy bars, Kentucky Derby winners, and so forth. To her endless questions of whether she would survive, he always answered in the affirmative, thereby assuring both her and himself. Borden never complained of his role as a caregiver. The only indication of the toll it was taking on him was when Laura overheard him sobbing one night, when he thought that she was asleep.

In September, Borden had to return to graduate school. Before he left, he gave her a silver ring with the French inscription, "*Vous et nul autre*," which translates to "You and no other."

Laura finally got a correct diagnosis of her illness, so that it could be properly treated. Her affliction was chronic fatigue syndrome, which had been triggered by food poisoning. She also heard about the story of the Depression-era horse Seabiscuit, a discovery that would change her life. Her passion to write a book about him gave her a new lease on life. Just as the racehorse had given hope to a country mired in the Great Depression, he did the same for Laura. In 2001, Random House made her dream a reality when they published the story of the horse that had given inspiration to a nation in the tragic decade of the 1930s. When her publisher and agent phoned her and yelled simultaneously that her book had topped the bestseller list, Borden opened a window and screamed the same amazing words to the neighborhood.

In June 2004, when there was an oasis in the desert of her disease, Borden rented a hotel room. They had a romantic dinner, which Laura was well enough to enjoy. When they returned to their room, Borden had arranged for it to be strewn with rose petals, and there were candles and champagne. When he went down on one knee, they both began to cry when she accepted the proposal from her lover and steadfast best friend. His love and loyalty had saved her; it had also been the source of her strength, which, in turn, had allowed Seabiscuit to gallop once more.

45

The Da Vinci Code

DAN BROWN

2003

FOR BLYTHE…AGAIN,

MORE THAN EVER.

VERY little is known about the reclusive wife of Dan Brown, Blythe, except that just as Brown extols the sacred feminine in *The Da Vinci Code*, his wife symbolizes the sacred female in his life. Lisa del Giocondo inspired Da Vinci to paint the *Mona Lisa*; Blythe inspired Dan to write *The Da Vinci Code*.

In the early 1990s, Dan Brown left his native New Hampshire for Los Angeles, seeking to make a name for himself as a song-writer. To help pursue his musical aspirations, Dan joined the National Academy of Songwriters. There the former choir boy met Blythe Newlon, a woman from Palmdale, California, twelve years his senior, who was employed as the academy's director. She soon became involved, on more than a mere professional level, in promoting Dan's work. She began writing press releases on his behalf and set up meetings with people in the industry who could advance Brown's career. After the release of his debut CD, Blythe publicly stated, "We fully expect Dan Brown will someday be included in the ranks of our [the Academy's] most successful members, talents like Billy Joel, Paul Simon and Prince."

After the CD's release, Blythe became his official manager and secret lover. On the release of his next recording, Dan thanked Blythe for "being my tireless co-writer, co-producer, second engineer, significant other and therapist." However, not finding the success that had lured him to California, in 1993 he returned to New Hampshire, accompanied by Blythe. Four years later they were married at Pea Porridge Pond, a remote area of New Hampshire, not far from his parent's home.

After their marriage the Browns turned from Dan's musical career to a literary one. In 1994, they took a vacation to Tahiti, where Dan read Sidney Sheldon's novel *The Doomsday Conspiracy*. Brown felt that he could write an even better book. Acting on this belief, he wrote *Deception Point*. When it was completed, Blythe, as she had done years earlier with his music, set out promoting her husband's novel. She wrote its press releases, booked Dan on talk shows, and set up interviews with the press. In the novel's acknowledgments he thanked "Blythe Brown for her tireless research and creative input." Although the book was only moderately successful, the Browns were not disheartened.

Dan Brown said that the inspiration for his *Da Vinci Code* was Blythe. He explained that she imparted to him her passion for art history, especially for the work of da Vinci, whetted even further when they went to Europe on a tour of the major galleries. Brown wrote about his wife's influence: "She became passionate about the history of the church's suppression of women and she lobbied hard to make it a primary theme of the novel." It was Blythe who introduced Dan to the theory that Jesus's bloodline survived his crucifixion. They both became fired with enthusiasm for their new project. Dan woke up at 4:00 a.m. seven days a week to work on it. At the same time, Blythe voraciously read articles, searching for information that Jesus was in actuality married to Mary Magdalene, who was pregnant with their child at the time of his crucifixion. She emailed her husband whenever she had finished her research (email, even when they are in the same place, is an important part of their communication).

The finished novel became one of the bestselling books of all time, spawned scores of other works and merchandising, made the couple multimillionaires, and placed the Roman Catholic Church on public trial.

Another offshoot of the book was a plagiarism trial in England. Brown was accused of copying portions of *Holy Blood, Holy Grail* into his novel. The trial and ensuing publicity were hell for the reclusive writer. And, although Blythe's name came up dozens of times because of her role as researcher, she herself was not present. Brown explained her absence by stating, "My wife and I are very close. I firmly believe that I can answer any questions regarding her assistance to me in the research of my book." He then elaborated by claiming that his wife greatly disliked public attention and that he did not want her troubled by it. What became clear during the proceedings was that Blythe was as essential to Dan's work as the Mona Lisa was to *The Da Vinci Code*. Moreover, by her very absence, she became as mysterious as La Gioconda herself.

During the trial, the curtain on the Browns' reclusive lives was partially raised. Those in the courtroom learned that Blythe encourages Dan to rise at 4:00 a.m., seven days a week, to write, and that as an antidote to the dreaded writer's block, he hangs upside down like a bat until the creative juices commence flowing. The trial concluded with Dan being acquitted of publishing's scarlet letter: *P*.

The Browns lived in an old converted mill in New Hampshire for ten years, until the low-key multimillionaires moved to a modest house. They are planning to relocate to a large home on a secluded plot of land, in the middle of a private wooded area. Their new home is going to be equipped with cutting-edge security devices. The latter is to protect both their privacy and their safety.

It is in their majestic retreat that Dan will continue work on his next novel, *The Solomon Key*, with a plot that will revolve around the Masons. We do not yet know the story behind the key, but what we do know is that it will be faithfully researched by his wife. It will come as no surprise if the future dedication is, once more, a tribute to his sacred female, Blythe Brown.

46

Suite Française

IRÈNE NÉMIROVSKY

2004

I dedicate this novel to the memory of my mother and father, to my sister, Elisabeth Gille, to my children and grand-children, and to everyone who has felt and continues to feel the tragedy of intolerance.

—DENISE EPSTEIN

THE history behind the dedication to *Suite Française* is so intriguing that it rivals the plot of the most unbelievable of novels. The story, as a variation on the theme of a message in a bottle, came about because of a journal in a suitcase, its secrets lying silenced for half a century.

The author of *Suite Française*, Irène Némirovsky, was born in Kiev, in a section of the city known as Yiddishland, where Russia's Jews were forced to congregate. Her father, Leon, was one of the country's wealthiest bankers, and his only child and wife led a life of extreme luxury, which included vacations on the French Riviera and Biarritz. However, the family was not a happy one. Leon was often away on business, and his wife Faiga (Fanny, as she called herself) was a vain, self-centered socialite who virtually ignored her daughter. To remedy the lack of maternal care, a French governess was hired. The result was that Irene could converse and write fluently in both Russian and French.

When the Bolsheviks executed the czar, as members of the upper class and as Jews, the family was forced to abandon their palatial home. In order to elude capture by the Red Army, they disguised themselves as peasants, and ultimately settled in France. There, Irène attended the Sorbonne, and Leon, again a prominent banker, once more was able to provide his family with a lavish lifestyle. At age eighteen, at a Parisian ball, Irène met and fell in love with Michel (Mikhail) Epstein, a fellow Russian Jewish émigré, who worked in a bank.

During the early years of their marriage, Irène wrote her first novel, *David Golder*, and became the golden child of literary society, especially when the book was adapted into a film. The Epsteins' apartment on the Left Bank was filled with writers, who discussed their novels till all hours of the night. Although Irène was thrilled with her career and the love of her husband, she was even more ecstatic at the birth of her daughters, Denise and Elisabeth, the latter nicknamed Babet. Unlike her own mother, the most important people in her life were her children.

Irène and Michel Epstein were content with their marriage, their daughters, and their careers. Then the Nazis marched into Paris. Having lost her home in Russia to the Bolsheviks, Irène dreaded losing her present one to the Germans. Therefore, rather than flee once more, she devised a plan to escape the net that was falling on Europe's Jews. Henri IV had converted to Catholicism to inherit the throne of France. He explained his actions by stating, "Paris is worth a Mass." Similarly, Irène, to evade persecution, along with Denise and Elisabeth, converted to Catholicism.

The baptism was performed in February 1939, by a Romanian bishop who was a friend of the family. Denise, who was thirteen at the time, was given her first communion instead of a bat mitzvah. Bizarrely, she attended the ceremony wearing the yellow Star of David that the Nazis decreed those of Jewish ancestry had to wear.

Despite the conversion, the Third Reich still considered them Jewish. Hoping to spare Denise and Elisabeth the horror of the Occupation, the children were sent to live with their nanny's family in the Burgundy countryside. A year later, because they were Jewish, Michel was dismissed from his position in the bank and Irène could no longer publish books. Their Left Bank apartment was deserted by their former friends. It was then that they rejoined their children.

The family was thrilled to be reunited, and Denise remembers her mother would go for long walks in the woods, where she would feverishly write in her notebook. She would take breaks to read from *Anna Karenina* and the works of Katherine Mansfield. On July 13, 1942, there was a knock at the door of the family home. The inevitable had come to call. The Germans had a list of names of those who had to leave immediately for "resettlement" in the east. Irène Némirovsky was chosen to be on the first transport. To the Nazis she was a Russian, a Jew, and an intellectual, all of which they both despised and feared. At age thirty-nine, she was arrested as a "stateless person [she had never been granted French citizenship] of Jewish descent" by French policemen under a German edict. As she was being led away, she told her daughters, "I am going on a journey now." Her last act was to leave a locked suitcase with her elder daughter.

She was first deported to a camp at Pithiviers and then, on

July 17, along with 928 other Jews, to Auschwitz. Irène was a loving wife, devoted mother, and talented author, but to the Nazis she was no more than the number they tattooed on her arm. Denise remembers that her father was so distraught that he set a place at the table every meal for his wife. Michel did everything in his power to bring his wife home. He wrote letters to the German ambassador in Paris and Marshal Pétain, the leader of Vichy France, Hitler's puppet government. He explained that Irène was a fierce anticommunist and a Catholic, but his efforts were futile. Indeed, his intervention may only have hastened his own deportation, for a month later he, too, was sent to Auschwitz. The Epstein children would have also been on their way to the concentration camp, but their nanny delivered them to a convent. For the rest of the war, they were shuffled from one hiding place to another. During each move, Denise carried with her the locked suitcase her mother had entrusted to her care.

When the war ended, every day the two sisters would go to the train station with signs around their necks, awaiting the return of their mother and father. Finally, they were informed that Irène died of typhus in the Auschwitz hospital and their father had gone to the gas chamber upon arrival at the concentration camp. Devastated, they made their way to the south of France, where their grandmother had lived out the war in safety. She would not answer the door, and when the two girls called to her through the mail slot that they were orphans, she just yelled back that if that were the case then they should go to an orphanage.

Denise stayed close to her sister until Elisabeth passed away in 1996. Elisabeth had worked as a publisher and written a book titled *The Watchtower*, which was an imaginary biography of the mother she had been too young to know. Both of them, unlike their own grandmother, had children and grandchildren they loved as dearly as Irène had loved her daughters.

In the 1970s Denise's home flooded, and she placed the suitcase on a shelf to protect it. Then she at last unlocked the suitcase. She had not done so before because by opening it she felt that she would be overwhelmed by painful memories of the past. Her childhood had been filled with the confusion of converting from Judaism to Catholicism, having both her parents murdered, and having to spend years in hiding, in fear. In the suitcase she saw family photographs and a notebook. The pages were onionskin thin, and the words, written in a blue ink, were so small it was almost impossible to decipher. Seeing the pages filled with her mother's writing, she remembered her sitting in the woods. She had always believed what her mother was writing was her diary, and that the reason that she had written so feverishly was that she was putting down the emotions of a woman who was not just writing about her life, but preparing to say good-bye to it. Once more, for emotional survival, Denise put the manuscript back into the suitcase, where it remained unopened for another twenty years.

In the late 1990s, over fifty years since her mother had handed it to her on the day of her arrest, Denise decided to donate her mother's papers to a French archive that was compiling artifacts from the Holocaust. Before she parted with them, she decided at long last to read her mother's last words. When she started to do so, the truth about the manuscript finally came to light. It was not a diary after all, but rather a novel about the German occupation of Paris. The first part, *Storm in June*, dealt with the exodus of the French in the face of the advancing German army. The second part, *Dolce*, dealt with daily life under the Occupation. The notes in the margins included her plan for future novellas, ones that would deal with later events of the war as well as its aftermath. Denise Epstein said, "I never opened it until 1995. It made me angry to read it. Seeing my mother's wonderful lucidity just gave me a tremendous sensation of abandonment."

Over the course of the next decade, with the aid of a magnifying glass, Denise read and typed out her mother's final novel, which Irène had named *The Suite Française*. She wrote, "She could look inside the human soul and make music with her words. But it is only now that I can look at it as a reader rather than as my mother's daughter." When she was finished, she sent it to a publishing house, and it became a bestseller in 2004. Denise told an interviewer, "For me, the greatest joy is knowing that the book is being read. It is an extraordinary feeling to have brought my mother back to life. It shows that the Nazis did not truly succeed in killing her. It is not vengeance, but it is a victory." Paradoxically, she had given birth to her mother; because of her daughter, Irène Némirovsky's voice, although smothered for sixty years, was not silenced forever.

Denise Epstein, who, given the circumstances of her life, could understandably have condemned in her dedication, instead used it as a tribute to her mother and father, as well as "to everyone who has ever felt and continues to feel the tragedy of intolerance."

47

The Year of Magical Thinking

JOAN DIDION

2005

This book is for John and Quintana

JOAN Didion discovered firsthand the veracity of the statement "God never sends us more than we can endure" during her year as Job's female counterpart, when she experienced two devastating blows, recounted in her memoir, *The Year of Magical Thinking*. It has become a guide for the bereaved needing a companion in dealing with death, and life.

Joan Didion met her soul mate when they were both staff writers in New York City; John Dunne worked for *Time*, Joan for *Vogue*. They lived together for a year before they decided to make it legal, perhaps because of John's Catholicism, with which he had a lifelong attraction–repulsion relationship. Joan bought a short white silk wedding dress in San Francisco, which she associates with John F. Kennedy, as he was assassinated on the day she purchased it. The afternoon ceremony, which included forty guests, was held at the Catholic Mission of San Juan Bautista. Joan decided not to have a bridal entrance or a procession, and during it she wore her trademark oversize dark sunglasses. The reception was held in the Pebble Beach Lodge with its sweeping view of the Pacific, and the couple spent their honeymoon in the Beverly Hills Hotel. They decided to make California their permanent home, where they hoped to become screenwriters. Although they had no experience in this field, they felt that their lifelong addictions to movies gave them ample qualifications. Moreover, they hoped that John's older brother, Dominick Dunne, who was a Hollywood producer, would help open studio doors.

Joan was deeply in love and what completed their circle of love was the adoption of their baby daughter, Quintana Roo. The first time Joan saw Quintana was in the nursery of St. John's Hospital in Santa Monica, on the day she was born. Seeing the newborn infant, she told her, "You're safe, I'm here." John's first words to his daughter were "I love you more than even one more day." When they took her home they placed her in a bassinet overlooking the Pacific, so that her first impressions would be of the majesty of the ocean. Joan wrote of those early years, "In fact I had no idea how to be a wife. In those first years I would pin daisies in my hair, trying for a 'bride' effect. Later I had matching gingham skirts made for me and Quintana, trying for young mother... both John and I were improvising, flying blind."

Hollywood status came with their screen adaptation of *A Star Is Born*, which cost six million to produce and grossed seventy million. However, art did not imitate life. In their screenplay, Esther Hoffman's—Barbra Streisand's character's—singing success so overshadows her husband's that he becomes known as Mr. Hoffman. However, in reality, although Didion's career eclipsed John's, he was proud of, rather than threatened by, her success. A friend of the couple, David Halberstam, said, "John was so proud of her. He had this joke he used to tell. He comes back from walking the beach at Malibu. 'You'll never guess who I ran into— Jesus Christ! Guess what He told me? He loves Joan's books.'" On one occasion the couple had lit a fire, something that Joan always found comforting. She wrote, "Fires said we were home, we had drawn the circle, we were safe through the night." Sitting by it, John read aloud from her recent work, *A Book of Common Prayer*. When he finished he told her, "Goddamn. Don't ever tell me again you can't write. That's my birthday present to you." A comment worth more than a world of karats.

Joan and John were the literary toast of both the East and West Coasts, and their professional lives were complemented by their private ones. They adored each other and Quintana, whom they nicknamed Q Roo. A photograph taken in Malibu on the deck of their home overlooking the ocean in 1976 encapsulates this golden time. Joan is standing behind them, leaning on the rail, while father and daughter are staring into the camera. Quintana's long hair is white gold, tinged with green from chlorine because of days spent swimming. Standing above the sea, a tight family unit, a moment of magical reality.

Quintana got married in the Church of St. John the Divine. Although she was dressed traditionally in a long dress and a veil, her hair was worn in a long braid down her back, just as she used to wear it when she was a child in Malibu. The reception included peacocks on the lawn and young barefoot girls with leis. Proving to be her mother's daughter, she removed her veil and kicked off her expensive shoes. When she called her parents that evening she said, "Wasn't that just about perfect?"

In *The Year of Magical Thinking* Didion writes, "Everything changes in an instant." Five months after her wedding, Quintana fell into septic shock on Christmas night as a result of a pneumonia infection and was in New York's Beth Israel North in a coma. On each of their five consecutive visits, John repeated as an invocation, as a prayer, "I love you more than even one more day." He hoped that on some level his daughter could hear his words. Returning home, John was drinking Scotch by the fire, while Joan was at the dinner table, making a salad. John was talking to her, and then, all of a sudden, he wasn't. He had slumped to the floor; they were rushed by ambulance to the hospital. When she was told that she had been assigned a social worker, Joan knew. It was her time to face the dreaded part of her wedding vows, "Till death do you part." In the blur that was the weeks following John's death, Joan kept recalling a poem that she had studied at Berkeley, one by Walter Savage Landor, "Rose Aylmer, whom these wakeful eyes / May weep, but never see / A night of memories and sighs / I consecrate to thee."

This was the beginning of Joan Didion's "year of magical thinking." She initially encountered this term when she was reading about anthropology. Primitive cultures used to operate on magical thinking, *if* thinking; for example, if one sacrifices the virgin, the rains will come. Similarly, Joan started thinking her own *ifs*, trying to fend off emotional pain by doing what early people did, resorting to superstition and a belief in magic. *The Year of Magical Thinking* is an exploration of the grieving process.

When Quintana was out of the hospital, Joan arranged John's memorial service, which was held at St. John the Divine, where her daughter had been married eight months earlier. According to John's wishes, his ashes were interred with those of his mother-in-law. Throughout the memorial ceremony, just as with her wedding ceremony, Joan's eyes were hidden behind her large sunglasses. Quintana read a poem for her father, "I love you more than even one more day." After she had finished she added, "As you used to say to me."

As a cruel postscript to Joan's memoir, after it was published, Quintana was readmitted to a hospital after she had gone to California with her husband. Quintana passed away despite Joan's endless incantations of "I'm here, you're safe" as she stroked the few tufts that were left of her daughter's hair after the surgeries. Her ashes were interred with those of her beloved father. Joan recalled that there was a tradition in Honolulu that when someone was departing the island, residents would throw leis on the water, which was to ensure that the person would return. Joan wanted to take Quintana home, and place her once more in the window overlooking the sea.

In 1968, Joan Didion wrote *Slouching towards Bethlehem*. Its title is an allusion to Yeats's poem "The Second Coming." The poet wrote, "Things fall apart; the center cannot hold; / Mere anarchy is loosed upon the world." With the passing of her beloved husband and child, things fell apart for Joan. However, with her magical thinking, she is endeavoring not to slouch, but to stride. After all, it was what John and Quintana would have wanted, and expected, of their beloved wife and mother, Joan Didion.

48

The History of Love

NICOLE KRAUSS

2005

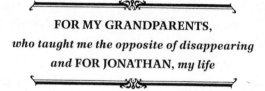

FOR MY GRANDPARENTS,
who taught me the opposite of disappearing
and **FOR JONATHAN,** *my life*

NICOLE'S "history of love" began with her European grandparents, whose four passport photos are included on the dedication page of her novel. All Nicole's Jewish grandparents were able to flee Europe before Hitler's deadly net caught and annihilated them. However, the same good fortune did not hold true for their families, who perished in the Holocaust.

Growing up in affluence on Long Island, New York, in the 1970s, Nicole was regaled by her grandparents with stories of their lost world: the world of their *shetls*, their families, their youth. Nicole's great-grandparents perished in concentration camps, and her great aunt (Nicole's Hebrew name is the same as hers) died in the Warsaw Ghetto. One story that made a deep impression upon Nicole was her grandmother's recollections of how her own father had been rounded up with other Jews and taken to a field outside of Nuremberg. There he was forced to kneel down and mow the lawn with his teeth. Her grandmother also recalled the concentration camp, located on the border of Germany and Poland, where she caught the last glimpse of her parents.

Nicole's grandmother ended up in a transit camp in Poland. While there, she met a doctor who was to become instrumental to her survival. He arranged for her to obtain papers that allowed her to sail to London, in the capacity as a chaperone, on the last Kindertransport (a boat that ferried Jewish children out of Nazi-occupied Europe and sent them to live with foster families). Her grandmother stayed in England, eventually immigrating to the United States. Years later, her grandmother, who had assumed the doctor had not survived the Holocaust, received a letter from his home in South America. Her grandmother never responded to those letters. Even though this may seem the epitome of ingratitude, those who were not victims of the Holocaust should never presume to judge those who were. The reason she gave for not responding was that she did not want to complicate her devotion to her new family with old allegiances to her past, one fraught with horror.

Although all four grandparents came from different countries, Hungary, Poland, Germany, and White Russia, their harrowing tales had the common threads of love and loss, the two forming the backbone of *The History of Love*. Indeed, the novel could just as aptly have been titled *The History of Loss*.

Love and loss come together in the novel's protagonist, eighty-year-old Holocaust survivor Leo Gursky. In Poland, as a boy, he had fallen in love with Alma Mereminski, and he had vowed to love her and no other all the days of his life. He told the teenaged Alma this, and she asked him what he would do if she died; his response was "even then." At age sixteen, he bought an English dictionary and tried to learn the new language by discovering the names of body parts. He would kiss Alma and then, for example, repeat its English word: *elbow*. When she escapes to America before the war, he is determined to survive, with the sole purpose of reuniting with her. He does this by disappearing into the woods of Poland for three years, thereby eluding the Nazis. When he comes to America, he discovers that Alma calls another man her husband, and his baby (she had been pregnant with Leo's son) calls another man his father. Leo has lost his soul, and becomes invisible once more. Krauss writes, "I put in the photographs and the dedication line because of the scene in the book where Leo . . . realizes that he has lost the ability to be seen by other people. He is a person who thinks a lot about his invisibility. And for that reason I wanted to use passport photographs of my grandparents." Similarly, Leo's last wish as an old man is "All I want is not to die on a day when I went unseen." The opposite of disappearing is survival; it is the theme of her grandparents' lives and of *The History of Love*.

The event that started Nicole on her own odyssey in the history of love was meeting author Jonathan Safran Foer. The two were introduced in 2001 when their Dutch publisher fixed them up on a blind date. He played matchmaker because his two clients shared a number of commonalities: age, religion, nationality, Ivy League educations, interest in Joseph Cornell, and occupation. The literary couple was wed in June 2004.

Jonathan grew up in Washington, DC, and had a number of jobs before his breakthrough debut novel, *Everything Is Illuminated*, was published. Some of his positions were: morgue assistant, math tutor, receptionist, ghostwriter, jewelry salesman, and archivist. Ironically, he was turned down, every summer, when he applied for a job in his local bookstore.

Hamlet said, "When sorrows come / They come not in single spies / But in battalions." However, the same is true of joy. Nicole and Jonathan are New York's crown jewel of literary couples. With the monies earned for their successful books, the couple purchased a multimillion-dollar brownstone on three lots near Prospect Park in Brooklyn, New York, which they share with their enormous female dog, George, a Great Dane mix. Their mansion was turned into a home with the arrival of their son, Sasha. Their baby was named (as was Leo's lost love) after Nicole's grandmother, Sasha Mereminski.

In *The History of Love*, one of the characters says, "We met each other when we were young, before we knew enough about disappointment, and once we did we found we reminded each other of it." However, what keeps "everything illuminated" for Nicole and Jonathan is that rather than disappoint, they nourish each other. Their second novels' respective dedications are testament to this: *For Nicole, my idea of beautiful* and *For Jonathan, my life.*

49

World Without End

KEN FOLLETT
(KENNETH MARTIN FOLLETT)
2007

For Barbara

THERE is an ancient Chinese proverb that states "May you live in interesting times." Whether or not the saying is a curse or a blessing is a matter of opinion. Ken Follett's wife, Barbara, has had an interesting life whose events rival those of Ken's novels. Her biography is replete with exotic locales, a tyrannical regime, historic figures, racism, murder, and multiple marriages. Obviously ennui was never one of her demons.

The adventure began for Daphne Barbara Hubbard on Christmas Day 1942, in Kingston, Jamaica. Her parents were British but had immigrated to the West Indies, where her father sold insurance policies. When Barbara was three, the family returned to Essex via a banana boat, as post–World War II modes of transportation were scarce. Six years later, when Barbara came home from school, her mother handed her a choc ice and said, "Oh, we're going to Ethiopia."

As most nine-year-olds are traumatized by moving to a new neighborhood and having to attend a different school, one can only imagine her childhood trauma of relocating to a new continent. Barbara's father, Vernon, had been asked to set up Ethiopia's first insurance company, in partnership with Emperor Haile Selassie. He took the three-week trip first, and his wife followed, carting along their three children and twenty-two pieces of luggage. Barbara recalls that they traveled in a very old steamship whose other passengers consisted mainly of missionaries bound for the Far East, who spent their time in constant prayer.

Despite Barbara's fears of leaving England, her expatriate life was a happy one, at least at first. She experienced the novelty of riding horses to school, and recalls once sitting on Emperor Selassie's knee to get a better view of a visiting magician. She recalls that behind the ruler were security guards, complete with disemboweling knives.

Barbara's problems started when her father became overly dependent on alcohol. Because of this, the money started to dry up and his wife, Charlotte, had to get a job working at a hospital in Addis Ababa.

When Barbara was fifteen, her father's alcoholism spiraled out of control. At a banquet given by the emperor to entertain Yugoslavia's president Tito, Mr. Hubbard became so intoxicated that he fell into the drink trolley while Selassie was making his royal toast. The emperor was extremely insulted and told the offending party to leave his country. That is how the family, in 1957, found themselves in Cape Town. Barbara recalls of their new city, "I moved from a land where blacks ruled to one where a minority of whites were ruling, and I suddenly realized what racism was." In her new school she was introduced to "an ethnic pecking order" and was made uncomfortably aware of the fact that she was Jewish. However, always a tomboy and always self-confident, she was able to hold her own.

The rampant racism of South Africa under Apartheid galvanized fourteen-year-old Barbara, and she began volunteering in the black townships. Two years later, she met a seventeen-year-old like-minded activist, Rick Turner, when her sister took her along to a wedding anniversary party. Rick and Barbara were married two days after her twenty-first birthday. Jane, her new mother-in-law, showed her disapproval of her son's choice by boycotting their wedding. That day the newlyweds sailed for Paris, where they lived for three years while Rick worked on his doctorate on Sartre at the Sorbonne and Barbara worked at the Berlitz School of Languages to support them and their new baby, Jann.

They returned to Cape Town in 1966 and took over Rick's mother's Stellenbosch fruit farm, and there Barbara had an experience that altered the course of her life. A worker's wife came to their door, holding her child. Barbara took the baby, who died in her arms. The doctor who examined the baby wrote *bronchial pneumonia* on the death certificate. However, that was merely a euphemism for malnutrition. Barbara then came to the realization that South Africa was bereft of a heart with regard to its black population. In response, Barbara went to work for Kupugani (Zulu for "uplift yourself"). This fired Barbara's zeal to embark on lifelong political activism. At the same time, Rick turned heavily to communism. He started raising wages on his farm and set up literacy classes and a first aid clinic. Despite the birth of their second daughter, Kim, their marriage began to unravel. Barbara explains, "I think we were just in different places. I was into children and making sure the farm ran properly and he was feeling encumbered by domesticity." She adds, "He had a couple of affairs—it was the 1960s, remember. He was talking about free love and I said, 'No, that's not for me,' but we never really fell out." They divorced in 1971 but the commonalities of their children and social activism and mutual affection left them on good terms. Turner became even more involved in radical causes, such as setting up trade unions and active campaigning to give blacks the right to vote. For these activities he was eventually placed under a five-year house arrest. Politically, Barbara fought against social injustice by joining the Domestic Worker's Union and Women for Peace. Feeling lonely, Barbara joined the Leaderless Couples Commune, where she met her next two husbands: Gerald Stonestreet, a psychologist she married in 1971, and Les Broer, an architect she married in 1974. With the latter she had a son, Adam.

The most traumatic night of her life occurred at midnight, sometime in 1978. Barbara received a phone call that something was going on at her ex-husband's home, where her two daughters, aged eight and thirteen, were visiting. Barbara right away went into a state of high anxiety. She knew that Richard's five-year house arrest was almost up, and that he had continued to be politically active all the same. After the phone call, she became apprehensive that the authorities were not pleased that Turner would soon be freed. Barbara began to feverishly pack. At 3:00 a.m. she received another call, this time from Jann. Her child said, "Daddy's dead," followed by, "I'm standing next to his body." Barbara recalls that she must have screamed upon hearing her daughter's message because then Jann continued, "Don't lose your head, otherwise I'll lose mine."

Rick had been in his daughters' bedroom when he had gone

to the window to investigate a noise. He was shot through the chest by an Apartheid agent. The bullet had traveled through him and exited just above Kim's head. He had then stumbled to the living room, where Jann, kneeling in a pool of blood, attempted to revive her dying father with mouth-to-mouth resuscitation. When Barbara burst on the scene, both of her daughters' hair was caked with their dead father's blood. Recalling this time, Barbara stated that she forever associates South Africa with the smell of drying blood.

Barbara was able to ascertain that Rick's death was a state-sponsored one, and that she, along with several other white activists, had been targeted for death. Phone calls threatening both her and her children followed. Understandably, Barbara was desperate to flee South Africa. Remembering her own childhood trauma of leaving her country of birth, she told her children that they "were going to Britain where people were not detained without trial or put under house arrest." Four months later she attempted to do so, but was detained at the airport. Finally a security officer threw her passport at her and shouted "Go!" Barbara (with three-year-old Adam), Kim, Jann, and her husband did not need further encouragement. As her England-bound plane flew over Zimbabwe's airspace, Barbara downed two gin and tonics and vowed, "I'm not going back there again. I am not going back." Arriving in England, Barbara was to encounter the person who was to become "the pillar of her earth."

Because of her experiences, Barbara was committed to political activism and became heavily involved in the local branch of the Labour Party. Three years later, in her capacity as its secretary, she met author Ken Follett at a political meeting. He had secured his reputation with his bestselling novel *The Eye of the Needle*, which was being made into a film starring Donald Sutherland. Barbara Broer and Ken did not immediately hit it off. Ken thought of her as "bossy boots," and Barbara thought "he was very arrogant and very irritating." Moreover, she felt that he resembled a weasel. Of their first encounters, Barbara said, "It was dislike at first sight." However, curiosity about his novel got the best of her, and she bought *The Eye of the Needle*. She recalls that she sat up all night reading it and subsequently phoned its author and said, "You know, you can write." That comment must have opened the door to a mutual respect, as Barbara appointed Ken the Labour Party press officer. Soon after, they fell in love.

The attraction posed something of a problem, because both of them were married: Barbara, to her third husband, Les Broer, and Ken, to Mary, whom he had married when they were both eighteen and who was the mother of his two children. Of their affair, Barbara says, "It's not something that I'm proud of, but that's what happened." They both left their respective spouses. Barbara continued to rise in the Labour Party, and she is currently its MP for Stevenage in Herefordshire. One of her many platforms as a politician is increasing the number of women in the Parliamentary Labour Party. Despite political opposition, Barbara, with her childhood self-confidence still intact, is still able to hold her own.

Ken's latest novel is *World Without End*, and if one were to substitute the word *world* for *happiness*, it would paint a portrait of the current lives of Ken and Barbara Follett. They spend their time among their homes in London, New York, and Antigua, their chief residence being a two-hundred-year-old riverside mansion in Chelsea that overlooks the Thames. They live with their two Labrador retrievers, Custard and Bess, and receive visits from their five children and two grandchildren, as well as host some of the most glittering soirees of the year. All of which is rather a far cry from being on an Apartheid assassination list. In fact, the horrors of the first act of Barbara's life served as a prologue to help her fully appreciate its epilogue, "a world without end" of contentment.

50

The Yiddish Policemen's Union

MICHAEL CHABON

2007

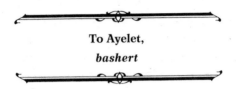

To Ayelet,

bashert

BASHERT is a Yiddish term that means finding one's preordained soul mate. Because it is a union created in heaven, even if all the forces of the world were to conspire against the meeting, it would still take place. Michael Chabon found his *bashert* in Ayelet Waldman.

Ayelet's father was born in Montreal but, as an ardent Zionist, had left Canada to fight in Israel's war of independence. He married a native of Brooklyn, and they settled in Jerusalem, where Ayelet was born in 1964. Three years later, by the time of the Six-Day War, Ayelet's mother was tired of her adopted homeland's constant struggle for survival. Waldman says, "I have a memory of the war, of my mother, opening a can of hummus, and eating it in the bomb shelter." The family moved to Ridgewood, an affluent suburb of New Jersey. Ayelet describes her hometown as "having little to offer but drug and liquor stores, which must have explained why everyone was always filling prescriptions and drinking gin and tonics." Ayelet felt alienated, as Ridgewood was wealthy and waspy, and she was neither.

In junior high, she was an outsider. She recalls, "I was off the coolness scale. I didn't even rate a mention." For solace, she found a refuge from bullies at the school library, where she could read in peace. A voracious reader, she consumed Holocaust novels or anything else where "terrible things happened to children and they survived." High school was just a miserable continuation, and, as a reprieve, when she was in the tenth grade, her parents sent her to Israel to live on a kibbutz in the Galilee for a year. She returned with more confidence, and found friends by involving herself with the drama crowd and acting in plays. Although the popular blonde girls always received the leading roles, at least she had people to hang out with and a social identity.

After the purgatory that was high school, she went to Wesleyan University, after which she decided to go to law school, a decision based on financial reasons. She needed a career because at that time she was dating a man who was "purely unemployable."

Ayelet met the man who was her *bashert*, Michael Chabon, on a blind date in 1992, when he was a young novelist and she was a Harvard-educated attorney working for a large New York firm. Michael was born in Washington, DC. His father, Robert, was a physician and an attorney; his mother was also a lawyer. When he was eleven, his parents divorced. He spent three months a year with his father; the rest of the time he lived with his mother. It was during his childhood that he developed his lifelong love of comics. In 1987, he married the poet Lollie Groth; however, they divorced four years later. Part of the reason for the failure of his marriage was the success of his novel *The Mysteries of Pittsburgh*. He stated, "I was married at the time to someone else who was also a struggling writer, and the success created a gross imbalance in our careers, which was problematic."

Before their date, like any competent lawyer, Ayelet researched her setup. She did so by reading Chabon's novel *The Mysteries of Pittsburgh*, where the male protagonist has sexual encounters with men. When he showed up, holding a bouquet of irises, the first words she said were "Thank you for the flowers, and are you gay?" Something that Michael either said or did must have convinced her otherwise, because she was smitten. She recalls that seeing Michael in a blue shirt that made his blue eyes pop out, she thought, "Now I can stop dating."

Three weeks later, waking up one morning, Michael told Ayelet that she had proposed to him in her sleep. Mortified, she asked him what he had answered, to which he replied, "Yes." Chabon also knew right away that Ayelet was "the one" and said that he felt, even on that first date, that he'd known her all his life. He says, "It was love at first sight. I just saw her, and she looked so beautiful, and it was…the thunderbolt!" A year later they were married in the Brazil Room in Tilden Park. Ayelet recalls, "Even at my wedding, my friends were coming up and saying, 'Are you sure he's not gay? Have you read *The Mysteries of Pittsburgh*?'"

Michael and Ayelet have now been married for thirteen years and have four children: Sophie, Ezekiel "Zeke" Napoleon Waldman, Ida Rose, and Abraham Wolf Waldman; the children are the ultimate answer to the question Ayelet posed on their first date. The couple live in Berkeley, California, where they write in a backyard cottage filled with Michael's comic book collection. It is there that Ayelet wrote her 2006 novel (her ninth), *Love and Other Impossible Pursuits*, and Michael wrote *The Yiddish Policemen's Union*.

Ayelet describes her husband as "the feminist fantasy dad," who equally partakes of all parenting tasks, with the exception of breastfeeding. Because of her own sad experiences at school, she has run down the street after the camp bus, yelling at her oldest daughter to remember to be nice to the nerdy girls.

Ayelet created a flap when she wrote the essay *Because I Said So*. In it she said, "If I were to lose one, or God forbid, even if I lost all my children, God forbid, I would still have him, my husband. It simply fails me when I try to picture a future beyond my husband's death." Women across the nation were enraged, and started viewing the now stay-at-home mother as a variation of "Mommy Dearest." Complete strangers have gone up to her and informed her that she has no business raising children. So great was the uproar that Oprah Winfrey herself invited Ayelet to her show, where she defended the outspoken author. The word *uxorious* is defined as "excessively submissive or devoted to one's wife." However, there is no word that means when a woman is slavishly enamored of her spouse. However, if there is not a word, there is a woman who embodies that concept.

Sometimes when couples meet they play the game of "what if?" If one were to do that with Michael and Ayelet, one could ask, What if the Israeli-born Ayelet had not left her native country? What if Ayelet's Canadian-born father had brought his family back to Montreal rather than settle in New Jersey? What if their mutual friend had not set them up on a blind date? However, these are not questions for this literary couple, because their meeting was, as Michael states in his dedication, preordained. The love story between Michael and Ayelet proves that sometimes "love does not have to be an impossible pursuit; that sometimes the gods let mortals meet their *bashert*."

References

ADAM BEDE / George Eliot

Adams, Kathleen. 1998. George Eliot. The Coventry and Warwickshire Network. www.coventry.org.uk/heritage2/people/eliot/kaeliot.htm (accessed April 17, 2007).

Burton, Sir Frederic William. 1865. Mary Evans. Oxford University Press. www.seniornet.org/gallery/bookclubs/middlemarch/MarianEvans.htm (accessed April 17, 2007).

George Eliot: Biography. http://etext.lib.virginia.edu/collections/projects/eliot/middlemarch/bio.html.

HistoryMole. 2006. George Eliot. www.historymole.com/cgi-bin/main/results.pl?theme=10004009 (accessed April 16, 2007).

Literature Collection. George Eliot: Biography and works. Art Branch Inc. www.literaturecollection.com/a/george-eliot (accessed April 17, 2007).

The Literature Network. 2007. George Eliot. Jalic Inc. www.online-literature.com/elbert-hubbard/little-journeys/2 (accessed April 21, 2007).

Middlemarch. George Eliot: A brief biography. PBS. www.pbs.org/wgbh/masterpiece/archive/programs/middlemarch/tg_biography.html (accessed April 17, 2007).

Perdue, David A. 2007. David Perdue's Charles Dickens page: Family and friends. http://charlesdickenspage.com/family_friends.html.

Wikipedia. 2008. George Eliot. http://en.wikipedia.org/wiki/George_Eliot.

THE ADVENTURES OF TOM SAWYER / Mark Twain

Applebaum, Alex. Olivia Clemens. http://etext.virginia.edu/railton/projects/applebaum/olivia.html (accessed April 29, 2007).

Harris, Haskell. The other Mark Twain. http://etext.virginia.edu/railton/enam482e/reviews/harris.html (accessed April 28, 2007).

MT Biography. Mark Twain. http://library.advanced.org/27864/data/twain/mtbio.html (accessed April 29, 2007).

Paine, Albert Bigelow. The boys' life of Mark Twain. www.authorama.com/boys-life-of-mark-twain-28.html (accessed April 29, 2007).

Sam Clemens: A life. About Mark Twain. www.geocities.com/swaisman/samclemens.htm (accessed April 29, 2007).

Steinbrink, Jeffrey. 1991. Getting to be Mark Twain. University of California Press. http://ark.cdlib.org/ark:/13030/ft7779p19g (accessed April 28, 2007).

Timeline. 2004. The Mark Twain House & Museum. www.marktwainhouse.org/theman/timeline.shtml (accessed April 29, 2007).

Wikipedia. 2008. Mark Twain. http://en.wikipedia.org/wiki/Mark_Twain.

AFTER THE FALL / Arthur Miller

Andrews, Suzanna. 2007. Arthur Miller's missing act. *Vanity Fair*, September.

Brooks, Zan. 2005. Death of a playwright: Legend Arthur Miller dies aged 89. *Guardian* (UK), February 11, Culture.

CNN. 2005. Arthur Miller dead at 89. February 14, Entertainment.

Daily Mail (UK). 2007. Arthur Miller and the son he hid away for 40 years. August 31.

Galvin, Rachel. Arthur Miller biography. www.neh.gov/whoweare/miller/biography.html (accessed February 7, 2007).

Grade Saver. Biography of Arthur Miller. www.gradesaver.com/classicnotes/authors/about_arthur_miller.html (accessed February 7, 2007).

Hurwitt, Robert. 2005. Arthur Miller: 1915–2005. *San Francisco Chronicle*, February 12.

Liukkonen, Petri. 2003. Books and Writers: Arthur Miller (1915–2005). www.kirjasto.sci.fi/amiller.htm (accessed February 7, 2007).

Samra, Esther. Remembering Inga Morath. www.pixelpress.org/contents/ingemorath/ingemorath_home.html.

St. Clair, William. 2002. Obituary: Inge Morath. *Independent* (London), February 5.

Telegraph (UK). 2002. Obituary: Inge Morath. February 1.

Wikipedia. 2008. After the Fall (play). http://en.wikipedia.org/wiki/After_the_Fall_%28play%29.

Wikipedia. 2008. Arthur Miller. http://en.wikipedia.org/wiki/Arthur_Miller.

Wikipedia. 2008. Inge Morath. http://en.wikipedia.org/wiki/Inge_Morath.

Wikipedia. 2008. Rebecca Miller. http://en.wikipedia.org/wiki/Rebecca_Miller.

ALICE'S ADVENTURES IN WONDERLAND / Lewis Carroll

Wikipedia. 2008. Alice Liddell. http://en.wikipedia.org/wiki/Alice_Liddell.

Wikipedia. 2008. Alice's Adventures in Wonderland. http://en.wikipedia.org/wiki/Alice%27s_adventures_in_wonderland.

Wikipedia. 2008. Lewis Carroll. http://en.wikipedia.org/wiki/Lewis_Carroll.

ATLAS SHRUGGED / Ayn Rand

The Atlasphere: About Ayn Rand. www.theatlasphere.com/about/about-ayn-rand.php (accessed May 20, 2007).

Ayn Rand and the Brandens: A chronology. Objectivism Reference Center. www.noblesoul.com/orc/bio/brandens.html (accessed May 18, 2007).

McLemee, Scott. 1999. Lingua franca: The heirs of Ayn Rand. www.mclemee.com/id39.html (accessed June 18, 2008).

Naumann, Friedrich. Ayn Rand: The modern revival of the liberal concept. www.africa.fnst-freiheit.org/webcom/show_page.php/_c-1032/_nr-15/i.html (accessed May 20, 2007).

Spayde, Jon. 1999. Aynal fixation. *UTNE Reader*, May/June.

Turner, Jenny. 2005. As astonishing as Elvis. *London Review of Books*, December 1.

Voice of America. 2007. Ayn Rand, 1905–1982: Americans still debate her books and ideas. March 11.

Wikipedia. 2008. Ayn Rand. http://en.wikipedia.org/wiki/Ayn_Rand.

THE BELL JAR / Sylvia Plath

The art of writing and making films from real life to reel life. The Writing Studio. www.writingstudio.co.za/page543.html (accessed June 8, 2007).

Carey, John. 2006. Their fatal attraction. *Sunday Times* (London), October 8.

Carrell, Severin. 2006. One call from Ted Hughes's mistress led to a literary tragedy. *Independent* (London), September 10.

Carrell, Severin, and Robin Stummer. 2003. Sylvia Plath film has lost the plot, says her closest friend. *Independent* (London), December 28.

Feinstein, Elaine. 2007. Fatal blade. *Times Literary Supplement* (London), January 19.

Fraser, Caroline. 2001. Plather. *LA Weekly*, June 13.

Grice, Elizabeth. 2006. A new biography of Ted Hughes's secret mistress has sparked a furious debate as to who was to blame for the affair that ended in tragedy. *Telegraph* (UK), September 24.

Grice, Elizabeth. 2006. No longer just a tragic footnote. *Telegraph* (UK), September 21.

Guardian (UK). 1999. I realised Sylvia knew about Assia's pregnancy—it might have offered a further explanation of her suicide. April 23.

Kirby, Terry. 2006. The other tragic woman in the life of Ted Hughes. *Independent* (London), March 6.

Macdonald, Marianne. 2004. I paid for the gas that killed Sylvia Plath. *Sunday Telegraph* (UK), January 31.

Mathieson, Amy. 2006. Sorry affair. *Scotsman* (UK), October 28.

Millar, Anna. 2006. Ted Hughes treated mistress like a tyrant before her suicide, claims new biography. *Scotland on Sunday* (UK), September 10.

Negev, Eilat, and Koren Yehuda. 2006. The invisible woman. *Guardian* (UK), October 28.

Negev, Eilat, and Koren Yehuda. 2006. Written out of history. *Guardian* (UK), October 19.

Reynolds, Nigel. 2006. Ted Hughes revealed as a domestic tyrant who laid down law to mistress. *Telegraph* (UK), September 9.

Smith, David. 2006. Ted Hughes, the domestic tyrant. *Observer* (London), September 10.

Thorpe, Vanessa. 2001. Ted Hughes's secret mistress named. *Guardian* (UK), May 6.

Wikipedia. 2008. The Bell Jar. http://en.wikipedia.org/wiki/The_Bell_Jar.

Wikipedia. 2008. Sylvia Plath. http://en.wikipedia.org/wiki/Sylvia_Plath.

THE BROTHERS KARAMAZOV / Fyodor Dostoevsky

Coulehan, Jack. 2003. Annotations of *Summer in Baden-Baden*, by Leonid Tsypkin. New Directions. http://litmed.med.nyu.edu/Annotation?action=view&annid=12077.

Gocsik, Karen. 2003. The brothers Karamazov. Dartmouth College, April 9. www.dartmouth.edu/~karamazo.

H2G2. 2003. Fyodor Dostoevsky: Novelist. BBC. December 9. www.bbc.co.uk/dna/h2g2/A1920593.

Wilcox, Lance. 1999. Dostoyevsky's gamble: A play in two acts. Elmhurst College.

CARRIE / Stephen King

Dubner, Stephen J. 2000. What is Stephen King trying to prove? *New York Times Magazine*, August 13.

Jeffries, Stuart. 2004. Dark rider. *Guardian* (UK), September 18.

King, Stephen. 2003. National Book Awards Acceptance Speeches. National Book Foundation. www.nationalbook.org/nbaacceptspeech_sking.html.

Liukkonen, Petri. 2003. Books and Writers: Stephen King. www.kirjasto.sci.fi/sking.htm (accessed June 28, 2007).

Stephen King's biography. Stephen King bookstore. www.stephenkingshop.com/biography.htm (accessed June 28, 2007).

Wikipedia. 2008. Stephen King. http://en.wikipedia.org/wiki/Stephen_King.

THE CONSTANT GARDENER / John le Carré

Dillon, Matt. 2005. She went where she was needed, helping refugees who had lost everything. *Reader's Digest*, April.

Feature film *The Constant Gardener* dedicated to former Refugees International advocate Yvette Pierpaoli. 2004. Refugees International. www .refintl.org/content/article/detail/6572 (accessed July 6, 2007).

Guardian (UK). 2001. The constant Muse. February 25.

Gussow, Mel. 2000. In a plot far from the cold, Le Carré sums up the past. *New York Times*, December 19.

Honan, William H. 1999. Yvette Pierpaoli, 60, aid worker who devoted life to refugees. *New York Times*, April 20.

Horowitz, Craig. 1999. Kosovo's unlikelist casualties. *New York Magazine*, June 14, News and Features.

Jeffries, Stuart. 2005. Into the darkness. *Guardian* (UK), November 12.

A love story, and a dedication. AllMoviePortal.com. www.allmovieportal .com/m/2005_The_Constant_Gardener_production_information .html (accessed July 6, 2007).

Refugees International at 25: A look back, part 4. 2004. Refugees International. www.refintl.org/content/article/detail/1582 (accessed July 8, 2007).

Refugees International congratulates Rachel Weisz for her Academy Award. 2004. Refugees International. www.refugeesinternational.org/content/ article/detail/8106 (accessed July 6, 2007).

Shi'an, Shen. 2006. Dharma inspired movie review. *Buddhist Channel*, March 18.

Trivia for *The Constant Gardener*. 2008. IMDb. www.imdb.com/title/ tt0387131/trivia (accessed July 6, 2007).

Turan, Kenneth. 2005. Movie review: *The Constant Gardener. Los Angeles Times*, April 31.

THE DA VINCI CODE / Dan Brown

Allen, Vanessa. 2006. Exclusive: The weird world of Mrs. Da Vinci Code. *Mirror* (UK), March 18.

Biblio. 2008. Dan Brown. www.biblio.com/authors/558/Dan_Brown_ Biography.html.

Button, James. 2006. Da Vinci author finds his marriage on trial. *Age* (Australia), March 16.

Lauer, Matt. 2003. Author Dan Brown, "The Da Vinci Code" talks about the success of his book and the research he did in order to write it. *Today* (NBC), June 9.

O'Keeffe, Alice, and Joanna Walters. 2006. How Dan Brown's wife unlocked the code to bestseller success. *Observer* (UK), March 12.

Stritoff, Bob, and Sheri Stitoff. 2008. Dan and Blythe Brown marriage profile. http://marriage.about.com/od/thearts/p/danbrown.htm.

Wikipedia. 2008. Blythe Brown. http://en.wikipedia.org/wiki/Blythe_ Brown.

DE PROFUNDIS / Oscar Wilde

Anarchopedia. Lord Alfred Bruce Douglas. http://eng.anarchopedia.org/ Lord_Alfred_Douglas (accessed October 21, 2007).

Graham, Eamon. 2005. Eamon's bookmark: De Profundus. *Boheme Magazine*, March 17.

Gribben, Mark. 2007. All about Oscar Wilde. www.crimelibrary.com/ gangsters_outlaws/cops_others/oscar_wilde/1.html (accessed October 21, 2007).

Gross indecency: The three trials of Oscar Wilde. Court Theatre. www .courttheatre.org/home/plays/9899/gross/PNgross.shtml (accessed October 22, 2007).

The Knitting Circle. 2002. Lord Alfred Bruce Douglas. www.knittingcircle .org.uk/alfreddouglas.html (accessed October 21, 2007).

Koymasky, Matt, and Andrej Koymasky. 2001. Lord Alfred Douglas. http:// andrejkoymasky.com/liv/fam/biod3/doug2.html (accessed October 21, 2007).

LudditeAndroid. 2002. Lord Alfred Douglas. Everything2, July 28. www .everything2.com/index.pl?node_id=1338515 (accessed October 21, 2007).

Neurotic Poets. Oscar Wilde. www.neuroticpoets.com/wilde (accessed October 21, 2007).

Stanton, Michael N. Douglas, Alfred Bruce (1870–1945). GLBTQ. www .glbtq.com/literature/douglas_a.html (accessed October 22, 2007).

Wikipedia. 2008. Lord Alfred Douglas. http://en.wikipedia.org/wiki/Lord_Alfred_Douglas.

Wikipedia. 2008. Oscar Wilde. http://en.wikipedia.org/wiki/Oscar_Wilde.

DR. ZHIVAGO / Boris Pasternak

Bellamy, Edward. Literary daybook, May 30. *Salon* May 30. http://dir.salon.com/story/books/today/2002/05/30/may30/index.html (accessed January 13, 2008).

Blake, Patricia. 1978. The other Lara. *Time,* March 6.

Corness, Patrick. 2003. Review: *Olga: Pasternak's Last Love*, by György Dalos. www.new-books-in-german.com/spr2000/book08c.htm (accessed January 12, 2008).

Darrow, Siobhan. 1996. Love letters from Boris Pasternak to be auctioned. CNN, November 26.

DeLaine, Linda. 2007. Doctor Zhivago and Khrushchev. Russian Life. www.rispubs.com/article.cfm?number=518 (accessed January 12, 2008).

Lara: My years with Boris Pasternak. German Films. www.german-cinema.de/app/filmarchive/film_view.php?film_id=612 (accessed January 13, 2008).

Liukkonen, Petri. 2003. Books and Writers: Boris (Leonidovich) Pasternak. www.kirjasto.sci.fi/pasterna.htm (accessed January 12, 2008).

New York Times. 2008. Olga Ivinskaya, 83, Pasternak Muse for "Zhivago." January 12.

Olga Vsevolodovna. Helene Celmina: Women in Soviet Prisons. http://vip.latnet.lv/LPRA/celmina/14.html (accessed January 13, 2008).

Smirnova, Svetlana. 2006. The sparkling soul of Boris Pasternak. *Neva News* (St. Petersburg), July 8.

Time. 1961. A lost lady. January 27.

Vronskaya, Jeanne. 1995. Obituary: Olga Ivinskaya. *Independent* (London), September 13.

Wikipedia. 2008. Boris Pasternak. http://en.wikipedia.org/wiki/Boris_Pasternak.

EMMA / Jane Austen

Austen-Leigh, William and Richard Arthur Austen-Leigh (Deirdre LeFaye, ed.). *Jane Austen: a family record.* New York: Simon and Schuster, 1989.

Austen, Emma, and the prince. Today in Literature. www.todayinliterature. com/print-today.asp?Event_Date=3/29/1815 (accessed April 19, 2008).

Clark, Robert. 2001. The Literary Encyclopedia: Jane Austen, January 8. www .litencyc.com/php/speople.php?rec=tru&UID=5167 (accessed April 19, 2008).

Liukkonen, Petri. Books and Writers: Jane Austen. www.kirjasto.sci.fi/jausten. htm (accessed March 23, 2008).

Perlstein, Arnold. 2007. Why did Jane Austen keep it all secret? Sharp Elves Society, September 14. http://sharpelvessociety.blogspot.com (accessed March 23, 2008).

Sheehan, Colleen A. 2006. Jane Austen's "tribute" to the Prince Regent. Jane Austen Society of North America. www.jasna.org/persuasions /on-line/vol27no1/sheehan.htm (accessed May 21, 2009).

Wikipedia. 2009. George Augustus Frederick. http://en.wikipedia.org/wiki /George_Augustus_Frederick.

Wikipedia. 2009. Jane Austen. http://en.wikipedia.org/wiki/Jane_Austen.

THE END OF THE AFFAIR / Graham Greene

Conroy, Ed. 2004. Essential Graham Greene. *National Catholic Reporter*, November 19. http://ncronline.org/NCR_Online/archives2/2004d/ 111904/111904a.php (accessed February 21, 2008).

Graham Greene. American Society of Authors and Writers. http://amsaw. org/amsaw-ithappenedinhistory-100203-greene.html (accessed February 21, 2008).

Graham Greene. 2004. www.leninimports.com/graham_greene.html (accessed February 21, 2008).

Graham Greene. BiblioUnbound. www.biblio.com/author_biographies /2044418/Graham_Greene.html (accessed February 21, 2008).

Hastings, Selina. 2000. The unquiet American. *The Spectator*, February 19.

http://findarticles.com/p/articles/mi_qa3724/is_200002/ai_n8878561 (accessed May 1, 2009).

Independent (UK). 2000. A hell of an affair. January 7. www.independent.co.uk/news/media/a-hell-of-an-affair-728643.html (accessed March 8, 2008).

Pearce, Joseph. 2005. Graham Greene: doubter par excellence. *Catholic Authors.* www.catholicauthors.com/greene.html (accessed February 21, 2008).

Rosenbaum, Danny. 2009. Biogs: Graham Greene's biography. www.biogs.com/famous/greenegraham.html (accessed May 21, 2009).

Times (UK). 2007. Extract from Graham Greene. September 13. http://entertainment.timesonline.co.uk/tol/arts_and_entertainment/books/article2439198.ece (accessed February 21, 2008).

Wikipedia. 2009. Graham Greene. http://en.wikipedia.org/wiki/Graham_Greene.

FOR WHOM THE BELL TOLLS / Ernest Hemingway

Benfey, Christopher. 2006. Covering her century. New Republic, September 12, Books and the Arts.

Houston Chronicle. 1998. Noted war correspondent Martha Gellhorn, 89, dies.

Kerrane, Kevin. 1998. Martha's quest. *Salon*, March 12. www.salon.com/media/1998/03/12media2.html.

Liukkonen, Petri. 2003. Books and Writers: Martha Gellhorn. www.kirjasto.sci.fi/gellhorn.htm.

Skloot, Rebecca. 2006. A war reporter's private life. Critical Mass. http://bookcriticscircle.blogspot.com/2006/09/war-reporters-private-life.html.

Wikipedia. 2008. Martha Gellhorn. http://en.wikipedia.org/wiki/Martha_Gellhorn.

FRANKENSTEIN OR THE MODERN PROMETHEUS / Mary Shelley

Answers.com. 2008. William Godwin. www.answers.com/topic/william-godwin.

Biographies of people in Mary Shelley's family tree. The Bakken Library and Museum.www.thebakken.org/Frankenstein/biographies.htm (accessed January 19, 2008).

Buzzing Bee. 2007. Mary Shelley. http://buttercupelffly.blogspot.com/2007/10/mary-shelley.html.

H2G2. 2007. Mary Shelley: The formative years. BBC, October 26. www.bbc.co.uk/dna/h2g2/A28234857.

University of Pennsylvania. Biography: William Godwin. www.english.upenn.edu/Projects/knarf/Godwin/bio.html (accessed January 19, 2008).

Wikipedia. 2008. Mary Shelley. http://en.wikipedia.org/wiki/Mary_Shelley.

Wikipedia. 2008. Mary Wollstonecraft. http://en.wikipedia.org/wiki/Mary_Wollstonecraft.

Woodbridge, Kim. The life of Mary Shelley. www.kimwoodbridge.com/maryshel/life.shtml.

GONE WITH THE WIND / Margaret Mitchell

Margaret Mitchell (1919–1925). www.geocities.com/athens/6098/margaret3.html?200826 (accessed January 26, 2008).

Quoteland. 2003. Margaret Mitchell. http://forum.quoteland.com/1/OpenTopic?a=tpc&s=586192041&f=4511947895&m=6151978576 (accessed January 26, 2008).

Wikipedia. 2008. Margaret Mitchell. http://en.wikipedia.org/wiki/Margaret_Mitchell.

THE GRADUATE / Charles Webb

Associated Press. 2006. "Graduate" author to write sequel. May 31.

Charles Webb to write sequel to "The Graduate." 2006. Damox's Literature Blog. http://damox.com/2006/05/charles-webb-to-write-sequel-to.html (accessed July 16, 2007).

Finke, Nikki. 2004. Say it ain't so, Mrs. Robinson. *LA Weekly*, June 24.

Huck, Peter. 2002. Life as a post-Graduate. *Age* (Australia), August 19.

An interview with Charles Webb. 2006. Thoughtcat. http://thoughtcat.blogspot.com/2006/07/thoughtcat-exclusive-interview-with.html.

Lawless, Jill. 2006. "Mrs. Robinson" returns in sequel. Associated Press, May 31.

Norman, Philip. 2003. "The Graduate" author, Charles Webb: Scrawl on the wild. *Time*, January 5.

Preston, John. 2007. The post-Graduate lifestyle. *Age* (Australia), June 23.

Turpin, Adrian. 2001. How we met: Charles Webb & Fred. *Independent* (London), April 8.

Wikipedia. 2008. Charles Webb. http://en.wikipedia.org/wiki/Charles_Webb.

THE GREAT GATSBY / F. Scott Fitzgerald

Prigozy, Ruth. F. Scott Fitzgerald and Zelda Fitzgerald background. F. Scott Fitzgerald Society. www.zeldafitzgerald.com/fitzgeralds/index_text .htm.

Wikipedia. 2008. F. Scott Fitzgerald. http://en.wikipedia.org/wiki/F_Scott_ Fitzgerald.

Wikipedia. 2008. Zelda Fitzgerald. http://en.wikipedia.org/wiki/Zelda_ Fitzgerald.

HARRY POTTER AND THE PHILOSOPHER'S STONE / J. K. Rowling

A brief history of J. K. Rowling. www.thesevenpotters.com/jkrowling.php.

McGinty, Stephen. 2003. The J. K. Rowling story. *Scotsman* (UK), June 16.

McGinty, Stephen. Life after Harry. www.india-forums.com/forum_posts .asp?TID=174026.

White, Claire E. J. K. Rowling and the extraordinary life. *Internet Writing Journal*. www.internetwritingjournal.com/aug05/rowling.htm.

THE HEART IS A LONELY HUNTER / Carson McCullers

Carson McCullers Center for Writers and Musicians. Columbus State University. www.mccullerscenter.org/bibliography.htm (accessed March 13, 2007).

Geissler, Kim. A life of confusion. The Carson McCullers Project. www .carson-mccullers.com/html/confusion.html (accessed March 13, 2007).

LitLinks. Carson McCullers. www.bedfordstmartins.com/litlinks/fiction/mccullers.htm (accessed March 13, 2007).

Liukkonen, Petri. 2004. Books and Writers: (Lula) Carson McCullers. www.kirjasto.sci.fi/carsonmc.htm (accessed March 13, 2007).

Wikipedia. 2008. Carson McCullers. http://en.wikipedia.org/wiki/Carson_McCullers.

THE HISTORY OF LOVE / Nicole Krauss

Authors Jonathan Safran Foer and Nicole Krauss welcome a son. 2006. Celebrity Baby Blog, April 26. www.celebrity-babies.com/2006/04/authors_jonatha.html.

Aviv, Rachel. 2005. Written with invisible ink. *Village Voice* (New York), April 25.

Bernard, Sarah. 2002. The natural surrealist. *Independent* (London), April 21.

Birnbaum, Robert. 2005. Birnbaum v. Jonathan Safran Foer. *Morning News* (Dallas), April 19.

Conversations with my thirteen-year-old self. 2007. Blog of Z Lite. http://zarine.i.ph/blogs/zarine/2007/04/14/conversations-with-my-13-year-old-self.

Freeman, John. 2005. The history of Nicole. *Age* (Australia), September 10. www.theage.com.au/news/books/the-history-of-nicole/2005/09/08/1125772645233.html.

Jonathan Safran Foer. www.literaturfestival.com/bios1_3_6_790.html (accessed December 26, 2007).

Kachka, Boris. 2005. Bio hazards. *New York Magazine,* May 21.

Marsh, Ann. 2005. With her bestseller, *The History of Love,* a young novelist makes a case for literature that simmers with emotion. *Stanford Magazine*, September/October.

Mostly Fiction. 2005. Review: *The History of Love*, by Nicole Krauss. www.mostlyfiction.com/contemp/krauss.htm (accessed December 27, 2007).

Mudge, Alden. 2005. The strength to survive. Bookpage.com, May. http://www.bookpage.com/0505bp/nicole_krauss.html.

On forgetting and remembering. 2007. http://zarine.i.ph/blogs/zarine/2007/04/15/on-forgetting-and-remembering.

On the Same Page. *The History of Love*, by Nicole Krauss. San Francisco Public Library. http://sfpl.org/news/sanfranreads/picksmay.htm.

Reading Group Guides. *The history of love,* by Nicole Krauss. www.reading groupguides.com/guides3/history_of_love2.asp.

Solomon, Deborah. 2005. The rescue artist. *New York Times,* February 27.

Thousand Oaks reads: One city, one book. http://thousandoaksreads.org/the-author (accessed December 26, 2007).

Wood, Gaby. 2005. Have a heart. *Guardian* (UK), May 15.

I KNOW WHY THE CAGED BIRD SINGS / Maya Angelou

African American Literature Book Club. 1998. About the author: Guy Johnson. Archived by Barnesandnoble.com, December 10. http://aalbc.com/authors/guyjohnson.htm

Alpha Kappa Alpha Authors. http://dickinsg.intrasun.tcnj.edu/akaauthors2/Maya.htm (accessed September 18, 2007).

Angelou, Maya. 1981. *The heart of a woman.* New York: Bantam Books.

Angelou, Maya. "Phenomenal woman." www.feminist.com/resources/art speech/insp/maya.htm.

Angelou, Maya. "Still I rise." www.poemhunter.com/poem/still-i-rise.

Kellaway, Kate. 1993. Poet for the new America. *Observer* (UK), January 24.

Maya Angelou: From brothel to books. www.cyberlearning-world.com/nhhs/project/1998/mayaa.htm.

McElrath, Jessica. 2008. Maya Angelou. http://afroamhistory.about.com/od/mayaangelou/p/bio_angelou_m.htm.

Moore, Lucinda. 2003. A conversation with Maya Angelou at 75. *Smithsonian Magazine,* April.

Thomson, Sedge. 2006. Maya Angelou and Guy Johnson: Mother and son poets become themselves. www.prx.org/pieces/8243.

Trip Atlas. 2008. Maya Angelou. http://tripatlas.com/Maya%20Angelou.

Wikipedia. 2008. Maya Angelou. http://en.wikipedia.org/wiki/Maya_Angelou.

IN COLD BLOOD / Truman Capote

AllExperts. Truman Capote. http://en.allexperts.com/e/t/tr/truman_ capote.htm (accessed April 1, 2007).

Hogan, Ron. 2006. Marc Weingarten remembers Jack Dunphy. *Beatrice,* March 5. www.beatrice.com/archives/001905.html.

Truman, Capote. 2005. *FYNE Times.* www.fyne.co.uk/index.php?item=230 (accessed April 1, 2007).

Truman Capote, his life and works. The New York Times & Sony Pictures Classics. www.nytimes.com/ads/capote/capote_e.html.

Wikipedia. 2008. Jack Dunphy. http://en.wikipedia.org/wiki/Jack_ Dunphy.

Wikipedia. 2008. Truman Capote. http://en.wikipedia.org/wiki/Truman_ Capote.

IN THE TIME OF THE BUTTERFLIES / Julia Alvarez

Alvarez, Julia. 2008. Julia Alvarez. www.juliaalvarez.com/about.

Brown, Jill. 2004. In the Time of the Butterflies. www.stolaf.edu/orgs/ bookreview/In%20the%20Time%20of%20the%20Butterflies%20_ %20Julia%20Alvarez%20_%20Jill%20Brown%20'04.html.

Daily Dispatch Online (South Africa). 2000. Three women who said "no." www.dispatch.co.za/2000/10/28/features/women.htm.

Dugan, Eileen. Mirabel Museo. http://semdom.50megs.com/mirabal_ museo.htm.

Fratini, Mary Elizabeth. 2006. Truth trumps fiction. *Vermont Guardian,* November 17.

Guardian (UK). 2006. Vivan las Mariposas. February.

Michniewicz, Margaret. 2006. The legendary butterflies: The Mirabal sis- ters' legacy of resistance. *Vermont Woman.*

The Mirabal Sisters. El Bohio Dominicano. http://el-bohio.com/mirabal (accessed June 19, 2008).

Notes on Novels: *In the Time of the Butterflies.* 2006. Answers.com. www .answers.com/topic/in-the-time-of-the-butterflies-novel-5.

Petra. Review: *In the Time of the Butterflies*, by Julia Alvarez. Epinions.com. www.epinions.com/content_66759528068.

Wikipedia. 2008. Mirabal sisters. http://en.wikipedia.org/wiki/Mirabal_sisters.

JANE EYRE: AN AUTOBIOGRAPHY / Charlotte Brontë

Bookyards. William Makepeace Thackeray. www.bookyards.com/biography .html?author_id=1297&author_name=Thackeray%2C%20William%20M.

Kaye, Richard A. 1995. A good woman on five thousand pounds. *Studies in English Literature 1500–1900* 35 (4).

A sampling of text and images from the collector's edition of *Jane Eyre*. 2004. New York Public Library. www.nypl.org/publications/abouted.cfm.

THE JOY LUCK CLUB / Amy Tan

Academy of Achievement. 2005. Amy Tan. www.achievement.org/autodoc/ page/tano bio-1 (accessed March 9, 2007).

Adams, Bella. 2001. Amy Tan. *The Literary Encyclopedia*, March 17.

Beason, Tyrone. 2003. Tan's musings blend dark and light, past and present. *Seattle Times*, October 31.

The biography of Amy Tan. 2007. Pennsylvania State University. www .personal.psu.edu/users/s/u/sul140/asn3.htm (accessed March 10, 2007).

De Bertodano, Helena. 2003. A life stranger than fiction. *Daily Telegraph* (UK), November 11.

Free Study Guide: *The joy luck club*, by Amy Tan. www.pinkmonkey.com/ booknotes/monkeynotes/pmJoyLuckClub13.asp (accessed March 10, 2007).

Gale, Thomson. 2006. Amy Tan. *Encyclopedia of World Biography*.

Gray, Paul. 2001. The joys and sorrows of Amy Tan. *Time,* February 19.

Guy, David. 2003. Wheel of fortune. *Washington Post*, November 2.

Harleman, Ann. 2003. Destiny's runaway. *Boston Globe*, November 30.

Hoggard, Liz. 2003. Death as a source of life. *Observer* (UK), November 23.

The Joy Luck Club book notes summary. BookRags. www.bookrags.com/ notes/jlc/BIO.htm (accessed March 10, 2007).

Lyall, Sarah. 1995. At home with Amy Tan: In the country of the spirits. *New York Times,* December 28.

Mason, Deborah. 2003. "The opposite of fate": A not-so-dutiful daughter. *New York Times,* November 23.

Messud, Claire. 2003. What's safe to say. *Daily Telegraph* (UK), November 17.

Prentice Hall Literature: Timeless voices, timeless themes. Author biographies: Amy Tan. www.phschool.com/atschool/literature/author_biographies/tan_a.html (accessed March 10, 2007).

Rollyson, Carl, ed. 2007. Notable American novelists, revised. Salem Press. http://salempress.com/Store/samples/notable_american_novelists/notable_american_novelists.htm (accessed March 10, 2007).

Scheider, Katie. 2003. The novelist tells (almost) all in her first nonfiction book. *Oregonian* (Portland, OR), November 9.

Shilling, Jane. 2003. What the memory box holds. *Daily Telegraph* (UK), November 17.

Simon, Clea. 2003. Amy Tan explores the interweaving of fate, fact and fiction: Tan takes a look at her work, life. *San Francisco Chronicle*, December 7.

Sylva, Bob. 2001. Soul mates: When author Amy Tan lost her mother, she also lost her inspiration. Now, she's digging deep to cover. Bee Book Club, April 11.

Walsh, Bryan. 2003. Family phantoms. *Time*, December 7.

Yahoo! Education. CliffsNotes: *The joy luck club*, by Amy Tan. http://education.yahoo.com/homework_help/cliffsnotes/the_joy_luck_club/1.html (accessed March 10, 2007).

LADY CHATTERLEY'S LOVER / D. H. Lawrence

Lady Chatterley's Lover. http://encyclopedia.jrank.org/articles/pages/732/Lady-Chatterley-s-Lover.html (accessed March 31, 2009).

Lawrence, D. H. *Lady Chatterley's lover.* New York: Barnes & Noble Books, 2005.

Sunday Herald (UK). 2003. Lady Chatterley's Lover obscenity trial of 1960. January 26. http://findarticles.com/p/articles/mi_qn4156/is_20030126/ai_n9627069/ (accessed March 27, 2009).

Wikipedia. 2009. D. H. Lawrence. http://en.wikipedia.org/wiki/Under_the
    _Volcano.

Wikipedia. 2009. Lady Chatterley's Lover. http://en.wikipedia.org/wiki
    /Lady_Chatterley%27s_Lover.

LOLITA / Vladimir Nabokov

Davydov, Sergei. 1990. The passions of young "Sirin." *New York Times*,
    October 14, sec. 7.

Knorr, Katherine. 1999. Behind the mask of Mrs. Vladimir Nabokov. *Inter-
    national Herald Tribune*, April 8. www.iht.com/articles/1999/04/08/
    nab.2.t.php.

Lowery, George. 2006. Woman behind "Lolita." *Cornell Chronicle Online*,
    June 23. www.news.cornell.edu/stories/June06/Nabokov.biographer
    .gl.html.

McGraw, Eliza R. L. 1999. Review: *Véra (Mrs. Vladimir Nabokov): Portrait
    of a marriage.* Nonfiction BookPage. www.bookpage.com/9905bp/non
    fiction/vera.html.

Slaight, Wilma. 2001. Vladimir Nabokov. *Anniversary* (Wellesley College
    newspaper), January 8. www.wellesley.edu/Anniversary/nabokov.html.

Zembla. 1999. Summary of *Véra (Mrs. Vladimir Nabokov),* by Stacy Schiff.
    Pennsylvania State University. www.libraries.psu.edu/nabokov/vera
    .htm.

LONG DAY'S JOURNEY INTO NIGHT / Eugene O'Neill

Albert, Janice. Eugene O'Neill (1888–1953). www.cateweb.org/CA_Authors/
    oneill.html (accessed October 16, 2007).

Barker, Matthew Jude. 2003. The Maine summer of Eugene O'Neill. *Port-
    land's Maine City Magazine.*

Black, Stephen A. 1999. *Eugene O'Neill: Beyond mourning and tragedy.* Lon-
    don: Yale University Press.

Cape, Jonathan. 1932. *Mourning becomes electra.* The Sharaff-Sze Collection
    at the New York Society Library. www.nysoclib.org/collections/oneill_
    eugene.html (accessed October 17, 2007).

Encyclopedia of World Biography. Eugene O'Neill. BookRags. www.bookrags.com/biography/eugene-oneill.

Eugene O'Neill's children. 2006. PBS: People and Events. www.pbs.org/wgbh/amex/oneill/peopleevents/p_children.html (accessed October 16, 2007).

Eugene O'Neill's Tao House. San Jose State University. www.sjsu.edu/depts/english/tao.htm (accessed October 16, 2007).

Eugene O'Neill's wives. 2006. PBS: People and Events. www.pbs.org/wgbh/amex/oneill/peopleevents/p_wives.html (accessed October 16, 2007).

Fitzgerald, Brian. 1999. The iceman stayeth: Eugene O'Neill's ghost a permanent resident of Shelton Hall? *Boston University Bridge,* October 29. www.bu.edu/bridge/archive/1999/10-29/features4.html.

Goodwin, Evan. 2007. Little blue light: Eugene O'Neill. October 14. www.littlebluelight.com/lblphp/intor.php?ikey=21 (accessed October 16, 2007).

Liukkonen, Petri. 2004. O'Neill biography. Literature Post. www.literaturepost.com/authors/O'Neill.html.

Maddocks, Melvin. 1973. Family disasters. *Time*, November 26.

O'Neill, Eugene. 2002. *Long day's journey into night.* London: Yale University Press.

Time. 1946. The ordeal of Eugene O'Neill. October 21.

Virtual Tour of Tao House. 2007. Eugene O'Neill Foundation, Tao House. www.eoneill.com/eof/tao_house/tour.htm (accessed October 16, 2007).

Wilkins, Frederick. 1987. Taasinge or tharsing? *The Eugene O'Neill Newsletter* XI. www.eoneill.com/library/newsletter/xi-1/xi-1g.htm (accessed October 18, 2007).

Wikipedia. 2008. Eugene O'Neill. http://en.wikipedia.org/wiki/Eugene_O'Neill.

LOOK HOMEWARD ANGEL / Thomas Wolfe

Connelly, Sharon. The Thomas Wolfe website. http://library.uncwil.edu/wolfe/aliner.htm (accessed July 24, 2007).

Donald, David Herbert. 2007. The troubled career of Thomas Wolfe. *New York Times*, July 24.

Enotes.com. 2007. Thomas Wolfe. www.enotes.com/contemporary-literary-criticism/thomas-wolfe (accessed July 24, 2007).

Fantastic Fiction. 2008. Thomas Wolfe. www.fantasticfiction.co.uk/w/thomas-wolfe.

Kanfer, Stefan. 1987. Lit. *Time,* March 16.

Moore, Mark A. A brief biography of Thomas Wolfe. www.ah.dcr.state.nc.us/sections/hs/wolfe/bio.htm (accessed July 24, 2007).

Powell, William S., ed. 1996. *Dictionary of North Carolina biography.* Chapel Hill: University of North Carolina Press.

Smith, Liz. 2007. Bits of nuptial news. *New York Post*, June 19.

Thomas Wolfe (1900–1938). Stanford University. www.stanford.edu/~evans/LitLondon/wolfe.htm.

Thomas Wolfe biography. The Thomas Wolfe Society. http://library.uncwil.edu/wolfe/bio.htm (accessed July 24, 2007).

Thomas Wolfe timelines. North Carolina Historic Sites. www.wolfememorial.com/life.html (accessed July 24, 2007).

Wagner, Christopher. 1999. Biographies: Thomas Wolfe. Historical Boys' Clothing. http://histclo.com/bio/w/bio-wolfe.html.

Wikipedia. 2008. Thomas Wolfe. http://en.wikipedia.org/wiki/Thomas_Wolfe.

Williams, Margaret. 2000. Love letters. *Mountain Xpress* 6 (26), February 9.

LOVE IN THE TIME OF CHOLERA / Gabriel García Márquez

Anderson, Jon Lee. 1999. The power of Gabriel García Márquez. *New Yorker*, September 27.

Associated Press. 2007. People: Gabriel García Márquez, Lindsay Lohan, Paula Abdul. May 31.

BBC News. 2007. García Márquez home to Colombia. May 31.

Biography of Gabriel García Márquez. Oprah's Book Club. www2.oprah.com/obc_classic/featbook/oyos/author/oyos_author_main.jhtml (accessed June 12, 2007).

The business of unsold magazines. 2007. Bibliostructures. http://bibliostruc
tures.wordpress.com/category/luxury-paper (accessed June 13, 2007).

Crowe, Darcy. 2007. Nobel Prize–winning novelist Gabriel García
Márquez visits hometown after 25-year absence. *Laredo Morning Times*,
June 3. http://airwolf.lmtonline.com/living/archive/060307/living5.pdf.

GABO: A brief history of Colombia's native son, Gabriel García Márquez.
2008. Hippodrome State Theatre. www.thehipp.org/perspectives/2005_
2006/wings/gabo.php (accessed June 12, 2007).

Iran Daily. 2007. Márquez delights fans. April 7.

Mirza, Afzal. 2006. Outsized reality: A profile of Gabriel García Márquez.
The News International (India), June 18.

Ruch, Allen B. 2003. Gabriel García Márquez. www.themodernworld.com/
gabo/gabo_biography.html (accessed June 14, 2007).

Walker, Berenice. Gabriel García Márquez. http://eprentice.sdsu.edu/S055/
bwalker/gabrielgarciamarquez.html.

Wikipedia. 2008. Gabriel García Márquez. http://en.wikipedia.org/wiki/
Gabriel_Garc%C3%ADa_M%C3%A1rquez.

MOBY DICK / Herman Melville

Bronski, Michael. 2003. When Nathaniel met Herman. *Boston Phoenix*,
August 22.

Kesterson, David B. Hawthorne and Melville: Hawthorne in Salem. www
.hawthorneinsalem.org/page/10179.

Koymasky, Matt, and Andrej Koymasky. 2001. Herman Melville. http://
andrejkoymasky.com/liv/fam/biom3/melv1.html (accessed March 25,
2007).

The Life and Works of Herman Melville: Melville and Nathaniel Hawthorne. www.melville.org/hawthrne.htm (accessed March 25, 2007).

Norton, Rictor. Gay History and Literature: Herman Melville. www.infopt
.demon.co.uk/melville.htm (accessed March 25, 2007).

Russo, Maria. 2000. *Herman Melville*, by Elizabeth Hardwick. *Salon*, July
26. http://archive.salon.com/books/review/2000/07/26/hardwick.

Wikipedia. 2008. Herman Melville. http://en.wikipedia.org/wiki/Herman_
  Melville.

Wikipedia. 2008. Moby Dick. http://en.wikipedia.org/wiki/Moby-Dick.

THE MURDER ON THE LINKS / Agatha Christie

Cade, Jared. 2007. Then and now. *The Times Literary Supplement*, October 3. http://entertainment.timesonline.co.uk/tol/arts_and_entertain-
  ment/the_tls/article2583582.ece (accessed April 3, 2009).

Hobbs, J. D. 2008. Hercule Poirot Central: Agatha's disappearance. www.
  poirot.us/disappear.php (accessed April 3, 2009).

Hobbs, J. D. 2008. Hercule Poirot Central: Archie Christie. www.poirot.
  us/archie.php (accessed April 3, 2009).

S.P. 2008. The mystery of the disappearing author. *Quazen*, January 14.
  www.quazen.com/Reference/Biography/The-Mystery-of-the-Disap-
  pearing-Author.74075 (accessed April 3, 2009).

Time. 1976. Dame Agatha: queen of the maze. January 26. www.time.
  com/time/magazine/article/0,9171,913961-3,00.html (accessed April 3,
  2009).

ORLANDO: A BIOGRAPHY / Virginia Woolf

McManamy, John. Virginia Woolf and her madness. Suite101.com. www
  .suite101.com/article.cfm/depression/31450 (accessed January 26, 2008).

Shaw, Guinevere. Virginia and Vita. www.geocities.com/CollegePark/
  Hall/1170/orlando.html (accessed January 26, 2008).

Virginia and Vita (1927). 2005. Woman-Stirred, July 31. http://woman-stirred
  .blogspot.com/2005/07/virginia-and-vita.html (accessed March 7, 2007).

Vita Sackville-West. 2007. The Bloomsbury Group: Mantex. www.mantex
  .co.uk/ou/a319/vs-west.htm.

Wikipedia. 2008. Orlando: A biography. http://en.wikipedia.org/wiki/
  Orlando:_A_Biography.

Wikipedia. 2008. Virginia Woolf. http://en.wikipedia.org/wiki/Virginia_
  Woolf.

PEYTON PLACE / Grace Metalious

Wikipedia. 2008. Grace Metalious. http://en.wikipedia.org/wiki/Grace_ Metalious.

Wikipedia. 2008. Peyton Place (novel). http://en.wikipedia.org/wiki/ Peyton_Place_%28novel%29.

THE PROFESSOR OF DESIRE / Philip Roth

Biography for Claire Bloom. IMDb. www.imdb.com/name/nm0001954/bio (accessed January 3, 2008).

Bloom, Claire. 1996. *Leaving a doll's house: A memoir.* Boston: Little, Brown and Company.

Claire Bloom. Yahoo! Movies. http://movies.yahoo.com/movie/contribu tor/1800014825/bio (accessed January 3, 2008).

Epinions.com. Review: *Leaving a doll's house: A memoir,* by Claire Bloom. www.epinions.com/book-review-7A6A-910668B-39DE1BC6-prod1 (accessed January 6, 2008).

Garner, Dwight. 2008. Philip Roth is his mother's son. *New York Times,* March 25.

Gleick, Elizabeth. 1996. Claire Bloom's complaint. *Time,* September 30.

Independent (London). 2004. Claire Bloom: The human pain. May 12.

O'Malley, Peter J. 2000. I can't believe no one ever told me about this book. Amazon.com. www.amazon.com/review/RZYD1SFK2NL4L (accessed January 6, 2008).

Robertson, Nan. 1984. The many faces of Claire Bloom. *New York Times,* January 15.

Roth, Philip. 1999. Slight revision. *New York Review of Books* 46 (4).

Senior, Jennifer. 2000. Philip Roth blows up. *New York Magazine,* April 24, Arts & Events.

Shoales, Ian. Ill humor. www.salon.com/oct96/shoales961028.html (accessed January 3, 2008).

Smith, Dinitia. 1996. Claire Bloom looks back in anger at Philip Roth. *New York Times,* September 17.

Telegraph (UK). 2006. When real life is like a Greek drama. November 22.

Walzer, Philip. 1995. Sullied Sabbath glimmers of Philip Roth's greatness are obscured by the vulgarity of his novel. *Virginian-Pilot*, September 17, Commentary.

Whittamore, Katharine. 1996. Review: *Leaving a doll's house: A memoir*, by Claire Bloom. *Salon*, October 22. www.salon.com/sneaks/sneak peeks961022.html (accessed January 6, 2008).

Wikipedia. 2008. Claire Bloom. http://en.wikipedia.org/wiki/Claire_Bloom.

Wikipedia. 2008. Philip Roth. http://en.wikipedia.org/wiki/Philip_Roth.

THE SATANIC VERSES / Salman Rushdie

Biography for Salman Rushdie. IMDb. www.imdb.com/name/nm0750723/bio (accessed February 12, 2008).

BookBrowse. 2007. Marianne Wiggins. www.bookbrowse.com/biogra phies/index.cfm?author_number=1478 (accessed February 12, 2008).

Daum, Meghan. 1998. Hide and speak. *Village Voice* (New York), October 6.

Dougary, Ginny. 2005. The incredible lightness of Salman. *Time*, August 20.

Featured couple. www.re-marriage.com/rservices/fc-rushdie-padma.htm (accessed February 15, 2008).

IBNLive.com. 2008. Salman Rushdie and Riya Sen? January 14.

James, Caryn. 1989. The ayatollah's other victim. *New York Times*, February 28.

James, Caryn. 1991. Marianne Wiggins and life on the run. *New York Times*, April 9.

Johnson, Pamela J. 2006. Painting words on a canvas. *USC College News*, July.

Joyful Rushdie steps out from the shadows. 1998. http://users.deltanet.com/~cybrgbl/burning/rushdie-free.html

Kennard, Paul. Who is Salman Rushdie, a man caught between two worlds. http://ezinearticles.com/?Who-is-Salman-Rushdie,-A-Man-Caught-Between-Two-Worlds&id=450103 (accessed February 12, 2008).

Liukkonen, Petri. 2003. Books and Writers: Salman Rushdie. www.kirjasto .sci.fi/rushdie.htm (accessed February 11, 2007).

Maus, Elizabeth. 2000. Salman Rushdie's 1,001 Manhattan nights. *New York Observer*, April 16.

New York Times. 2008. Salman Rushdie and wife living apart. February 11.

Salman Rushdie. Brain-Juice. www.brain-juice.com/cgi-bin/show_bio .cgi?p_id=114 (accessed February 11, 2008).

Salman Rushdie. Exclusive Books. www.exclusivebooks.com/features/ authors/srushdie2.php?PHPSESSID=fbgh655fd2a1riu4q6dnrqh3g4 (accessed February 12, 2008).

Salman Rushdie. NNDB. www.nndb.com/people/317/000022251 (accessed February 12, 2008).

Shur, Cherri L. Marianne Wiggins. Novelguide.com. www.novelguide.com/ a/discover/aww_04/aww_04_01294.htm (accessed February 12, 2008).

Sunday Times (London). 2007. Knight stripped of colour: Women in Salman's life. July 8.

Sunday Tribune (Dublin). 2007. Salman Rushdie: The dark knight. June 24. www.tribune.ie/2007/06/24/104126.html (accessed February 12, 2008).

Thorpe, Vanessa. 2004. Uxorious genius. *Observer* (UK), April 11.

Wikipedia. 2008. Marianne Wiggins. http://en.wikipedia.org/wiki/Mari anne_Wiggins.

Wikipedia. 2008. Salman Rushdie. http://en.wikipedia.org/wiki/Salman_ Rushdie.

SCHINDLER'S LIST / Thomas Keneally

Doti, James L. The "1939" club. Chapman University. http://1939club.com/ 1939%20Chapman.htm (accessed March 20, 2007).

The handbag studio. Granta. www.granta.com/extracts/2135 (accessed March 20, 2007).

Keneally, Tom. 2007. *Searching for Schindler.* Sydney: Knopf.

Oskar Schindler: The riddle of an enigma. Who is Oskar Schindler? www.michaeldvd.com.au/Articles/WhoIsOskarSchindler/WhoIs OskarSchindler.html (accessed March 20, 2007).

Pfefferberg, Poldek. Schindler survivor. www.auschwitz.dk/Panzuck/id4 .htm (accessed March 20, 2007).

Pottinger, Susan. 2008. Oskar Schindler. The American-Israeli Cooperative Enterprise: Jewish Virtual Library. www.jewishvirtuallibrary.org/ jsource/biography/schindler.html (accessed February 20, 2008).

Searching for Schindler: A memoir. Booktopia. www.booktopia.com.au/ searching-for-schindler-a-memoir/prod9781740512015.html (accessed February 2, 2008).

Steinhouse, Herbert. 1994. The real Oskar Schindler. Literature of the Holocaust. www.writing.upenn.edu/~afilreis/Holocaust/steinhouse.html (accessed February 20, 2008).

Thomas Keneally and Leopold Page. www.muc.edu/academics/lecture_ series/the_schooler_lecture/thomas_keneally_leopold_page (accessed March 20, 2007).

Trotterman. 2000. He who saves one saves the world entire. Epinions.com, July 16. www.epinions.com/book-review-196C-1BECC9F9-39726D90- prod5 (accessed March 20, 2007).

Tugend, Tom. 2001. Survivor who spread word of Schindler's list dies at 87. Jewish Telegraphic Agency, March 16.

Wikipedia. 2008. Oskar Schindler. http://en.wikipedia.org/wiki/Oskar_ Schindler.

Wikipedia. 2008. Poldek Pfefferberg. http://en.wikipedia.org/wiki/Poldek_ Pfefferberg.

Wikipedia. 2008. Thomas Keneally. http://en.wikipedia.org/wiki/Thomas_ Keneally.

SEABISCUIT: AN AMERICAN LEGEND / Laura Hillenbrand

Hillenbrand, Laura. 2003. A sudden illness: How my life changed. *New Yorker*, July 7.

Jacobs, Sally. 2002. Against all odds. *Boston Globe,* October 24.

Jaffe, Jody. 2006. Brave hearts. *Bethesda Magazine,* March/April.

SUITE FRANÇAISE / Irène Némirovsky

BookBrowse. 2006. Irène Némirovsky. www.bookbrowse.com/biographies/ index.cfm?author_number=1293 (accessed June 3, 2007).

Brawarsky, Sandee. 2006. Her mother's keeper. *Jewish Week*, July 7.

Durant, Erin. 2005. Writing in the dark: The story of Irène Némirovsky. *Brooklyn Rail*, September.

Guardian (UK). 2006. The novel in the suitcase. March 9.

Irène Némirovsky. www.services.ex.ac.uk/cmit/modules/web_design/sample_ work/nemirovsky/web-project/daughters-biography-2.html (accessed June 3, 2007).

Némirovsky's unburied treasure. 2007. The Scrivener. http://prochoros .blogspot.com/search/label/Irene%Nemirovsky (accessed June 3, 2007).

Pryce-Jones, David. 2007. Discovering Némirovsky. *Commentary Magazine*, March 26.

Randall, Par Colin. Auschwitz victim's book causes a stir in France. Presse Internationale. http://pagesperso-orange.fr/guillaumedelaby/3_pi_tele graph_041023.htm (accessed June 3, 2007).

Self, John. 2007. Irène Némirovsky: *Suite Française*. Asylum. http://theasy lum.wordpress.com/category/nemirovsky-irene (accessed June 3, 2007).

Stoffman, Judy. 2006. Lost tales of war. http://fanset4.blogspot.com/2006/ 05/lost-tales-of-war.html (accessed June 3, 2007).

Taylor, John. 2005. Suit Française. *France Magazine* 74, Summer.

Wikipedia. 2008. Irène Némirovsky. http://en.wikipedia.org/wiki/Irene _Nemirovsky.

Wyatt, Caroline. 2005. French novel survives Auschwitz. BBC News, January 27.

THE THIN MAN / Dashiell Hammett

Dashiell Hammett. Crimeculture.com. www.crimeculture.com/Contents/ Dashiell%20Hammett.htm.

Liukkonen, Petri. 2004. Books and Writers: Lillian Herman.www.kirjasto .sci.fi/lhellman.htm (accessed April 6, 2007).

Marling, William. Dashiell Hammett. Case Western Reserve University. www.detnovel.com/Hammett.html.

Wikipedia. 2008. Dashiell Hammett. http://en.wikipedia.org/wiki/Dashiell
    _Hammett.

Wikipedia. 2008. Lillian Hellman. http://en.wikipedia.org/wiki/Lillian
    _Hellman.

Wikipedia. 2008. The Thin Man. http://en.wikipedia.org/wiki/The_Thin_Man.

TO KILL A MOCKINGBIRD / Harper Lee

Shields, Charles J. 2006. *Mocking bird: A portrait of Harper Lee*. New York:
    Owl Books.

Wikipedia. 2008. Harper Lee. http://en.wikipedia.org/wiki/Harper_Lee.

UNDER THE TUSCAN SUN / Frances Mayes

Bee, Adrianne. 2003. It takes a villa. *SFSU Magazine*, Fall/Winter.

Cornelisen, Ann. 1969. Once there was a woman. *Time*, March 7.

Cornelisen, Ann. 2002. *Torregreca*. Vermont: Steerforth Italia.

Cornelisen, Ann. 2001. *Women of the shadows*. New Hampshire: Steerforth
    Press.

Cornelisen, Ann, and Frances Mayes. 2008. *Torregreca*. Random House, Inc.
    www.randomhouse.com/catalog/display.pperl?isbn=9781586420444
    &view=excerpt.

Guide to the Ann Cornelisen papers. 2007. Archives and Special Collec-
    tions. Vassar College Libraries. http://specialcollections.vassar.edu/
    findingaids/cornelisen_ann.html.

Maddocks, Melvin. 1971. Erosion of souls. *Time*, November 15.

Martin, Douglas. 2003. Ann Cornelisen, 77, writer on impoverished
    Southern Italy. *New York Times*, November 14.

Randall, Fredericka. 1990. Learning to be Italian. *New York Times*, February 18.

UNDER THE VOLCANO / Malcoln Lowry

BC Author Bank: Lowry, Malcolm. www.abcbookworld.com/view_author.
    php?id=2870 (accessed March 30, 2009).

Books of the World: Lowry, Malcolm. www.booksfactory.com/writers/
    lowry.htm (accessed April 20, 2009).

Duguid, Lindsay. 2000. Malcolm in the middle. *New York Times*, December 10, Books. www.nytimes.com/books/00/12/10/reviews/001210.10duguidt. html (accessed March 31, 2009).

Edwards, Robert. 2004. Find a Grave: Margerie Bonner Lowry. October 11. www.findagrave.com/cgi-bin/fg.cgi?page=gr&GRid=9584458 (accessed March 30, 2009).

Gale, Thomas. 2004. Encyclopedia of World Biography: Malcolm Lowry. www.encyclopedia.com/doc/1G2-3404707397.html (accessed March 31, 2009).

Howard, Jennifer. 1995. By words obsessed. *Washington Post*, October 15. www.washingtonpost.com/wp-srv/style/longterm/books/reviews/pursued.htm (accessed March 30, 2009).

Internet Movie Database: Biography for Marjorie [sic] Bonner. www.imdb. com/name/nm0094918/bio (accessed March 31, 2009).

Liukkonen, Petri. 2008. Books and Writers: (Clarence) Malcolm Lowry. www.kirjasto.sci.fi/mlowry.htm (accessed March 30, 2009).

Martin, Tim. 2008. Malcolm Lowry, killed by his own book. *Telegraph* (UK), January 11. www.telegraph.co.uk/culture/books/non_fiction-reviews/3670166/Malcolm-Lowry-killed-by-his-own-book.html (accessed March 31, 2009).

Max, D. T. 2007. Day of the dead. *The New Yorker*, December 17. www. newyorker.com/reporting/2007/12/17/071217fa_fact_max (accessed March 30, 2009).

New York Times. 1988. Margerie Lowry, 83, actress and a writer. October 4. www.nytimes.com/1988/10/04/obituaries/margerie-lowry-83-actress-and-a-writer.html (accessed March 30, 2009).

Preschel, Bill. 2008. Reader's almanac 6/26. June 26. www.planetpeschel. com/index?/site/comments/readers_almanac_6_26 (accessed March 30, 2009).

Rolfe, Lionel. Notes of a California bohemian: down and out at the brown derby. www.dabelly.com/columns/bohemian52.htm (accessed March 31, 2009).

Time. 1965. One man's volcano. December 31. www.time.com/time/magazine/article/0,9171,842368-1,00.html (accessed March 30, 2009).

Time. 1968. Death of the optimist. June 28. www.time.com/time/magazine/article/0,9171,841362,00.html (accessed March 30, 2009).

Under the Volcano: A Brief Lowryan Chronology. http://home.istar.ca/~stewart/time.htm (accessed March 30, 2009).

Wikipedia. 2009. Malcolm Lowry. http://en.wikipedia.org/wiki/Malcolm_Lowry.

Wikipedia. 2009. Under the Volcano. http://en.wikipedia.org/wiki/Under_the_Volcano.

VALLEY OF THE DOLLS / Jacqueline Susann

Lehrman, Karen. 1998. The original "Valley" girl. *New York Times*, January 4.

Tennenbaum, Ray. 2000. Lovely me: The life of Jacqueline Susann. Ray Tennenbaum's text. www.ray-field.com/SUSANN.HTM (accessed March 16, 2007).

Wikipedia. 2008. Jacqueline Susann. http://en.wikipedia.org/wiki/Jacqueline_Susann.

THE WONDERFUL WIZARD OF OZ / L. Frank Baum

Allen, Brooke. 2002. The man behind the curtain. *New York Times*, November 17.

Roesch Wagner, Sally. 2005. The mother of Oz. The Matilda Joslyn Gage Foundation. www.matildajoslyngage.org/motherofoz.htm.

Willingham, Elaine. 1998. The story of Dorothy Gage: Beyond the rainbow to Oz. 1998. www.beyondtherainbow2oz.com/dorothygage.html.

WORLD WITHOUT END / Ken Follett

Barbara Follett. BBC News: Vote 2001: Candidates. http://news.bbc.co.uk/hi/english/static/vote2001/candidates/candidates/5/53704.stm (accessed December 16, 2007).

BookBrowse. 2007. Ken Follett. www.bookbrowse.com/biographies/index.cfm?author_number=238 (accessed December 16, 2007).

CBS News. 2007. Ken Follett's monumental new novel. October 7.

Evans, Gavin. 1997. "Champagne socialist" pulls the cork on Tory whip's safe seat. *Independent* (London), May 4.

Evans, Gavin. 1996. You've been Folletted. *Observer Life Magazine* (UK), February 25.

Ken Follett: Biography and bibliography. www.ken-follett.com/media/bio/KF_bio_en_0709.pdf.

Sparrow, Andrew. 2005. Follett tells of husband's death under house. *Telegraph* (UK), February 24.

Stinson, Jeffrey. 2007. Author Ken Follett follows through to "End." *USA Today*, October 8.

Time. 2006. Best of times, worst of times. December 3.

THE YEAR OF MAGICAL THINKING / Joan Didion

Answers.com. 2008. Biography: Joan Didion. www.answers.com/topic/joan-didion.

Brockes, Emma. 2005. Interview: Joan Didion. *Guardian* (UK), December 16.

Callahan, Tom. 2007. Review: *The Year of Magical Thinking*. Bookreporter .com. http://bookreporter.com/reviews2/140004314X.asp.

Columbia, David Patrick. 2004. Remembering John Gregory Dunne. *New York Social Diary*, January 7.

Delehanty, Adam. 2005. Review: Joan Didion's *The Year of Magical Thinking*. *The College Hill Independent* (Brown/RISD), October 20.

Feeney, Mark. 2005. Amid unbearable sorrow, she shows her might. *Boston Globe*, October 26.

Frances. 2005. Joan Didion's Magical Thinking. November 2, http://frances dinkelspiel.blogspot.com/2005/11/joan-didions-magical-thinking.html.

Gerrie, Anthea. 2007. Interview: A stage version of Joan Didion's painfully honest account of her husband's death comes to London. *Independent* (London), September 1.

Gross, Jane. 2004. John Gregory Dunne eulogized at cathedral. *New York Times*, March 24.

Gwinn, Mary Ann. 2005. Joan Didion shares what she's learned about grief, mourning. *Seattle Times*, November 18.

Homberger, Eric. 2004. Obituary: John Gregory Dunne. *Guardian* (UK), January 2.

Italie, Hillel. 2005. Joan Didion remembers husband in acclaimed new memoir. Associated Press, November 13.

Leonard, John. 2005. Review: *The Black Album. New York Review of Books* 52 (16).

Lim, Dennis. 2005. The last thing she wanted. *Village Voice* (New York), October 3.

Manister, Diana. 2008. The year of magical thinking. http://contemporary lit.about.com/od/memoir/fr/yearMagical.htm.

Matousek, Mark. 2007. Writing to live. *AARP Magazine*, March/April.

Messud, Claire. 2005. Dark irony. *LA Weekly*, September 19.

Miller, Kerri. 2005. Author Joan Didion deals with grief through "magical thinking." *Minnesota Public Radio*, October 20.

O'Connor, Anne-Marie. 2005. Joan Didion's memoir, steeped in grief. *Los Angeles Times*, October 16.

Pinsky, Robert. 2005. *The year of magical thinking:* Goodbye to all that. *New York Times*, October 9.

Rosenheim, Andrew. 2004. Obituary: John Gregory Dunne. *Independent* (London), January 12.

Sandimck. 2006. If you're in a life partnership, read this book! Epinions. com, April 21. www.epinions.com/content_227614822020.

Scott. 2007. *The year of magical thinking*, by Joan Didion. January 12. http://scoboco.blogspot.com (accessed October 30, 2007).

Severo, Richard. 2004. John Gregory Dunne, novelist, screenwriter and observer of Hollywood, is dead at 71. *New York Times*, January 1.

Smith, Sid. 2006. Review: *The Year of Magical Thinking*, by Joan Didion. *BC Books*, September 4.

Stritoff, Bob, and Sheri Stitoff. 2008. Joan Didion and John Dunne marriage profile. http://marriage.about.com/od/thearts/p/dideondunne.htm.

Van Meter, Jonathan. 2005. When everything changes. *New York Magazine*, October 2.

Waugh, Jessica. 2006. Review: *The year of magical thinking*, by Joan Didion. *Book remarks*, June 16.

Wesselmann, Debbie Lee. 2007. Review: *The year of magical thinking*. Mostly Fiction Book Reviews. www.mostlyfiction.com/adventure/ didion.htm.

Wikipedia. 2008. Joan Didion. http://en.wikipedia.org/wiki/Joan_Didion.

Wikipedia. 2008. John Gregory Dunne. http://en.wikipedia.org/wiki/ John_Gregory_Dunne.

Williams, Alan. 2005. Thinking magically about Joan Didion. TheSimon .com, October 28. www.thesimon.com/magazine/articles/between_ the_covers/01004_thinking_magically_about_joan_didion.html.

Yardley, Jonathan. 2005. A celebrated writer recalls the devastating emotions unleashed by death and illness. *Washington Post*, October 2.

Yardley, Jonathan. 2006. In memory of a writer who was the very definition of professional. *Washington Post*, January 22.

THE YIDDISH POLICEMEN'S UNION / Michael Chabon

Behe, Regis. 2002. Chabon, Waldman share lives as writers, parents. *Pittsburgh Tribune-Review*, October 1, Entertainment.

Behe, Regis. 2007. Michael Chabon and Ayelet Waldman: A novel romance. *Fanfare Magazine*, May 7.

Benson, Heidi. 2003. Ayelet Waldman. *San Francisco Chronicle*, October 22.

Biography. The amazing website of Kavalier & Clay. http://gawker.com/ news/smug-marrieds/how-ayelet-waldman-stole-christmas-327058.php (accessed January 8, 2008).

CBS News. 2002. Michael Chabon makes a living. January 13.

Giles, Gretchen. 2006. God forbid. *Metroactive*, February 1.

Gould, Emily. 2007. Smug marrieds: How Ayelet Waldman stole Christmas. Gawker.com, November 27. http://gawker.com/news/ smug-marrieds/how-ayelet-waldman-stole-christmas-327058.php (accessed January 8, 2008).

Kirschling, Gregory. 2007. The new adventures of Michael Chabon. *Entertainment Weekly*, May 4.

New York Magazine. 2006. Michael Chabon, defender of the acknowledgment. December 11, News & Features.

Reese, Jennifer. 2005. Mammamia! *Entertainment Weekly*, August 12.

Seligman, Katherine. 2005. Ayelet, unfiltered. *San Francisco Chronicle*, July 24.

Siegel, Jennifer. 2007. Michael Chabon and Ayelet Waldman: Raising $25K for Obama. *Forward*, April 30.

Waldman, Ayelet. 2005. Truly, madly, guiltily. *New York Times*, March 27.

Wikipedia. 2008. Ayelet Waldman. http://en.wikipedia.org/wiki/Ayelet_Waldman.

Wikipedia. 2008. Michael Chabon. http://en.wikipedia.org/wiki/Michael_Chabon.

Ybarra, Michael J. 2003. Taking on the law. *Los Angeles Times*, October 5.

Acknowledgments

The acknowledgments page is the most heartfelt one of the book, as it involves introspection. It takes a village to make a book, and the following were the ones who guided me along the way.

Caren Johnson, my literary agent, immediately comes to mind. Thank you for not consigning my manuscript to the slush pile, and believing in its merit. If it were not for you, Zelda would have remained just the name of Fitzgerald's wife.

Meg Leder, my editor at Penguin/Perigee, was all that I could hope for—and more. From the first to the last she was insightful and enthusiastic. I would also like to mention my publicist at Penguin, Catherine Milne, for arranging my inclusion at booksellers' conventions in Los Angeles and Oakland, as well as bookstore signings.

When I emailed my colleagues at my school about the forthcoming publication of my book, several people responded with their variations of *mazel tovs*: Hilda Paul, Jill Shapira, Araceli Vaca, John Arguilez, Jason Josafat, Manuel Narvaza, Meg Garcia, Jesus Moreno, Lysabeth Luansing-Garcia, Maureen Rymer, Robert Jackson, Anthony Garcia, Robert Bonilla, Christina Campbell, Debbie Domenie, Donna Matthews, Jerome Kocher, Sergio Quintero, Reid Buns, Alan Nakano, Yolanda Rocha, Nancy

Hokenson, Ellen Schrier, Javier Nunez, and Georgia Wapnowski. Thank you for not subscribing to the Gore Vidal philosophy of "Every time a friend succeeds, something in me dies." Vicky Urias, my school librarian, was kind enough to offer to email all the librarians in the district about *Zelda*. We have been there for each other through the years, and through the tears. I am indebted to Stephen Scanlan (my ex-roomie, when he was a traveling teacher) for his invaluable assistance with the bibliography. In the lexicon of our students, "U R da bomb." I am excited to see my website, which is being crafted by webmaster (and friend) extraordinaire Jerome Kocher.

The road of life would be so much harder without the companionship of fellow musketeers, and here are mine: Karen Brody, Elisa Landau-Bloom, Brenda Vernon, and Kane Handel. Thank you for always standing by with your emotional first-aid kits. In the spring, I was in Toronto with my mother at United Bakery when she asked me if I recognized anyone. I was about to say no, as having been away for twenty years all faces were those of strangers. It was at that point that I saw Donna Kotzer Jacobs, a friend from Forest Hill Collegiate. She was gracious enough to arrange for a reunion with three other friends from our alma mater: Mary-Anne Harnick, Cynthia Blackman, and Lilie Zendel. We had a wonderful dinner followed by Starbucks, where we reminisced until closing. Thank you for not equating "gone" with "forgotten."

I wrote to Dean Koontz asking him to elaborate on Father Jerome Molokie, and he was gracious enough to send me a letter of explanation, as well as the book *Life Is Good!: Lessons in Joyful Living,* by Trixie Koontz, an eight-page tribute to his late dog, and a newsletter, *Useless News*. From the correspondence I was able to glean that he is as gracious a human being as he is talented an author.

Lois Lowry also was kind enough to respond. She explained that her dedication, *tusind tak,* is Danish for "a thousand thanks." She also gave an explanation of the title, *Number the Stars.* She stated that it was derived from Psalm 147 and "describes the individual value of each person, and that they should *not* be classified as a group."

My home away from home is the Barnes & Noble booksellers located in the Grossmont Center (with its adjoining Starbucks). Holly Golightly, to fight off her "mean reds," went to Tiffany; I go to Barnes & Noble. She said of Tiffany, "Nothing very bad can happen to you there." Holly's Tiffany is my Barnes & Noble.

One's family members are the nucleus around which one's life revolves, and now I will acknowledge my own. I want to thank my husband, Joel Geller, whose conviction that I would never publish a book proved the wind beneath my writer's wings. I also want to thank my daughter, Jordanna (Jordi) Geller, without whose constant demands the book would have been finished in half the time. Lastly, I want to thank my mother, Gilda Wagman. Although she never read a word I wrote, she believed in my book wholeheartedly. In addition, despite all odds, nothing has ever conquered her indomitable spirit. And that, to me, is the true test of courage.

To the ones I have mentioned, and to the ones I have not, I send all my gratitude, all my love.

My *tusind tak*,
Marlene